# THE
# PRUNER'S
# HANDBOOK

# THE PRUNER'S HANDBOOK

practical pruning advice for healthy, beautiful plants

JOHN MALINS

David & Charles

**FRONTISPIECE:**

*Wisteria sinensis* is a superb wall climber with few problems once established in an appropriate site.
Here is an old plant in flower, encouraged by the previous hot summer.
Pruning takes place in two stages: in midsummer the long (up to 6m/20ft) extension growths are
cut back to 15cm (6in), then, in winter, these shortened growths are cut back to two buds.
Look out for any branches which are twisting together and remove one of them

A DAVID & CHARLES BOOK

First published in the UK in 1992 as *The Essential Pruner's Companion*
This completely revised edition published 1995

Colour photographs © Andrew Lawson except:
pp50, 59, 63 (Author)
pp159, 171, 183 (Photos Horticultural)

Line drawings by Maggie Redfern

Copyright © Professor John Malins 1992

The estate of Professor John Malins has asserted his right to be identified as
author of this work in accordance with the Copyright, Designs and Patents Act,
1988.

A catalogue record for this book is available from the British Library.

ISBN 0 7153 0399 6

Printed in the UK by BPC Paulton Books Ltd
for David & Charles
Brunel House   Newton Abbot   Devon

# Contents

# Introduction

Most of us think we know what pruning is, but would find it difficult to define. Let us forget a modern use of the word prune in which 'cut down' in any context is meant – an example of this use being provided by publishers who say 'Prune your manuscript', meaning 'Cut it by half, including your favourite passages'. The verb 'to prune' is derived from the Old French 'prounier', meaning to cut back the vine, and this became 'prouyne' in Middle English. By the end of the sixteenth century 'to prune' was to 'lop off branches, boughs or shoots'.

From the seventeenth century onwards, the introduction to Britain of trees and shrubs, especially from America, drew attention to their manner of growth and the way in which they could be trained for the best effect. Fruit bushes were pruned and trained according to set plans, with splendid results. Scientific study in this century has, in the main, confirmed the principles which trained gardeners had taught from long observation and experience. It is not surprising that the best understood and practised of all pruning tasks is the ancient craft of training the vine.

William Thiselton-Dyer was appointed Director of the Royal Botanic Gardens at Kew in 1885 and found that pruning had been neglected, many trees being 'unshapely'. There was nothing new about such complaints. The Scots gardener John Reid, in his influential book of 1683, wrote 'Some ignorants are against pruning, suffering their trees to run and ramble to such a head of confusion as neither bears well or fair.' W. J. Bean became Assistant Curator at Kew in 1900 and no doubt put things to rights there, if the work had not been done already. In 1914 he published his classic work *Trees and Shrubs Hardy in the British Isles,* in which he wrote 'Of all the arts that go to make up horticulture pruning is the one most frequently misapplied – hard pruning or pruning without aim is worse than none.' Even now, in places other than Kew, there is evidence of ignorance and carelessness where neither should exist. This book aims to help you prune with wisdom and skill.

**OPPOSITE**

'Old Blush China' (Parson's Pink China, The Monthly Rose) is an ancient rose, introduced to Europe in 1789. On a wall it grows to 2.4m (8ft) but makes a 1.2m (4ft) wide, 1.5m (5ft) high bush in the open. It flowers every month, always at Christmas at Tintinhull. The flowers are semi-double, two or three on a stem, beginning crimson then fading to pink. This wonderful old rose is hardy and free from disease and should be in every garden. Prune it early in the spring, cutting back stems by one-third of their length

PART ONE

# The Purpose
# *of* Pruning

Why should we bother to prune our plants? Doesn't nature do it? It's true that She – or is it He? – does eventually remove dead or diseased branches, but conditions in nature are different to those in even the most natural-looking garden. To achieve the kind of longevity, balanced, healthy growth and ornamental display that gardeners demand from their trees and shrubs, pruning is not only advisable, but essential.

As a tree grows in woodland, the lower branches are deprived of light and the crown takes more and more of the nourishment from the roots. Eventually this results in the lower branches dying and falling to the ground, but before they do so damage often occurs, with two branches rubbing together, damaging the bark and allowing infection to enter and sometimes spread to the main trunk. Shrubs competing for space and light grow tall and leggy, often bare at the base and dead in the centre. This is what happens in nature but no sane gardener would tolerate it in an ornamental plantation. There is every reason to cut back unhealthy limbs as soon as possible and to remove overcrowded shoots at the appropriate time. Problems of the sort described above can be pre-empted by correct training, formative pruning and regular maintenance thereafter. The aims of pruning trees and shrubs may be summarized as follows:

1. To keep the plant healthy by the prompt removal of diseased, damaged or dead wood. In some plants, this is all that is needed.
2. To restore overgrown and neglected plants to health and to a manageable and appropriate size and habit.
3. To maintain a good 'natural' shape by removing over-long or misshapen branches and by maintaining a single leader and removing any rivals, where

appropriate, to promote upward growth.
4. To encourage branching low down, where appropriate, and the formation of a strong framework of growths.
5. To allow light and air to reach the centre of the plant by removal of weak or crowded shoots there, thus improving the quantity and quality of flowers and foliage produced.
6. To remove dead flowers as soon as they fade before seed formation begins, and so save the energy which would otherwise be spent on reproduction. Dead-heading like this may not be appropriate when fruits are decorative or grown for the table, but in the latter case it is often worth thinning them out after the normal 'drop' in early summer, as those that remain will develop better size and flavour with less competition.
7. To remove old flowered wood at the appropriate time so that a good crop of flowers will be borne at the desired level on the plant, rather than appearing ever higher up on extension growth produced on top of years'-worth of mature wood.
8. To assist in the training of wall plants and some climbers, so as to take advantage of the sun and the extra heat reflected from the wall surface and the shelter the wall provides. You should maintain a horizontal position of shoots by tying them to supports. This checks the stimulus to upward growth and encourages the formation of flower buds.
9. To encourage fruit trees to form a framework of fruiting spurs (see p153), and to maintain fruit production by selective pruning of trees and bushes.

## PRUNING AND FEEDING

Pruning, as it is carried out in gardens, is far more radical than the rather gradual and haphazard form practised in nature. To remove a substantial number of stems, especially those bearing foliage which would normally produce nourishment for the roots, puts a considerable strain on the parts of the plants that remain. If pruning has been appropriate the plant should strive to produce replacement growth, especially when pruning has been severe, and it should be given plenty of help and encouragement in the form of mulching and feeding.

## EFFECTS OF PRUNING

As explained above, taking away the shoots and leaves of trees, shrubs or herbaceous plants reduces the amount of plant food that will be generated in the following season. Yet pruning normally stimulates growth. This is because the terminal bud of a stem or branch produces a chemical that inhibits the growth of any buds below it. Once the tip of a shoot or branch is removed, therefore, the lower buds can develop. Paradoxically, hard pruning results in more vigorous growth than light pruning, so cutting a large and overgrown shrub right back in the hope of limiting its growth and spread will actually have the opposite result. This phenomenon can be harnessed to help reshape an unbalanced shrub: by cutting the weaker growths back hard they can, in time, be encouraged to catch up with the stronger shoots.

Another effect of pruning, however, is that the reproductive phase of growth slows down as the vegetative growth is promoted. This can sometimes have unwanted results: when fruit trees in their early years are pruned too hard, for example, new growth is produced by fruit buds which fail to develop normally. This is why it is important to prune appropriately, both in terms of timing and extent.

## WHEN TO PRUNE

The time of year at which a specific plant should be pruned will depend on its habit of growth and the effect that is to be produced. It is easier to say when not to prune:

1. When the soil is sodden after rain; standing by and walking round a tree or shrub compacts the soil and prevents moisture from penetrating to the roots. In gardens much visited by the public this compacting of the soil and direct damage to the roots near the surface is quite a serious problem, and may require that a precious specimen be roped off.
2. When there is frost, actual or forecast, or icy wind – the only exception is the mature tree, which foresters will prune regardless of frost.
3. When you do not have time to do it properly (stolen from Christopher Lloyd).
4. In some cases, when the sap is actively rising, as

certain trees will then respond to cutting by 'bleeding'. This usually stops within hours or, if not, invariably ceases within a few days. Some writers suggest 'die back' will result, but this is not the case. Bleeding is quite harmless but it can be avoided by pruning in autumn rather than spring. The bleeding tendency is described most often in maples, birch, walnut, poplar and hornbeam.

Now, at last, when to prune: the best time is that which allows the longest period for the development and ripening of new growth before winter. This is the case for:

1. Flowering plants that carry their flowers on wood formed in the previous year, and which should be pruned as soon as the flowers have faded.
2. Flowering plants that carry their flowers on wood formed in the current year from early spring onwards and have the months until flowering begins in which to ripen their growth. It is now accepted practice to prune them at the end of winter, hoping that late frosts will not be severe.
3. Deciduous trees, which can be pruned at any time, but usually from midsummer until Christmas (with respect for the anti-bleeding school). An exception to this rule is the genus *Prunus*, in particular plums and a few related species. The reason is silver-leaf disease, which is caused by a fungus and is often fatal, resulting in a change in leaf colour from green to silvery. Next the shoots and branches die and finally fruiting bodies, usually bracket-shaped but sometimes flat, appear on the affected wood, which is purple-tinted when cut. Pruning wounds provide a route of entry for the disease, but infection is least likely to occur in summer, which is when plums should be pruned. There is no effective treatment for the fungus infection but some experts advise fungicidal applications to wounds and cut surfaces after diseased limbs have been amputated (see *Prunus* in A–Z of Trees & Shrubs).

## TOOLS

It is important that pruning tools should be kept sharp and clean, and good-quality tools will generally give the best results and last longest. One manufacturer even offers spare parts for secateurs and knives which can keep a much-loved tool in good condition for ten years or more.

### Pruning knives

The pruning knife is the badge of the professional gardener but is not much used by amateurs, though it is available in the major garden centres. It usually has a curved blade and a handle into which the blade folds. Particularly useful for tidying up ragged cuts sometimes made by secateurs, it must be kept clean and very sharp.

### Secateurs

Secateurs also need looking after and that is more difficult. Inevitably the blades are blunted sooner or later, but most problems arise from incorrect use – especially from cutting or trying to cut a stem which is too thick or too hard. To be on the safe side, make 1cm (½in) the maximum diameter of stem you tackle with secateurs, unless you are familiar with the plant. On some roses 2cm (¾in) would be quite easy to cut, but their old wood at the base would probably not be so amenable.

If you begin to cut and encounter firm resistance, give up at once. On no account use a twisting action, which can only cause an ugly and untidy cut and will probably damage the bearing of the blades and begin to loosen them. Instead, use a lopper or a pocket saw (see below).

There are two types of secateurs: bypass and anvil. The bypass type has two blades, one sharp and thin and the other stouter. The blades are curved, which helps to prevent the stem moving out of the jaws as they come together. It is probably wise, if cutting off

A view of the ancient yew topiary at Levens Hall, Cumbria, maintained continuously for three centuries. Box hedges enclose annual and perennial plants. The yew is trimmed with electric clippers in late summer

a small shoot from a branch on the trunk of a tree, to make sure that the sharp blade is pressed against the branch or trunk before cutting. The anvil type has a single blade which cuts on to a surface of soft metal. Both types have ardent supporters and there is evidently not much to choose between them. Some of the bypass models have refinements such as a rotating hand grip, which is comfortable and less tiring for the elderly or those who have a lot of pruning to do.

### Long-handled pruners

Long-handled pruners or loppers are secateurs with a handle about 45cm (18in) long. They are often not quite strong enough for stems more than 3.5cm (1½in) thick, but that difficulty is partially solved by the double-action lopper, which is a really sturdy tool. The pole pruner has lopper blades at the end of a pole about 3.9m (13ft) long. The cutting blade is operated by a strong wire running from the blade to the foot of the pole. It is not easy to use because a tool of this length

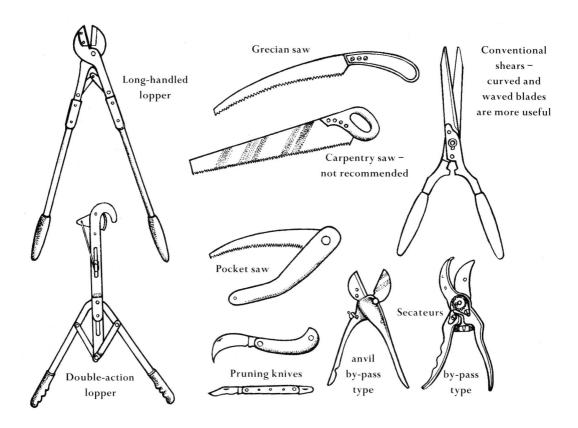

Long-handled lopper

Grecian saw

Carpentry saw – not recommended

Conventional shears – curved and waved blades are more useful

Pocket saw

Double-action lopper

Pruning knives

Secateurs

anvil by-pass type

by-pass type

is heavy, and awkward to control and to direct with any precision. You think you have at last got it to the correct position and triumphantly bring the blades together, only to find that they are not enclosing the target stem. With practice, however, it proves to be a most useful tool, unparalleled for cutting back climbers on house walls that threaten to invade the gutters.

## Saws

With saws, we move into an altogether more serious type of pruning for thicker or more resilient stems than the average pair of secateurs can cope with. The pocket saw has a straight blade 15cm (6in) long and folds into the handle, which is 19cm (7¹/₂in) overall. The teeth are not inclined but cut when the tool is pulled back towards the gardener. This type of saw makes a clean job of stems up to 7.5cm (3in) thick or a little more, if you hold the stem with your free hand to prevent it tearing off suddenly.

So we come to another saw which can be recommended wholeheartedly – the Grecian. It has a curved blade with teeth on one side only. These are disposed so that the cut is made as you pull the blade backwards, which is an advantage especially when working up a ladder. Cutting is rather slow, but be patient. For larger branches a bow saw with a narrow nose is very useful as it will fit into quite small spaces, and cuts as it is pushed away. A full-sized bow saw will cope with larger branches. Use a ladder to get as near as possible to the end of the branch, then begin a piecemeal removal, taking off 0.9–1.2m (3–4ft) at a time and hoping to avoid damage to any underplanting. If the underplanting is precious, the cut pieces of branch can be lowered to the ground using a rope.

## Shears

Shears are used for hedge-cutting, for topiary and for trimming some shrubs. They should have stainless steel blades and the nut and bolt holding the blades together must be easily tightened. Large shoots tend to slide along the blades as they are brought together, and at the tip it is difficult – or impossible – to make a cut. Curved blades help and, better still, waved blades are quite effective. Shears are satisfactory for trimming compact hedges such as *Buxus sempervirens* (box), or *Lonicera nitida* or low-growing shrubs, for instance *Hypericum calycinum* or ericas.

## Hedge-trimmers

Power hedge-trimmers are driven by electricity or petrol. Electricity may come from mains-charged batteries or directly from the mains. The mains-charged battery works with a light cordless machine which is easy to handle and effective for box (*Buxus sempervirens*), *Lonicera nitida*, privet (*Ligustrum*) and the trimming of yew (*Taxus*). The mains electric machine is available in a wide range of prices and a more expensive model will tackle tough and neglected hedges, but its efficiency is limited by the length of the cable, which loses power significantly at about 30m (33yd). This may suffice for a small garden, but otherwise a second power point may be necessary. For safety reasons, mains-powered hedge-trimmers should always be used with a circuit breaker, available from DIY stores or garden centres.

Petrol-driven cutters are more satisfactory than electric if the hedges are extensive and old, but the machine is heavy and calls for a fit and muscular person (I nearly said man) to operate it. Two hours' trimming at a stretch is the most one can ask, perhaps less when working up a ladder. Using extra-long blades is not helpful unless the operator has acquired the skill needed to make sure of a smooth result.

The noise of these engines is really loud and it is definitely necessary to use earmuffs. In towns the neighbours will not appreciate it, especially at the weekend. An ideal day of gardening does not include engine noise and the whine of someone else's electric machine is especially maddening. Young and fairly young gardeners do not seem to mind the engine noises, but perhaps they are conditioned by exposure to wallpaper noise on radio.

## Chain-saws

Chain-saws hardly enter into a discussion of pruning, except of large branches or in the case of a tree falling in your or your neighbour's garden. For everyday use they are exceptionally noisy and quite frightening. We are now in an area which requires professional help – and be sure that the help is professional. Saw-happy cowboys abound.

A final word of caution. For many years the author, in his capacity as a physician, paid a fortnightly visit to a cottage hospital in the Teme valley, an area famous for its fruit. At certain seasons he could be sure that he would find at least one patient per visit with a fracture of thigh, pelvis or arm suffered through a fall from a tree while pruning or picking. These people were not beginners – they were very experienced but somewhat over-confident. Be warned.

PART TWO

# The Practice
# *of* Pruning

## TREES
### FORMATIVE PRUNING

The major type of pruning required for trees is called formative pruning. Its purpose is to ensure that the tree develops healthily and with the desired shape and habit, and it usually takes place over a number of years.

A young tree, grown at home or received from a nursery in its first year, may be in the form of a 'whip', with a single stem and no side branches, or a 'maiden' with side branches known as 'feathers'. If the intention is to grow the tree with a single central leader, attention is focused on that stem, which must be protected from damage and from the competition of laterals forming near it.

In the first year it is unlikely that any pruning will be needed but a stake is desirable, not just to avoid damage from wind-rock but also to mark the site of the tree in winter, when it can sometimes be forgotten. A rabbit guard will also be useful. In the second year, look at the tree often, once a week at least, and make sure that the leader is still intact.

If it is damaged or broken remove it completely, cutting to just above a promising-looking bud on undamaged wood. The idea is to encourage the young tree to produce a replacement leader which you will then train upwards to take over from the original one. If you are skilled in using the pruning knife, this is the best tool to use as it makes it easier to avoid any damage to the replacement shoot. If using secateurs, start the cut on the side opposite the bud about level with its lower end, cutting slightly upwards to end 5mm (¼in) above it. Then the next shoot below is trained to take the place of the lost leader. This may involve tying it to a cane placed as near upright as possible.

In autumn cut back the lower laterals by half, but continue to watch out for any lateral threatening the leader, and remove such a lateral if necessary. In the next autumn cut away the lower laterals completely up to a height of 0.9–1.2m (3–4ft) on the tree, and reduce those above this height to half their length. In the next year these can be removed in autumn to leave a bare stem up to 1.8 (6ft), or whatever length is appropriate for the specimen in question.

From this point pruning can cease apart from general tidying, cutting away diseased or dead wood, and perhaps branches which get in the way of easy progress round the garden. All these procedures can be carried out using secateurs, graduating to a pocket saw and finally a bow saw. If any sizeable branches, 7.5cm (3in) or more across, have to be dealt with it will be necessary to reduce them piecemeal. Take off about 45cm (18in) at each cut. Start by cutting the underside off the branch until the saw begins to bind, then transfer to the upper side and complete the removal of that section. The initial undercut ensures that the section does not split away and perhaps damage the bark. The final cut is made not flush with the main stem but rather 1cm (½in) from it. There is a collar at the point where the branch takes off and this produces cambium which helps early healing of the wound.

The practice of painting all wounds to avoid infection has now been generally abandoned as experiments have shown no benefit and perhaps occasional harm resulting. Paints make the wound less obvious for the first year. Some old gardeners believe that rubbing earth on them does good.

## SHRUBS
The general instructions given above for the method of pruning apply equally to the pruning of shrubs – all cuts should be tidy (no whiskers) in order to

encourage rapid healing. The pruning of trees and shrubs differs only in as much as the aim with the former is to give height by removing the lower branches, and in the latter to promote branching and flowering and, in a few cases, to produce young leaves of good form and colour by cutting them to the ground in spring. The frequency and extent of pruning vary from shrub to shrub, and are discussed under individual entries. Remember always that pruning provokes growth from the stem that is cut. If a shrub becomes lopsided, prune the side which is the weaker and leave the overgrown side alone or prune very lightly (see also p17).

## CONIFERS

A conifer is the name given to a tree that bears cones, but it is also loosely applied to a group now consisting of eight families, some of which do not produce cones, such as *Ginkgo* (maidenhair tree) and *Taxus* (yew). There are only three species of conifer native to Britain – *Juniperus communis*, *Pinus sylvestris* and *Taxus baccata* – but owing to the activities of plant collectors from as long ago as the seventeenth century, a rich variety of conifers are grown.

### A CHOICE OF CONIFERS

The great majority of the conifers grown in the open in Britain are large species, suitable only for gardens of at least 0.4ha (1 acre). Even so, space can often be found in a smaller garden for one or even two sizeable trees, especially if slow-growing varieties are chosen. A grand tree such as *Picea brewerana* might seem a good choice; it will grow slowly to 15m (50ft) or more in 50 years. Even in tiny gardens there can be a place for conifers. The dwarf types rarely exceed 1.8m (6ft) and some are much smaller. They are regarded as alpines and are often planted as features, sometimes as exclamation marks in the rockery (a Victorian term now unfairly derided along with the 'shrubbery').

### PRUNING CONIFERS

Beyond initial care and training to maintain a healthy lead, no regular pruning is required for most conifers, although hedging varieties are, of course, trimmed to give a formal shape. When conifers are raised from seed or cuttings they tend to develop a single leader naturally, but any rivals should be removed and this process should be continued after planting out, spring being the best time for it. Laterals are retained, except for those low on the trunk; they will, in any case, die naturally but there is no harm done if they are cut off. As the tree grows larger, extra leaders may develop and grow close to the main leader without being

noticed: this is most common in the *Chamaecyparis* species and cultivars. In time they will be troublesome as they begin to grow outwards and are best removed, perhaps not an easy task. In the case of slender fastigiate trees such as *Cupressus sempervirens* the problem does not arise, a leader being naturally retained, but the Irish yew, *Taxus baccata* 'Fastigiata' (see p106), has upright growths which often need to be tied together. The best time for pruning conifers, if that becomes necessary because of irregular or excessive spread, is autumn or early winter. For all the dwarf conifers pruning is only needed to control spread or improve the outline. It can be carried out at any time, apart from during a prolonged frosty spell.

## CLIMBERS

All climbers have the urge to grow upwards, sooner or later needing the support of walls, pergolas, arbours, frames, pillars, trees or hedges. They differ, however, in how they climb:

1. By means of aerial roots which adhere to a surface – wall, timber, tree trunk branches and so on. Ivies are the most obvious example.
2. By means of tendrils which branch and end in small suckers, adhering as in Group 1. The prime example is *Parthenocissus* (Virginia creeper, Boston ivy).
3. By means of twining stems. Examples are *Wisteria* and *Lonicera* (honeysuckle).
4. By means of twining petioles. *Clematis* is a notable example.
5. By means of tendrils which are modified branch stems, arising opposite leaves and ending in spring-like coils which waft freely until they touch another object, which they then coil around. In this way,

The typical roots of
*Hedera helix* (ivy)

when repeated, the plant may reach a height of 1.8m (6ft). Examples are vines and garden peas, and among the weeds white bryony (Bryonia dioica).

All of these groups are true climbers. One more category is less convincing – the scrambler. This has long sinuous shoots often armed with thorns, which are able to attach the shoots firmly to other plants or to

*A border beneath a wall 3m (10ft) high. Trained against this wall are two spring-flowering* Ceanothus *and a* Clematis montana. *These plants need quite severe pruning once the flowers have faded. To their right in the picture is the evergreen shrub* Choisya ternata, *surprisingly hardy and also flowering in spring. It grows slowly and seldom needs pruning. In the foreground is the hardy perennial* Euphorbia characias *subsp.* wulfenii. *The stems which carry the flowers are cut away when the flowers fade*

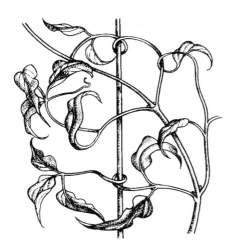

Another 'support' system:
twining petioles, most commonly seen in clematis

wires and trellis. Many of the roses and brambles fall into this category, as does *Clematis × jouiniana*. If cut back in winter it makes vigorous shoots, which spread along the ground unless given encouragement by being 'attached' to a neighbouring shrub, perhaps a climber such as one of the loniceras. Then it will rise to 1.8–2.4m (6–8ft). This hybrid plant (*C. vitalba × C. heracleifolia* var. *davidiana*) will spread over a stump and make ground cover. The flowers are white with blue shading.

## Supports

For wall climbers use coated wire stretched horizontally at 60cm (2ft) intervals and held by vine eyes driven into the wall, with straining bolts at one end to maintain tension. An alternative is trelliswork held

MAKING THE CUT — THE PRINCIPLES

Correct: cut
upwards to a
point 0.5cm (¼in)
above a bud

Cut too far from
bud and sloping
wrong way
(towards bud)

Cut too close
to the bud

Rough cut;
too far from
the bud

Cut sloping the
wrong way
(towards bud)

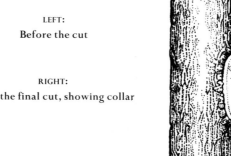

LEFT:
Before the cut

RIGHT:
After the final cut, showing collar

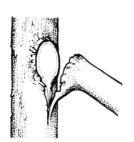

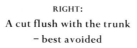

LEFT:
Effect of removing
a large limb with one cut

RIGHT:
A cut flush with the trunk
– best avoided

CORRECTING UNEVEN GROWTH

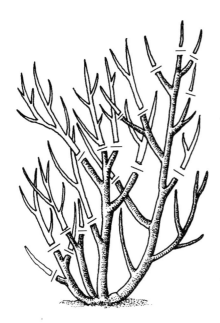

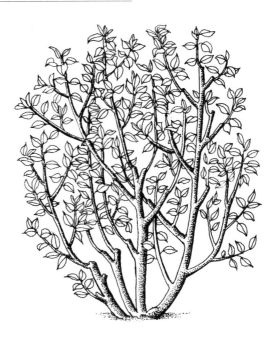

1 This shrub is overgrown on the right-hand side, undergrown on the left. The cure is to prune on the weaker side, to stimulate strong growth. The overgrown side should be pruned only lightly, if at all

2 The result: a nicely balanced shrub

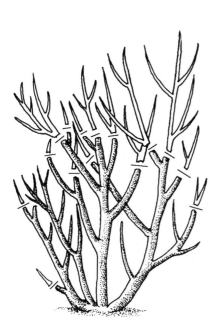

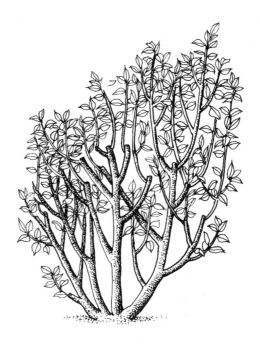

3 Here the shrub has been incorrectly pruned, by cutting back the overgrown side heavily

4 The result: an even more lop-sided shrub

---

### DECIDUOUS SHRUBS, TYPE A

Most evergreen shrubs will develop well if planted in the appropriate soil and will flower within a few years. The same is true of some deciduous shrubs, and nothing is gained by unnecessary pruning.

The following are good examples:

| | |
|---|---|
| *Aronia arbutifolia* | *Halimium* |
| *Berberis thunbergii* | *ocymoides* |
| *Chionanthus* | *Hydrangea* |
| *virginicus* | *quercifolia* |
| *Clethra*, all | *Ilex verticillata* |
| deciduous species | *Jasminum* |
| *Colutea arborescens* | *nudiflorum* |
| *Cornus mas,* | *Ligustrum quihoui* |
| *C. florida* | *Parrotia persica* |
| *Cotoneaster* | *Poncirus trifoliata* |
| *horizontalis* | *Prunus mume,* |
| *Euonymus* | *P. tenella* |
| *europaeus* | *Rhus typhina* |
| *Fothergilla major* | *Salix hastata* |
| *Genista tenera* | 'Wehrhahnii' |
| *Halesia carolina* | |

5–7.5cm (2–3in) from the wall surface. An expensive system is the use of square-headed nails with lead tags which lightly hold the plant stems.

### Planting

Most climbers should be planted at least 30cm (12in) from a wall, as the soil close to it dries out easily.

### CLIMBERS AS GROUND COVER

Some climbers trail on the ground as readily as they hoist themselves upwards, but others may be too rampant to be used in this way. The common ivy, *Hedera helix*, will need frequent trimming at busy times of the year. Its cultivar 'Sagittifolia' is neat and relatively slow-growing, and will need only annual clipping in spring. *Hedera colchica* is rather more vigorous and has leaves 20cm (8in) long, dark green and sombre in a well-planned garden with trees which will slow the ivy's growth. In a more open position between shrubs *Schizophragma hydrangeoides* or the larger *S. integrifolium* makes a dense carpet of good green foliage with flowerheads of creamy white in early summer. Extension growths can be cut back in the dormant period, avoiding the buds of the coming year's flowers. *Clematis × jouiniana*, already mentioned as a scrambling climber, bears white flowers in partial shade from late summer for several weeks.

---

### DECIDUOUS SHRUBS, TYPE B

**These plants produce extension growth from branches, but not from the base, so preparing a framework for further development. Once this framework has been achieved, little regular pruning is needed**

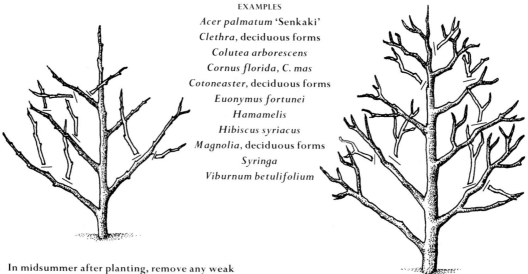

EXAMPLES
*Acer palmatum* 'Senkaki'
*Clethra*, deciduous forms
*Colutea arborescens*
*Cornus florida, C. mas*
*Cotoneaster*, deciduous forms
*Euonymus fortunei*
*Hamamelis*
*Hibiscus syriacus*
*Magnolia*, deciduous forms
*Syringa*
*Viburnum betulifolium*

1  In midsummer after planting, remove any weak and crossing branches, and those growing inwards. Pruning at this time allows for complete healing before winter

2  In future years minimal pruning is required: simply remove any dead, damaged or diseased growth

## DECIDUOUS SHRUBS, TYPE C

These mostly vigorous plants flower on wood of the previous year,
either on laterals or small shoots of the branches themselves. They require regular
pruning to maintain the production of flowering wood on a compact shrub

EXAMPLES
*Cytisus scoparius* and cultivars
*Deutzia*
*Forsythia*
*Hydrangea macrophylla*
(delay pruning until spring, see p65)
*Kolkwitzia amabilis*
*Philadelphus*
*Ribes sanguineum*
*Stephanandra*
*Tamarix*, spring-flowering forms

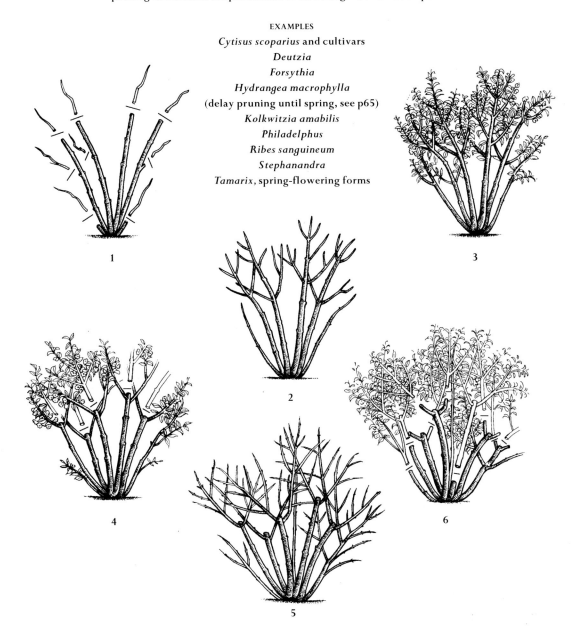

1 A typical three-year-old shrub at planting time.
  Remove weak shoots, prune strong stems by 15cm
  (6in)
2 By autumn of the first year, stems have grown well
  and laterals have formed
3 In the second year, moderate flowering occurs in
  early summer

4 Immediately after flowering, cut back the main
  stems which carried the flowers to strong young
  growth or buds
5 By autumn the young shoots have grown well.
  Mulch in winter
6 Repeat pruning after flowering in the following and
  subsequent years

## DECIDUOUS SHRUBS, TYPE D

These generally less vigorous plants bear flowers on the current year's growth. Regular pruning is required in spring to prevent a build-up of bare wood at the base of the plant

EXAMPLES

*Caryopteris × clandonensis*
*Ceanothus*, deciduous forms
*Spartium junceum*

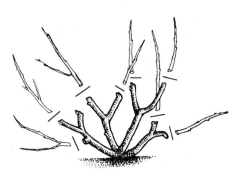

1 In the first year shorten main shoots by 2.5–5cm (1–2in) in early spring

2 Strong shoots bear the flowers in late summer

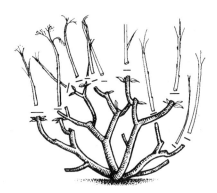

3 In the following spring the previous year's growth is cut back by one-half of its length. All weak growth is removed and in subsequent years all wood produced in the previous year is cut back to two buds

## DECIDUOUS SHRUBS, TYPE E

These vigorous plants produce a woody framework and flower on the current year's growth. They are pruned regularly to ensure a reasonably compact habit with flowers produced at a level where they can be appreciated

EXAMPLES

*Buddleja davidii*          *Sambucus nigra* 'Guincho
*Cornus*, many                  Purple'
*Cotinus coggygria*

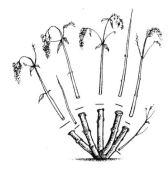

1 In early spring cut all healthy shoots back to 30cm (12in). Discard others

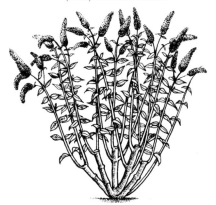

2 By summer the shrub will have doubled in size, and flowers are borne at the end of shoots

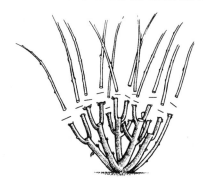

3 In late winter cut all shoots back to 30cm (12in) as before. Repeat annually, manuring well in spring

## DECIDUOUS SHRUBS, TYPE F

These plants flower on the previous year's wood and produce nearly all their new growth from ground level. They must be pruned to the ground regularly to prevent the build-up of old, flowered wood

EXAMPLES

*Kerria japonica*

*Spiraea × arguta*

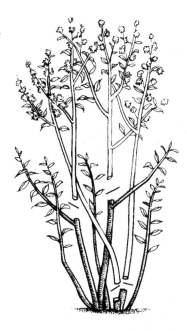

1  A young shrub at planting. Remove any weak stems; otherwise, do not prune

2  After flowering, cut all shoots to the base, except for one or two which have produced strong laterals

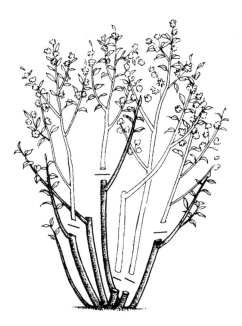

3  This pruning routine is repeated in subsequent years

## DECIDUOUS SHRUBS, TYPE G

These flower on the current year's growth but do not produce a woody framework. These shrubs often suffer winter damage and pruning is aimed at removing dead wood in spring

EXAMPLES
*Ceratostigma willmotianum*
*Dorycnium hirsutum*
*Fuchsias*, hardy
*Leycesteria formosa*
*Perovskia atriplicifolia*

1 In the spring after planting, cut back to one or two buds

2 The plant will flower in late summer to autumn

3 Prune again to two buds each spring. Leaving the shrub unpruned leads to weak stems and no flowers within a year or two

## DECIDUOUS SHRUBS, TYPE H

These plants are grown for their decorative young stems or leaves, or both. Pruning is aimed at producing these rather than allowing mature growths to form

1 After planting, cut back in early spring almost to ground level

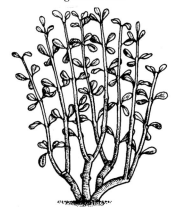

2 New growth creates a shrub to 1m (3ft) with good foliage

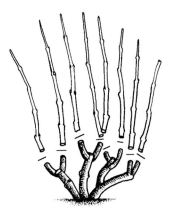

3 After leaf fall the stems remain attractive throughout winter. Repeat first-year pruning in early spring each year

## EVERGREEN SHRUBS

These do not need systematic pruning, provided sufficient space has been allotted for the mature plant. Growths which protrude from the plant in isolation should be removed in spring

EXAMPLES
*Arbutus andrachnoides*
*Artemisia*
*Berberis darwinii*
*Bupleurum fruticosum*
*Camellia*
*Cotoneaster lacteus*
*Daphne burkwoodii*
*Escallonia rubra* 'Apple
Blossom'
*Hebe*, many
*Hypericum kouytchense*
*Mahonia*, most
*Olearia macrodonta*
*Pieris formosa* 'Wakehurst'
*Rhododendron*, many
*Sarcococca*

1

2

3

## POLLARDING

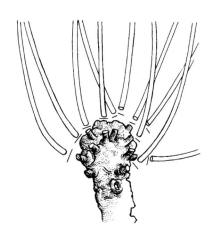

Plants of Type H may, alternatively, be pollarded by cutting back the year's growth by half rather than to ground level. This can be repeated for several years and will build up a woody base, from which new growths will arise and these may be cut back to their origin in early spring. Manuring is desirable, as this process eventually exhausts a plant which is not fed

1  A young camellia with failing leader. In the first spring, cut it back to a healthy bud. Apply a lime-free mulch
2  By summer there has been considerable improvement all over. Train in the new leader
3  A young plant with a rival leader. Cut it back in spring

# A–Z OF
# Trees & Shrubs

*Abbreviations:*
*(CL) – climber    (CO) – conifer    (D) – deciduous*
*(E) – evergreen    (S/E) – semi-evergreen*

### ABELIA × GRANDIFLORA (*Caprifoliaceae*) (S/E)

This shrub grows to 1–1.8m (3–6ft) high with arching branches and shining dark green leaves. The flowers are white, tinged pink, and produced from midsummer, often continuing until autumn. It is hardy in all but the severest winters and will grow to 3m (10ft) in the shelter of a wall. None of the species is better or as hardy as this garden-raised hybrid.

**Pruning**  No regular pruning required. The flowers are carried on wood of the current year and some shoots may be shortened after flowering, with some of the oldest wood removed.

### ABELIOPHYLLUM DISTICHUM (*Oleaceae*) (D)

Although hardy, this open shrub reaching 1.2m (4ft) is best grown against a south-facing wall to protect the fragrant, white, star-shaped flowers which appear in late winter before the leaves.

**Pruning**  Strong shoots develop to 3m (10ft) in height and are tied to supports. The laterals are allowed to remain and about one-third are cut back to 45cm (18in) after flowering to maintain vigorous growth. If the lower branches are allowed to touch the ground they will root easily, and should be removed to prevent them competing with the parent plant.

### ABIES (*Pinaceae*) (CO, E)

A genus of mostly tall conifers with usually soft needles and upright cones.

*A. grandis* (giant fir) would have to exceed 45m (150ft) to excite comment. Moderately lime-tolerant, it does best with heavy rainfall but good drainage.

*A. nordmanniana* (Caucasian fir) is a very handsome and robust tree, often exceeding 30m (100ft). It needs high rainfall but is lime-tolerant. The dwarf cultivar 'Golden Spreader', height and spread 90cm (3ft), is almost prostrate and has the dense foliage of its parent but coloured gold, reliably keeping a low profile.

*A. pinsapo* (Spanish fir) is a very good-looking tree that succeeds in dry areas and tolerates lime. The rigid dark green leaves radiate all round the branchlets and trees over 24m (80ft) are not rare.

*A. procera* is a great tree which does well in moist chalk-free soils. The cones are up to 25cm (10in) long, rich brown-purple in colour.

**Pruning**  No regular pruning required. A strong leader contributes greatly to the appearance of these conifers, but if damage occurs a new leader should be trained in to replace it. The lower branches should be retained if possible, but any that are seriously dying back can be cut back to the trunk.

### ABUTILON (*Malvaceae*) (D, E, S/E)

Grown for their attractive flowers and foliage, these shrubs do best in a sheltered position and in fertile well-drained soil.

*A. megapotamicum* is an evergreen that needs a south-facing wall, where it will grow to 1.8m (6ft). The flowers appear from late spring for several months; the calyx is red and the corolla yellow, an unhappy combination in this case not improved in the form with variegated leaves.

*A. × suntense* is deciduous and vigorous with abundant deep mauve flowers in spring.

*A. × vitifolium* is also deciduous and is best grown in the shelter of a wall, where it will reach 2.4m (8ft), producing mauve-lavender flowers for at least two months. *A. × v.* 'Album' is an attractive white form.

**Pruning**  Abutilons usually have a short life, sometimes dying for no obvious reason, but removing spent flowerheads can help. Shoots of *A. megapotamicum* damaged by frost should be cut back to live wood in spring. *A. × suntense* should be dead-headed and cut back after flowering. If the height is as intended no pruning of the leader is required, but laterals are reduced to 30cm (12in). If the plant has grown too tall, reduce the leader to the appropriate level; laterals should be reduced as before. It is best grown in the shelter of a wall. Pruning of *A. × vitifolium* is the same. Abutilons are easily propagated from cuttings.

## ACCA SELLOWIANA (formerly FEIJOA SELLOWIANA) (*Myrtaceae*) (E)

A large bushy shrub up to 3m (10ft), needing shelter near, but not too close to, a wall. The leaves are greyish-green with white undersides, the large flowers crimson and white, sometimes followed by edible fruits.
**Pruning** If pruned back directly after flowering each year it will build up a firm structure.

## ACER (*Aceraceae*) (D)

A very large genus of trees and shrubs, of which only a few can be included here. It is said that maples are very easily cultivated, and some are, but it is clear that a few are reluctant to develop in soils which suit most other plants. It seems that many species produce their best autumn colours on soils that are neutral to acid, although very few maples actually need lime-free soil.
*Acer campestre* (common field maple) is a fine tree, sometimes over 16m (50ft) high, but also serves as a hedge (see Hedges & Topiary). There is usually no difficulty in training a leader and producing a leg of 3m (10ft). The branching tends to be close and this need not be discouraged except in the case of erect shoots towards the end of a branch.
*A. forrestii* has striated bark, revealed by creating a leg of 1.8–2.4m (6–8ft). The young stems are coral red. This tree is almost certainly lime-hating.
*A. griseum* is a small tree occasionally reaching 12m (40ft), with bark which peels to reveal the cinnamon-coloured underbark. The leaves have three leaflets which colour red and scarlet in autumn. It is a most handsome tree, slow of growth and eminently suited to modest gardens. It seems to tolerate any good soil and is hardy.
*A. japonicum* forms a bushy tree or shrub reaching 10m (30ft). It is favoured for its cultivars, especially 'Vitifolium' with large leaves which produce autumn colours of purple, crimson, scarlet and orange.
*A. negundo* (box elder) is a fast-growing tree 15m (50ft) high, most often seen in one of its variegated forms.
*A. palmatum* is a small, round-headed tree reaching 6m (20ft) which has given rise to a large number of clones and cultivars, the best-known being the Dissectum group, of which the outstanding member is 'Senkaki', the coral bark maple. All the younger branches of this are coral red, and the deeply cut leaves are pale green turning to yellow in autumn.
*A. pensylvanicum* (moose wood) is a small tree, 6m (20ft) high, with brown bark striped with white lines. The cultivar 'Erythrocladum' is even more striking, with young shoots shrimp-pink in winter.
*A. platanoides* is immensely vigorous, reaching 25m (82ft) and not suitable for gardens under 4ha (10 acres), but the cultivar 'Drummondii' with white variegation of the leaves is so handsome that it would justify the loss of half a hectare or so.
*A. saccharinum* is very vigorous, reaching 25m (80ft), and very beautiful, not too common a combination. The bark is grey and gave it the name silver maple. It has five-lobed leaves and, following a mild winter, it produces yellow flowers in early spring. The only fault is some brittleness of the wood, not important when it is grown in an open space. As a rule, it makes a well-shaped crown without any training.
**Pruning** No regular pruning required. Pruning of maples follows the general indications and there are few specific requirements. One should be prepared for the possibility of 'bleeding' if pruning is undertaken early in the growing season, which may be taken to start in early to midwinter. The best time to undertake any pruning is late summer and early autumn. In some of the trees it is desirable to produce a leg which will display the bark, as has been noted for *A. forrestii* and *A. campestre*. The latter of these two sometimes produces upright shoots near the ends of the branches and these should be removed. The variegated forms of *A. negundo* are likely to produce green-leaved shoots if pruned and these should be removed at once, although they are likely to recur. Don't give up.

## ACTINIDIA (*Actinidiaceae*) (CL, D)

These vigorous and attractive twining climbers are suitable for growing on walls and pergolas.
*A. chinensis* is hardy and very vigorous, with a height and spread of 7.5m (25ft). The shoots are covered with red hairs, as are the veins and stalks of the leaves, and the flowers are white ageing buff in summer. Edible fruits may be produced. It is best (that is to say most orderly) against a wall.
*A. kolomikta* appeals to many but few have the conditions to suit it: a sheltered wall 4.5m (15ft) high by 6m (20ft) long. The foliage starts more or less purple, then develops a variegation, white on pink with some green. This lasts from late mid-spring until midsummer, when the leaves become dull green. Train it

LEFT *Abutilon × suntense*. A very successful, vigorous hybrid with the dark mauve flowers produced freely. Lateral growths are shortened by half in spring

RIGHT *Acer platanoides* 'Drummondii' is an elegant tree which develops a broad, spreading head over time. The leaves are margined with cream; occasional branches reverting to green should be removed

to cover the space. Later just cut back shoots which come forward.

**Pruning** Old shoots of *A. chinensis* can be replaced by young growth from low down in winter, though not after midwinter as the sap rises early and there is a risk of bleeding. Any growths of *A. kolomikta* that come forward can be pinched back to 15cm (6in) during the growing season to keep the plant tidy and compact.

### AESCULUS (*Hippocastanaceae*)
#### Horse chestnut, Buckeye (D)

Hardy trees or shrubs, all having compound palmate leaves and upright panicles of flowers. They do well in any good soil and transplant easily.

*A. × carnea* (red horse chestnut) is most often seen now as the cultivar 'Briotii' with red flowers in late spring and early summer. It branches low down, but ample space should be allowed for the effect to be seen. It can reach 9–12m (30–40ft) with a leg of 3m (10ft), provided the leader is maintained. This chestnut is apt to develop burrs on the trunk and main branches. Its nature is uncertain but often healing keeps pace with its development and only leaves an unsightly swelling.

*A. hippocastanum* (horse chestnut) is the most beautiful of large flowering trees, with panicles of white flowers, blotched red at the base, freely produced in late spring. Since it can grow to over 15m (50ft) tall, it should only be planted in gardens of not less than 0.2ha (½ acre). When mature, it makes a very large tree with heavy branches. In towns it is a target for collectors of 'conkers' in autumn, and they will stop at nothing.

*A. indica* produces white flowers tinged pale pink in early to midsummer and becomes a very large and graceful tree, up to 20m (70ft), with no problems, and that includes pruning.

*A. parviflora* grows to 2.4m (8ft) high but spreads widely and produces suckers. They help to produce a clump which looks splendid in midsummer, as may be seen at Westonbirt Arboretum in Gloucestershire. The flowers are white with pale pink stamens.

**Pruning** No regular pruning required. In mature specimens of *A. hippocastanum* the heavy branches are wide spreading, sometimes with a downward sweep, and to produce a well-shaped tree a central leader must be maintained from the nursery stage, with any rivals removed. As the tree grows there is a tendency to produce upright limbs from the laterals and these should be cut away if possible. Longitudinal cracks on the bark are a cause for concern but often they are due to rapid enlargement of the trunk and heal quite quickly. All in all, the horse chestnut maintains good health for many years without much attention. *A. parviflora* can be thinned out by removal of some of the oldest shoots in late winter, and its spread can be limited if it outgrows its allotted space.

### AILANTHUS ALTISSIMA (*Simaroubiaceae*)
#### Tree of heaven (D)

This hardy spreading tree is very common in London gardens because it is very tolerant of atmospheric pollution. Large clusters of small green flowers are produced in midsummer, followed by winged fruits on female trees.

**Pruning** If unpruned it can reach 25m (80ft), but it can be useful in small gardens if cut to the ground each spring. The emerging buds are reduced to two or three and produce handsome ash-like leaves 90cm (3ft) long that give an almost tropical effect.

AKEBIA QUINATA (*Lardizabalaceae*)
(CL, D, S/E)

A very vigorous twiner to 10m (30ft) or more, retaining most of its leaves in sheltered places. The vanilla-scented brown-purple flowers are produced in late spring, but the sausage-shaped fruits are rare in Britain. Though it is often recommended for scrambling into a tree it can be a nuisance, as the long shoots multiply and disfigure the tree if it is alive but hardly conceal it if it is dead. A wall can provide a sound support and the shoots can be allowed to fall forward from a coated wire at 1.8m (6ft) above the ground.

**Pruning** This involves shortening the sound growth and removing that which is weak or dead in winter or early spring.

ALNUS (*Betulaceae*) (D)

An unfairly neglected genus including several first-rate trees and shrubs, all hardy, healthy and undemanding plants that will enhance any garden of medium or greater size. The leaves are alternate, often toothed, with male and female flowers borne on the same plant. The fact that alders flourish in wet land of very little value may give them a poor reputation but they include some great trees and worthy shrubs. *A. cordata* (Italian alder) prefers a good soil and tolerates alkaline conditions. It is fast-growing and reaches 21m (70ft) in time.

*A. glutinosa* (common alder) is a waterside tree to 25m (80ft) with purple to deep yellow catkins in late winter. It is tolerant of alkaline conditions.

*A. incana* (grey alder) is remarkably vigorous, up to 15m (50ft) and completely hardy. The male catkins are 10cm (4in) long in late winter and very pretty. The cultivar 'Aurea' has red-yellow young wood, striking all through winter.

*A. maximowiczii* is a large shrub, growing to over 3m (10ft) high, with prominent fat yellow catkins in late spring.

**Pruning** No regular pruning required. These large species form pyramidal outlines with a definite lead and, when mature, can be enhanced by the trunk being cleared, say to a height of 1.5m (5ft). *A. glutinosa* will make a big tree with a fine bark but is seldom allowed to do so. Sadly but understandably, some river authorities cut it to the ground every few years.

AMELANCHIER (*Rosaceae*) Snowy mespilus (D)

A genus of hardy trees and shrubs with white, star-shaped flowers borne in spring and bright autumn foliage. Can be grown in sun or light shade, and in any good, moisture-retentive soil.

*A. canadensis*, *A. laevis* and *A. lamarckii* are often confused with each other in cultivation, but *A. canadensis* has a more suckering habit. All three can reach 6m (20ft).

**Pruning** *A. canadensis* is a suckering shrub and the oldest stems are cut away in winter. *A. laevis* and *A. lamarckii* can be trained to tree form by reducing the side shoots in spring.

AMORPHA FRUTICOSA (*Leguminosae*)
False indigo (D)

A deciduous shrub reaching 90cm (3ft) for a sunny position and well-drained soil, with pinnate leaves and racemes of small, violet-blue, pea-like flowers in midsummer.

**Pruning** No regular pruning required. A woody framework of branches is gradually formed with flowers being borne on the current season's growth. Some branches can be cut out in spring and will be replaced by the new growth from the base.

AMPELOPSIS (*Vitaceae*) (CL, D)

A genus of vigorous climbers with attractive foliage, suitable for growing in a sheltered position.

*A. brevipedunculata* climbs by tendrils. It is valued for its blue fruits and handsome leaves and should be planted on a south-facing wall. Growth is rapid and extensive, covering a large area to a height of 4.6m (15ft) or more.

*A. megalophylla* has leaves of 60 × 45cm (2 × 1½ft) and, although rather slow growing, will eventually reach over 6m (20ft).

**Pruning** A sufficient number of shoots is tied in, the rest being sacrificed and cut back to two buds in winter (not after midwinter as the sap rises early).

ANDROMEDA POLIFOLIA (*Rosaceae*)
Bog rosemary (E)

A hardy shrub 30cm (12in) high with narrow, glossy, mid-green leaves, white beneath, and terminal clusters of pink flowers in late spring. Needs a damp, acid soil.

**Pruning** No pruning needed, but semi-hardwood cuttings can be taken in autumn.

ANTHYLLIS HERMANNIAE (*Leguminosae*) (D)

A small, deciduous shrub, not more than 60cm (2ft) high, with crooked branches, having grey leaves and abundant yellow pea-like flowers in early summer. It needs a sunny position and is particularly suited to rock gardens.

**Pruning** Young plants are compact in habit, but can become looser with maturity. Discreet cutting back by about half after flowering will help maintain a well-shaped shrub.

ARALIA ELATA (*Araliaceae*)
Japanese angelica tree (D)

A deciduous shrub or tree with dark green, compound, tropical-looking leaves and small, off-white flowers in panicles over 30cm (12in) long. The strongest growth is achieved on light, well-drained soil. More or less hardy in most northerly areas, it is remarkable in Cornwall (south-west England), where the branches spread 6m (20ft) or more on a tree 9m (30ft) high.

**Pruning** If given plenty of space and good conditions, *A. elata* branches freely to become a large, crooked shrub or occasionally tree of character, which is best left unpruned. However, suckers often form and should be removed.

ARAUCARIA ARAUCANA (*Araucariaceae*)
Monkey puzzle (CO, E)

This large, hardy tree is unmistakable, with its long curving branches densely clothed with overlapping, dark green, scale-like leaves and large, globular cones. Eventually reaching over 15m (50ft), it is suitable only for large gardens where it can be grown as a specimen tree, and requires a moist, loamy soil.

**Pruning** No regular pruning required. If the central leader is damaged, new growth will be produced and can be trained in to replace it. Dead and damaged branches detract greatly from the appearance of this tree, and should be removed at the main trunk, although this is an unpleasant task because the leaves are tipped with spines.

ARBUTUS (*Ericaceae*) (E)

A genus of small trees with ornamental bark, panicles of white urn-shaped flowers and strawberry-like fruits. Most require acid soil.

*A. × andrachnoides*, including many plants sold as *A. andrachne*, is most desirable. Not requiring acid soil, it shows tenderness only in severe winters. Growth is quite fast up to 6m (20ft) and it should be allowed plenty of space to show the ruddy-brown bark and the flowers produced in late autumn and winter.

*A. menziesii* is only hardy in southern Britain and is extremely calcifuge. It flowers in late spring and should be trained with a clear trunk.

*A. unedo*, STRAWBERRY TREE, is a small tree which does well in south-west Britain and Ireland, to which it is native. Withstanding gales, it needs no pruning.

**Pruning** No regular pruning required. *A. × andrachnoides* and *A. unedo* require only the removal of dead shoots at the centre which hide the bark. Wood damaged by frost or storm may be cut out completely once new growth has started; all species regenerate freely and the new growth is obvious.

ARCTOSTAPHYLOS UVA-URSI (*Ericaceae*)
Bearberry (E)

One of a genus of evergreen prostrate shrubs which must have acid soil, this is the species most frequently grown in Britain and is particularly suited to a shady soil. It is useful for ground cover, with a height of 10cm (4in), and has plentiful green foliage and small pinkish flowers from early spring, followed by red fruits.

**Pruning** No regular pruning required. If it encroaches on neighbouring plants individual shoots may be removed with secateurs to preserve an informal appearance, rather than trimming the plant back with shears.

ARISTOLOCHIA DURIOR (*Aristolochiaceae*)
(CL, D)

A vigorous deciduous climber which needs a warm site but is suited to wall, pergola or pillar where it will reach 6m (20ft) or more. The leaves are 12.5–25cm (5–10in) long, and almost as wide. The early summer flowers are solitary, tubular, bent in the lower half like a syphon, and yellowish-green, with the mouth purple.

**Pruning** After flowering, thin out shoots and remove any that are wayward.

ARONIA (*Rosaceae*) (D)

Attractive, hardy shrubs related to *Sorbus*. They should be grown in full sun for the best autumn leaf colour to be produced.

*A. arbutifolia* (red chokeberry) is a vigorous shrub 1.5–3m (5–10ft) high. The leaves are narrowly obovate, toothed, dark green above, the lower surface covered by a white felt. White flowers appear in late spring and are followed by bright red fruits, then the leaves turn brilliant red until they fall.

*A. melanocarpa* (black chokeberry) is a small shrub, about 2.1 (7ft) high, with white flowers in spring, followed by black fruits.

**Pruning** These shrubs produce shoots from the base when well manured and, when necessary, old growth can be cut away entirely after the autumn display of foliage and fruits is over, although this may be as late as midwinter. They do not readily tolerate chalk in the soil although they do best in a well-drained site.

ARTEMISIA (*Compositae*) (E, S/E)

The shrubby species of this large genus are grown for their attractive, feathery, silver-grey foliage and are best grown in well-drained soil in a sunny position.

*A. abrotanum* is a hardy, long-lived, upright shrub which reaches 0.6–1.2m (2–4ft) and has sweetly aromatic, finely divided leaves.

*A. arborescens* is tender but has choice silver leaves and is worth risking in front of a wall. The cultivar 'Faith Raven' is hardier and a better plant.

*A. tridentata* (now known as *Seriphidium tridentatum*) (sagebrush) has silvery-grey leaves which give out a pleasant aroma even after a shower of rain. Reaching over 1.5m (5ft), it is fairly hardy.

**Pruning** To prevent mature plants becoming woody and bare at the base, and to remove any frost-damaged shoots, they should be cut back hard every spring, just as the new growth starts to appear.

### ATRIPLEX (*Chenopodiaceae*) (E, S/E)

Foliage plants, well suited to coastal areas in full sun and well-drained soil.

*A. canescens* is an evergreen growing to 1.2m (4ft) or rather more. The flowers are yellow and very small, borne in midsummer. The grey leaves are pleasant.

*A. halimus* (tree purslane) is a 1.8m (6ft) bushy shrub with 5cm (2in) long leaves, silvery and of excellent appearance. The flowers are negligible, often absent.

**Pruning** No regular pruning required. *A. canescens* tends to sprawl, especially in rich soil, and may be trimmed in spring to produce a regular shape. *A. halimus* is sometimes scorched by frost, but recovers in spring. Damaged growth tips can be cut back in spring, just as the new growth starts to appear.

### AUCUBA JAPONICA (*Cornaceae*) (E)

The green-leaved form of this strongly growing, large-leaved shrub, 1.8–3.7m (6–12ft) tall, is less common than the yellow-spotted 'Variegata'. The female plants of the former produce scarlet berries, but not regularly. Even without them, the green-leaved form is more stylish and worth a place in the garden. Both forms are hardy and endure the most unfavourable conditions of shade and competition.

**Pruning** No regular pruning required. Dead wood remains on the bush indefinitely without causing any ill effect other than ugliness. Removal with a Grecian saw is easy, and the informal shape is best preserved by cutting out whole growths to the base rather than removing small branches.

### AZARA (*Flacourtiaceae*) (E)

These bushy, strong-growing shrubs or small trees, up to 6m (20ft) tall, are best grown against a sunny wall except in the mildest areas.

*A. lanceolata* is moderately hardy and, after a hot summer, produces a spectacular display of yellow flowers in spring, small but crowded in corymbs.

*A. microphylla* is hardier, with small dark leaves with vanilla-scented yellow flowers in early spring.

**Pruning** No regular pruning required. Shoots that

**ABOVE** As this picture suggests, *Ampelopsis brevipendunculata* is a very vigorous climber, making a dense mat of lobed foliage. The main attraction is the colour of the fruits which is deep blue, but these only make a display if the plant is exposed to full sun and the summer is hot. Long, untidy shoots have to be removed throughout the summer and in early winter the whole plant is cut back to two or three buds on the strongest stems

**RIGHT** *Berberis thunbergii* 'Rose Glow' is a striking shrub, its young leaves being purple mottled with pink. Later in the summer the leaves become deep purple

have been damaged during winter can be removed once all danger of frost is past.

### BERBERIDOPSIS CORALLINA (*Flacourtiaceae*) (CL, E)

An evergreen climber twining to 6m (20ft). The leaves are ovate with spiny teeth, dark green above, glaucous beneath. The deep crimson flowers are borne in terminal racemes in midsummer, continuing for two months. It is not an easy plant to grow: it is not very hardy, needs a rich, moist loam and is intolerant of alkaline soil. It is best sited on the north side of a 1.8m (6ft) wall, protected from north and east winds.

**Pruning** Pruning is seldom necessary beyond shortening weak shoots in spring.

BERBERIS (*Berberidaceae*) (D, E, S/E)

These popular and easily grown shrubs illustrate the importance of finding out the height and spread to be expected of a plant before deciding to put it in the garden. There are dwarf berberis less than 90cm (3ft) high, others which reach 2.4m (8ft) high or more but remain neat, and some less high but which arch widely.

*B. darwinii* This 2.4–3m (8–10ft) plant is among the evergreens and is very hardy, flourishing in any good soil, including chalk, and producing a fine show of orange flowers in late spring, followed by luminous blue fruits. What more can one ask of any shrub?

*B. dictyophylla.* Of the deciduous shrubs, this 2.1m (7ft) species attracts by its slender branches, covered in their first year by a white bloom. The flowers are pale yellow, the fruits red. It is not perfectly hardy, and should be put in a sheltered place.

*B. linearifolia* is perhaps even better, reaching 2.1m (7ft), also evergreen with flowers of a more refined colour, and is equally hardy.

*B.* × *rubrostilla* is notable for abundant coral-coloured fruits. It is deciduous, a hybrid of *B. wilsoniae*, and probably *B. aggregata*.

*B.* × *stenophylla* makes a dense evergreen bush 2.4m (8ft) tall from which emerge arching stems covered with golden-yellow flowers.

*B. temolaica*, another deciduous species, grows rather slowly to 2.4m (8ft) with glaucous pale green leaves and pale yellow flowers, not abundant. When fully grown it is a magnificent sight.

*B. thunbergii* is a deciduous shrub of dense habit reaching 2.4m (8ft). It is valued for the fine red colour of the leaves in autumn and the bright red berries, but in Britain neither of these is as striking as in the USA and its native Japan. The cultivar 'Rose Glow' is not as large as the type, and has purple leaves with pink and white variegation.

*B. verruculosa* is an evergreen notable for its tidy form, slowly reaching 1.5m (5ft) high and 1.2m (4ft) across.

*B. wilsoniae* reaches 1.2m (4ft) high, rather more across. The flowers and fruits are abundant and the deciduous leaves colour well before they are shed in autumn, in tints too difficult to describe.

**Pruning** No regular pruning needed. Try to position plants so they will have ample space to achieve their natural habit of growth. Old stems can be removed at the base or cut back to healthy young growth, and straggly stems can be shortened to maintain the shape of the plant. Prune deciduous types in late winter and evergreens mostly after flowering. *B. darwinii* is admittedly rather untidy and needs some pruning. The temptation to do so after the flowers fade should be resisted if the fruits appeal. They will have disappeared by midsummer and any over-long shoots can then be cut back by two-thirds. On *B.* × *stenophylla* pruning can be carried out immediately after flowering (although the fruits will be sacrificed), preferably using secateurs and reducing long shoots by a half. *B. verruculosa* seldom needs any pruning, but with *B. dictyophylla* some of the older stems should be cut out each winter, followed by ample manuring.

BETULA (*Betulaceae*) Birch (D)

Deciduous trees and a few shrubs, nearly all of character and beauty, with attractive bark, male and female catkins borne on the same plant, and good autumn colour. Most need a good deep loam to thrive.

*B. albo-sinensis* makes a tree up to 15m (50ft) tall and has a trunk of bright orange to orange-red. *B. a.* var. *septentrionalis* was described by Wilson, who collected it in China, as having 'Bark orange-brown or orange to yellowish-orange or orange-grey . . . singularly beautiful'. The beauty is often marred somewhat by the old bark persisting on the tree.

*B. alleghaniensis* (formerly *B. lutea*), often a multi-stemmed tree 12m (40ft) tall, has shining amber-coloured bark with leaves turning rich yellow in autumn.

*B. lenta* (cherrybirch) with its smooth reddish-brown trunk and aromatic young bark does not make a tall tree in Britain, although in its native country it can reach 25m (82ft).

*B. maximowicziana* is very vigorous and makes a wide crown on a tree 18m (60ft) tall. The trunk is orange-brown becoming grey. The large leaves colour well in autumn.

*B. medwediewii* makes a large shrub over 3m (10ft) tall with stout branches and large terminal buds. Good autumn colour.

*B. papyrifera* (paper birch) does well in Britain, reaching 6–9m (20–30ft). It has clean white bark and good autumn colour.

*B. pendula* (common silver birch) can be 18–21m (60–70ft) tall under good conditions, but will also tolerate thin sandy soil. It is one of the best birches, particularly in its graceful outline. The cultivar 'Laciniata' (Swedish birch) with drooping shoots and cut leaves is nearly as good.

*B. utilis* (Himalayan birch) is a tree reaching 18m (60ft) with paper-thin orange or copper-brown peeling bark.

**Pruning** No regular pruning required. In specimens that are to become trees, it is important to maintain the leader and, if it is broken in the early stages, the replacement should be the strongest growing shoot, at whatever level it is situated. Any pruning necessary for birches should be carried out in autumn, as in spring there is a tendency for bleeding to occur. 'Witches' brooms', dense masses of twiggy shoots caused by fungal infection, are seen mostly on *B. pendula*. Their exact nature is obscure but they may be present and multiply for years without affecting the health of the tree.

### BROUSSONETIA PAPYRIFERA (*Moraceae*) (D)

Makes a round-headed tree about 10m (30ft) tall and is notable for the variable outline of the leaves, both in size and form. On young trees no two leaves may be identical but the difference becomes less obvious as the tree matures. The male tree bears catkins up to 7.5cm (3in) long, and the female tree has orange-red fruits.

**Pruning** Branches often grow low down and may need removing, or can be allowed to extend, according to the space available.

### BUDDLEJA (*Loganiaceae*) (D)

Medium to large shrubs, a few making small trees. They all like good soil but survive in a feeble state in rough ground. For the gardener they may be classified according to flowering pattern.

**1.** Those which flower mainly on wood of the previous year; the best-known is *B. alternifolia*, which produces arching stems bearing flowers freely in early summer.

**Pruning** These stems are cut back after flowering to new growth, which by then is appearing.

**2.** Those which flower at the end of shoots produced in the current year, including *B. davidii* and its many cultivars.

**Pruning** The shoots are left after flowering until late winter, when all are cut back to 30cm (12in). They can be relied on to produce a symmetrical arching bush each year, but must be well manured after pruning.

**3.** Those which develop strong shoots in one year and flower in the next on buds which develop from these shoots. Such is *B. globosa*, an erect shrub with handsome leaves and, in early summer, globular flower heads.

**Pruning** In early spring, weak growths may be removed. It is tempting to do no pruning after flowering but the shrub can grow to 6m (20ft) and become gaunt. If that happens it must be cut back drastically, perhaps to 90cm (3ft) all over, with the loss of a year's flowering.

### BUPLEURUM FRUTICOSUM (E)

A woody, evergreen sub-shrub which can be grown in mild areas or with a little shelter. With its sea-green foliage and heads of tiny yellow flowers borne from midsummer to early autumn, it looks tender but does very well in exposed coastal positions, even making a good hedge. It will grow 2.4–2.7m (8–9ft) high and rather more across.

**Pruning** Prune in spring, cutting back all shoots to about 90cm (3ft). More drastic pruning will only produce longer and weaker growth. For hedging purposes, trim annually in late spring.

### BUXUS (*Buxaceae*) (E)

Mainly used for hedging and the edging of borders, and ideal for providing a foil to flowering plants, with neat bushy foliage and insignificant flowers.

*B. balearica* makes a tree of character with good bright green leaves. It bears shade, even quite dense, and will reach 6–9m (20–30ft).

*B. sempervirens* (common box) can reach a height of 6m (20ft) but is rarely allowed to do so, as it is too slow in growth to encourage its use as an ornamental tree.

*B. wallichiana* took 50 years to reach a height of about 1.8m (6ft) at the Royal Botanic Gardens, Kew and is rather tender, both somewhat discouraging features.

**Pruning** *B. balearica* should never need pruning as its habit is compact. *B. sempervirens* can be grown as a shrub, in which case no regular pruning is required, but hedges and topiary specimens must be clipped regularly in late summer (see also pp116, 124).

### CALLICARPA BODINIERI var. GIRALDII (*Verbenaceae*) (D)

An erect, deciduous, hardy shrub reaching 2.4–2.7m (8–9ft). It must have plenty of sun and a good soil. The flowers are diminutive and lilac-coloured, borne in midsummer, and followed by abundant small violet fruits. The plant has at first an upright growth, but shoots extending outward from the base become almost horizontal.

**Pruning** Any pruning to maintain shape is carried out in spring. If the plant seems to be failing and flowering poorly, cut it to 30cm (12in) from the ground in autumn and manure well. It should recover and flower well the next year.

### CALLISTEMON (*Myrtaceae*) (E)

Natives of Australia, these evergreen trees and shrubs flourish in Britain only in mild maritime climates and even there benefit from protection from the north and east.

*C. glaucus* (formerly *C. speciosus*) makes a large shrub or small tree to 4.6m (15ft) high. If given wall protection it should be planted 60–90cm (2–3ft) from the wall, as it has a rounded shape. It does not like chalky soil but otherwise needs only plenty of

An arch of *Ceanothus thyrsiflorus*, which is vigorous and hardy with evergreen leaves about 2.5cm (1in) long and pale blue flowers in late spring to early summer. It should be pruned immediately after flowering, cutting the flowered growth back to 2.5–5cm (1–2in) from the old wood, but not into it. The cultivar 'Cascade' is very similar

sunlight. The flowers are borne in spikes 15cm (6in) long, the stamens rich crimson. The fruit is a capsule firmly attached to the branch, able to persist for years. The growing point continues to extend beyond this and in the next year produces a stem, leaves and eventually another flowerhead.

**Pruning** No pruning needed, except for correcting the shape of the plant.

### CALLUNA VULGARIS (*Ericaceae*)
### Heather, ling (E)

This hardy evergreen bears small bell-shaped flowers in spikes 15–30cm (6–12in) long from midsummer to late autumn, in shades of white or pink to red or crimson in the many cultivars. Foliage colour varies from green, grey and yellow to the more startling orange and red. Growth is vigorous at first but in the end results in lengths of bare stem and hardly any leaf.

*Calluna vulgaris*: cut back by at least half in spring, but do not cut into old wood

**Pruning** Annual pruning in spring is very effective in maintaining a compact, bushy plant and consists of cutting back all shoots by at least one-half but avoiding the old wood, which does not readily break into leaf. Secateurs produce the best effect but if shears have to be used, try not to produce a smooth civilized surface, but something which looks natural. Meanwhile, cuttings should be taken from midsummer to mid-autumn to provide replacement plants when old age at last prevails.

### CALOCEDRUS DECURRENS (*Cupressaceae*)
### Incense cedar (CO, E)

Although in the wild this conifer forms a large tree with spreading branches, most cultivated specimens are narrowly columnar, eventually reaching up to 15m (50ft). The sprays of aromatic, scaly leaves are dark green in the species, but there are golden-leaved forms such as 'Aureovariegata' and 'Berrima Gold', and a dwarf form called 'Intricata'. With adequate light it

retains its foliage down to ground level, so it is best grown as an isolated specimen.

**Pruning** Older specimens may be damaged by pollution, losing foliage and dying back. Cut out the dead wood as soon as it appears, water well and feed in spring to encourage recovery.

CALYCANTHUS FLORIDUS (*Calycantheaceae*)
Carolina allspice (D)

A hardy, good-looking deciduous shrub up to 1.8m (6ft), with no special needs except for ample sunlight – not unknown in Carolina, but uncommon in Britain. The leaves are glossy dark green and the fragrant flowers, borne on young wood in early to midsummer, are reddish-purple and brown. The leaves, wood and even roots have the fragrance of camphor.

**Pruning** This shrub has a stooling habit and old branches cut down in spring will quickly be replaced by new growth from the base.

CAMELLIA (*Theaceae*) (E)

A huge genus of mostly hardy flowering shrubs and trees provoking a sometimes obsessive interest in many gardeners who have the conditions to grow them well, and envy to many who have not. The many hybrids of the popular *C. japonica* vary greatly in size, from 90cm (3ft) to 10m (30ft), in flower colour, most commonly red, pink or white, and flower shape, from single to double, and there are many other species and cultivars. They must have a moist, neutral to lime-free soil and do well at planting if given some peat or a substitute and leaf mould. The spring-flowering types require protection from frost, which damages the flower buds.

## DEAD-HEADING

Camellias share with rhododendrons the capacity to flower with abandon and produce a lot of seed. It is logical to dispose of any seed that is not needed for reproduction and thus spare the plant the output of energy required for its production. This is achieved by removing the flower heads as the blooms fade, a tedious task with large bushes – desirable, but not vital

**Pruning** No regular pruning needed. Stems that spoil the shape of the plant may be cut back in the dormant season except for *C. sasanqua* and other autumn-flowering kinds, for which spring is the right time. The object is to produce a dense texture, allowing branches which develop low down to grow. Some

plants, when young, flower very freely and may be partly disbudded. On the other hand a worn-out shrub, hardly flowering, may be pruned heavily, removing up to half the total plant by cutting back stems by half. With liberal feeding regeneration should occur quite rapidly. Young flower buds damaged by late frost are best left until the level at which live tissue begins is revealed. This can be decided by scratching a small area of bark: the underlying tissue is pale and juicy if alive, brown and dry if dead.

### CAMPSIS RADICANS (*Bignoniaceae*)
### Trumpet vine (CL, D)

A strong-growing climber, best against a sunny wall where it will cling with aerial roots to a height of 12m (40ft). The pinnate leaves are up to 38cm (15in) long and the flowers, borne in small clusters in midsummer, are trumpet-shaped, scarlet, yellow and orange.
**Pruning** The lateral growths should be cut to two or three buds in early spring to encourage flowering.

### CARAGANA ARBORESCENS (*Leguminosae*) (D)

This very hardy, shrubby tree up to 6m (20ft) is the easiest species to grow and has several interesting cultivars. The dark green pinnate leaves are spine-tipped and yellow pea-like flowers are produced in clusters in spring.
**Pruning** No regular pruning required. Young plants left alone for one season may, in the spring of the following year, be reduced by rather more than a half, to encourage the formation of laterals and build up a sturdy, shrubby plant. To form a tree, a leader is selected and maintained in the usual way (see p13) with suckering and lower growths removed. Dead wood can be cut out in spring.

### CARPENTERIA CALIFORNICA (*Hydrangaceae*) (E)

In southern England this shrub is hardy when grown near a south- or west-facing wall, preferably 60–90cm (2–3ft) from it to allow the formation of a bush some 3m (10ft) high. The large, fragrant white flowers with golden-yellow anthers appear in midsummer and the leaves are glossy dark green. It is lime-tolerant and thrives in normal garden soil but should not be too heavily fed, since this encourages the formation of tender shoots.
**Pruning** Worn-out shoots may be removed, with straggly growths shortened after flowering, and young shoots from the base encouraged.

### CARPINUS (*Carpinaceae*) (D)

Only a few of the 45 known species are in cultivation. All are very hardy, do well in any good soil, not objecting to lime, and make good specimen trees or hedges.

***C. betulus*** (common hornbeam) a British native, can reach 21m (70ft) high but is usually not more than 18m (60ft). The trunk becomes fluted, which quickly distinguishes it from the beech. The leaves are ribbed and turn a good yellow in autumn. The fruiting catkins, 7.5cm (3in) long, are conspicuous in summer. The tree is very strong and not inclined to lose major branches. The cultivar 'Fastigiata' is a medium-sized tree, narrow in its early years and suitable for a garden, later broadening out.

***C. caroliniana*** (American hornbeam) does not make as fine a tree in England as in the USA, but its autumn leaves colour well. It reaches 10m (30ft).

**Pruning** No regular pruning required. In the stage of maintaining a leader, a clear stem 1.8–2.4m (6–8ft) should be formed. Dead wood can be removed from the centre of the crown. *C. betulus* can bleed, even from old wounds, in early spring but this seems not to harm the tree. For hedges see p117.

### CARYA (*Juglandaceae*) Hickory (D)

Fast-growing, large trees with good autumn colour and attractive grey bark.

***C. cordiformis*** (bitternut hickory) is a very large tree up to 25m (82ft) and, of all the hickories, the hardiest and most vigorous in Britain. It can be recognized by the yellow scales on the winter leaf buds which expand to form leaves 25cm (10in) long, usually with seven leaflets. It is best sown in a pot and later planted out into the permanent position as it transplants badly.

***C. ovata*** (shagbark hickory) is equally handsome but slower in growth, reaching 20m (70ft). The leaves are 25cm (10in) or more long, with five leaflets, and turn a striking yellow in autumn.

**Pruning** No regular pruning required. A leader must be trained and a clean trunk of 1.8–2.4m (6–8ft) exposed, the pruning for this taking place in summer.

### CARYOPTERIS × CLANDONENSIS (*Verbenaceae*) (D)

The aromatic leaves of these attractive shrubs are ovate-lanceolate and the late-summer flowers are bright blue. The cultivar 'Ferndown' has dark green leaves and flowers of deeper colour than the type, 'Kew Blue' has even darker blue flowers, and 'Heavenly Blue' has a compact habit and deep blue flowers.

**Pruning** *Caryopteris* repays annual pruning, which prolongs the useful life of the plant considerably as long as feeding is adequate. It involves cutting back all the shoots into living wood, although this is not easy to identify at the end of winter, during which

some die-back is inevitable. Therefore be patient; if your patience fails by mid-spring, but not your courage, cut back boldly and all should be well.

### CASSINIA FULVIDA (*Compositae*) (E)

This dense evergreen shrub, eventually up to 1.8m (6ft) high, has yellow shoots and crowded white flowers in midsummer.

**Pruning** Though it is normally erect, wayward shoots may appear and should be removed entirely.

### CASTANEA SATIVA (*Fagaceae*) Sweet *or* Spanish chestnut (D)

At its best, this is one of the greatest trees of Britain, thought to have been brought in by the Romans and certainly here before the Norman Conquest. It is suitable only for a large garden and is best in an open position in a park. It is easily raised from seed and self-seeds even in cooler areas. Somewhat intolerant of lime, it does well in light sandy soils. The leaves are long and lance-shaped with toothed edges, with pale yellow catkins borne in midsummer. At first growing slowly, after three or four years it develops rapidly and forms a good leader. A clean trunk up to 1.8–2.4m (6–8ft) is desirable as the bark is impressive, at first grey and smooth, later deeply fissured and dark brown with spirals of heavy ridges.

**Pruning** No regular pruning required, although on young trees a clear trunk of 1.8–2.4m (6–8ft) should be developed. Dying branches on old trees should be removed as there is a danger of them dropping. The vitality of the tree usually persists and some regeneration can occur. Sucker growth is common at all stages and is coppiced to provide fencing. The timber of large trees is of limited value.

### CATALPA (*Bignoniaceae*) (D)

These summer-flowering trees are best grown as specimens in isolation so that their attractive leaves and bell-shaped flowers can be admired. They are extremely tolerant of atmospheric pollution.

***C. bignonioides*** (Indian bean, southern catalpa) is a hardy tree that thrives in deep loam and some sun but not an exposed position, where wind may damage the large leaves. The flowers are white with yellow and purple markings in midsummer. W. J. Bean found that this tree often declined in its fifth decade and was best in southern England.

***C. speciosa*** (Western catalpa) seems to have several advantages over *C. bignonioides*: it makes a taller tree, its flowers have few purple spots and its timber, at least in the USA, is extremely durable and resistant to moisture.

**Pruning** No regular pruning required. If left to itself,

a young specimen of *C. bignonioides* quickly begins to branch low down and pruning is directed to achieving a clean trunk up to 1.8–2.4m (6–8ft), after which a crown is quickly established. If it becomes necessary to cut back damaged branches, regeneration is rapid and soon fills the space.

## CEANOTHUS (*Rhamnaceae*) (D, E)

A genus containing evergreen and deciduous shrubs of great beauty with a variable flowering habit, including the best blue-flowered shrubs available for garden use. They flourish in good soil, well drained and neutral. The evergreens are moderately tender though most will survive and flower well when grown against a south- or west-facing wall, on which they should be trained fanwise to create a framework.

C. 'Burkwoodii' is a splendid evergreen hybrid, 1.5m (5ft) tall, with glossy dark green leaves, grey beneath, and flowers of bright blue from midsummer to midautumn.

*C. thyrsiflorus* is perhaps the hardiest evergreen, and best in its form 'Cascade', reaching 4–6m (13–20ft). The nomenclature of the evergreens is confused and it is advisable to see a plant in flower before buying it, unless you know the nursery to be reliable.

The deciduous shrubs are almost hardy, including 'Gloire de Versailles', 1.5m (5ft), powder-blue flowers, and 'Topaz', 1.5m (5ft), light indigo flowers.

**Pruning** The evergreen types, such as *C. thyrsiflorus*

ABOVE Examples of *Cedrus libani atlantica* 'Pendula', a remarkable form of the majestic Atlas cedar, occur in the wild, but it is not known how it appeared in cultivation. This fine specimen in the National Botanic Garden in Dublin, Eire, was planted around 1875. The grey-glaucous foliage remains fresh and the steeply pendulous growth inhibits branches on the inner plant and makes pruning unnecessary

RIGHT The half-hardy shrub *Cestrum parqui* is in fact hardy against a sunny, sheltered wall. It is deciduous and can be cut down in winter, often growing to 1.8m (6ft) by early summer. The leaves are lanceolate and rather striking. The flowers are yellow or greenish-yellow and appear in midsummer, often carrying on into autumn. This picture was taken in October at Tintinhull

and cultivars, need no regular pruning but can be pruned immediately after flowering, with the laterals reduced to two or three buds from the old stem. The old wood, bare of leaves, will not regenerate if cut back. Use secateurs if possible – no, on reflection, use secateurs always, as shears leave an untidy surface. C. 'Burkwoodii' is pruned in spring, cutting back to two to three buds as with many evergreens. The deciduous types can be pruned severely in mid-spring with the previous season's growth cut back to two buds of the old wood, with plentiful feeding and mulching.

CEDRUS (*Pinaceae*) (CO, E)

A genus of hardy, long-lived evergreen trees of the grandest style, suitable as specimen trees on large lawns.

**C. deodara** has foliage that is usually grey or glaucous green, and dark green in the mature tree. It is particularly charming when only 0.9–2m (3–6ft) high, with drooping shoots, but is always graceful, with an ultimate height of 15–25m (50–82ft). Growth is quite rapid, 30cm (12in) a year in good conditions until around 70 years, when it gradually slows down.

**C. libani** (cedar of Lebanon) rarely grows over 25m (82ft) tall in Britain and its lateral spread predominates. It is apt to lose large branches in gales or when weighted down by snow and regeneration is very unlikely. Its large roots are superficial and undoubtedly suffer from the patter of large feet; if it is grown on a much-frequented lawn there is a case for roping off specimens at 10–12m (30–40ft). It has a dwarf cultivar 'Comte de Dijon' which, after many years, will reach 2.7m (9ft) high and 1.8m (6ft) across.

**C. l. atlantica** (formerly *C. atlantica*) will reach 15–25m (50–80ft) and has branches that are at first ascending but eventually spreading, as in *C. libani*. There is a popular cultivar, 'Glauca Fastigiata', with silvery-blue leaves, and a smaller weeping form, 'Glauca Pendula'. *C. l. a.* 'Pendula' is a very fine tree, and the photograph on p38 shows the specimen in the National Botanic Garden, Dublin, planted around 1875.

**Pruning** No regular pruning required. A single lead should be maintained for as long as possible, although vigorous mature trees may develop rival leads which may be susceptible to weather damage. If lower branches start to die back they should be cut out promptly and completely in midwinter to mid-spring. No pruning for dwarf forms.

CELASTRUS ORBICULATUS
(*Celastraceae*) (CL, D)

One of a small number of species which climb by twining and are grown for their long-persistent capsules which split open in autumn to reveal brightly coloured seeds. The leaves are obovate to orbicular, up to 12.5cm (5in) long, turning clear yellow in autumn; the flowers are inconspicuous. It is vigorous and able to reach 9m (30ft) high, particularly when grown into a tree such as a mature *Robinia pseudoacacia*, which has very durable wood.

**Pruning** This is limited to cutting back some of the longest shoots and, of course, any dead wood. This is done in summer as it is not easy to distinguish dead from living tissue when the plant is dormant.

CELTIS (*Ulmaceae*) Nettle tree (D)

Fast-growing elegant trees with attractive glossy foliage and small fruits. They need good growing conditions from an early stage, and some shelter.

**C. australis** is not a great success in Britain, presumably due to lack of sun to ripen the wood. It flourishes in Italy and Spain and makes a good street tree of 20m (60ft). The leaves turn bright yellow in autumn. The fruit is reputed to be the lotus of the ancients, making those who ate it forget their own country; not necessarily a bad thing.

**C. sinensis** grows well, if slowly, in milder areas and makes a pleasant tree with leaves of shining green.

**Pruning** No regular pruning required. If pruned or otherwise damaged, it regenerates freely.

CEPHALOTAXUS FASTIGIATA
(*Cephalotaxaceae*) (CO, E)

One of a small genus of shrubs growing well in shade. They differ from yews in their longer leaves, which have two broad white bands beneath, and in their large olive-like fruits.

**C. harringtonia** is a spreading shrub or small tree, reaching 4.6m (15ft), leaves dark green above, densely disposed along the branchlets in two ranks. The cultivar 'Fastigiata' is in habit like the Irish yew (*Taxus baccata* 'Fastigiata').

**Pruning** No regular pruning needed. Similar to yew in that new growth will form from the oldest wood if cut back hard. The branches of 'Fastigiata' become heavy and may pull the bush out of shape. Tying in may be tried but hard pruning may have to be used and regeneration, although reliable, will be slow.

CERATOSTIGMA WILLMOTIANUM
(*Plumbaginaceae*) (D)

A half-hardy deciduous shrub to 1.2m (4ft) high with bright blue flowers in summer and into autumn. The dark green leaves are tinted red in autumn. Best with some shelter.

**Pruning** The semi-woody stems usually die right back and can be cut off, but in mild areas they survive and should be hard pruned to a few inches in spring.

CERCIDIPHYLLUM JAPONICUM
(*Cercidiphyllaceae*) (D)

This exceptionally handsome hardy tree reaches 9m (30ft) or more. The young leaves are red but soon change to their summer colour of rich green before the autumn change to reddish-purple and yellow, particularly on acid soil. The fallen leaves smell of caramel. The young growth is often damaged by frost, but it should thrive on a sheltered southern slope as long as the soil is not dry.

**Pruning** No regular pruning required. The natural habit is for several leads to form near the base, and after early training the tree should be allowed to develop without intervention.

## CERCIS SILIQUASTRUM (*Leguminosae*)
## Judas tree (D)

A deciduous tree, not often much over 6m (20ft) in Britain. It needs a deep, well-drained loam and plenty of sun, but if satisfied will produce clusters of rosy-lilac pea-like flowers on the leafless shoots in spring followed by purple pods in summer as an additional bonus.

**Pruning** It is desirable, but not easy, to train a single leader. If attempts fail, branches should be shortened and some removed to make a stronger framework. The tree is seldom killed by frost but may be damaged enough to require extensive removal of small branches. It is very prone to attacks by the coral spot fungus (*Nectria cinnabarina*). As soon as the small but prominent spots of bright coral colour are seen the affected branch should be removed at a point 15–30cm (6–12in) away from the spots on the healthy side and burnt. If the main trunk is involved there is little chance of a cure and the tree must be sacrificed. A replacement should be planted on a different site.

## CESTRUM PARQUI (*Solanaceae*)

A deciduous shrub to 3m (10ft) high with long upright shoots from ground level. The lanceolate leaves are mid-green and the flowers yellow, rather than yellowish-green as often described, in panicles, from early summer to autumn and fragrant at night.

**Pruning** It is hardy with wall protection and can be cut to the ground in early spring.

## CHAENOMELES (*Rosaceae*) (D)

Popular and easily grown shrubs, bearing beautiful saucer-shaped flowers in spring in shades of scarlet, pink and white.

*C. japonica* remains one of the best, growing to 90cm (3ft) in height. Like the other species and cultivars, it needs a good loamy soil and a sunny position, and does best against a wall.

*C. speciosa* is more vigorous and can reach 3 × 3m (10 × 10ft), so space must be allowed. There are a large number of cultivars, of which 'Nivalis' (pure white flowers), 'Moerloosii' (white flowers with pink overlay), 'Crimson and Gold' and 'Knap Hill Scarlet' easily predominate.

**Pruning** Pruning of *C. japonica* is aimed at first at producing a framework of short branches. Any shoots coming forward from the wall are stopped during the growing season at four or five leaves, unless they are needed for extension of the bush. The sublaterals which may form are stopped at two leaves, and this is repeated if more growth occurs. The whole procedure is continued each year until spurs form and flowering is established. Thereafter, the shoots which have flowered are shortened to three buds and in late summer any branches which point outward are shortened by half, or rather more. The pruning of *C. speciosa* in the early stages is the same as for *C. japonica*, but in maturity nothing more than the shortening of overlong shoots is necessary.

## CHAMAECYPARIS (*Cupressaceae*) (CO, E)

A genus of only a few species of slow to moderate-growing evergreen trees, but containing a large number of cultivars.

*C. lawsoniana* Usually a broad pyramid with fern-like sprays of foliage reaching to the ground if there is sufficient space and light, making it a good hedging plant (see p117). It can reach 15–25m (50–80ft) but the forms and cultivars, too numerous to list here, vary considerably in size, foliage colour and habit.

*C. nootkatensis* One of the best of this genus, very hardy, healthy and not demanding of soil. Like *C. lawsoniana*, it too spoils the gardener for choice with the number of its forms and cultivars, but can reach 15m (50ft).

**Pruning** No regular pruning required, except the removal of rival leading shoots on young trees in early to mid-spring, unless used for hedging (see Hedges & Topiary).

## CHILIOTRICHUM DIFFUSUM (*Compositae*) (E)

This is a variable shrub 0.9–1.5m (3–5ft), but normally hardier than its relations the olearias. Grows slowly in good soil and the flowers in midsummer are white and daisy-like.

**Pruning** No regular pruning required provided an area 90cm (3ft) wide is allocated.

## CHIMONANTHUS PRAECOX (*Calycanthaceae*)
## Wintersweet (D)

An upright shrub to 1.8m (6ft) with no special soil requirements. It is commonly grown against a wall to gain the extra warmth reflected by the structure. It is hardy but flowers more freely in this situation. The leaves are glossy dark green, and strongly scented, many-petalled, yellow flowers with purple centres appear on the bare stems in winter.

**Pruning** This consists of shortening the secondary shoots to two buds to promote spur formation, and is carried out as soon as the flowers have faded to **give** as much time as possible for the new wood to mature before the next winter.

### CHIONANTHUS (*Oleaceae*) Fringetree (D)

A genus of two hardy, easily grown shrubs with abundant white flowers in summer on established plants. *C. retusus* and *C. virginicus* are alike, both about 3m (10ft) and both needing a deep, loamy soil and full exposure to sun. They are hardy in Britain but often fail to produce the very striking display of flowers which makes them so sought after in the USA; lack of heat is probably the reason. Nevertheless, they are handsome at all times and are among the latest shrubs to come into leaf.

**Pruning** No regular pruning required. *C. virginicus* often makes a small tree, and if it shows the vigour to do so a leader may be trained. However, it may be impossible to control the upward inclination of the branches. If so you should give in and await developments.

### CHOISYA TERNATA (*Rutaceae*) Mexican orange flower (E)

A rounded shrub with almost every virtue one could wish, and one of the greatest garden plants. It accepts an average soil and appreciates full sun. If in the shelter of a wall, it should be planted 1.8m (6ft) from it. The obovate leaves are dark green and are aromatic when crushed, although opinion is divided on whether the aroma is pleasant or not. The white flowers are borne in corymbs in late spring and sometimes again in autumn.

**Pruning** No regular pruning required. The plant is hardy in an average winter but is often damaged, though not severely, by early spring frosts. It regenerates vigorously if the damaged shoots are cut away in early spring.

### CISTUS (*Cistaceae*) Rock rose (E)

A very attractive genus, and moreover useful, an adjective usually reserved for unattractive plants, but this case is the exception. Rock roses like a dry, sunny position, are not affected by drought and, although the flowers last for less than a day, they are produced in a steady succession daily through midsummer. Few are really hardy but *C. laurifolius* and *C. × hybridus* (formerly *C. corbariensis*) are the most resilient. The former is rather untidy but reaches 1.8m (6ft) in a few years; the latter does not exceed 90cm (3ft) and is neat. Both bear white flowers. Of others *C. × cyprius* with large flowers, white with a red blotch near the base of each petal, is one of the best and quite hardy. Another is *C. × skanbergii* with grey-green leaves and pale pink flowers on a beautifully smooth shrub.

**Pruning** No regular pruning required. Members of this genus do not break freely from mature stems if damaged and mature plants will probably never recover if pruned. Any cutting back of the tips should be left until spring. Have a replacement ready from a cutting, which will root readily.

### CLADRASTIS LUTEA (*Leguminosae*) Yellow wood (D)

An attractive specimen tree, reaching 12m (40ft) or more, with a spreading crown. It does not require more than average soil. It bears long drooping wisteria-like panicles of white flowers in early summer and the leaves turn a good yellow in autumn.

**Pruning** No regular pruning required. The mature wood is brittle and, if a large branch breaks off, a mass of young growths will often appear on the rest of the tree, possibly causing further damage because of the extra weight. These growths should be thinned in late summer.

### CLEMATIS (*Ranunculaceae*) (CL, D, E)

A large genus including a few worthy herbaceous plants, but the majority are climbers which have twining leaf stalks (petioles) that attach themselves to stems of shrubs or trees; failing such support, they simply twine round each other. Commonly used supports include walls with wooden lathes or wire mesh attached, pergolas, trellises and arbours. Most clematis like plenty of sun on their flower-bearing part, but the blooms may fade if sunshine is prolonged. The lower part should be sheltered by a 60cm (2ft) plant to avoid drying out. The pruning of clematis is aimed at producing the maximum crop of flowers all over the plant. To do this it is important to know whether the plant produces flowers on the previous or current year's growth.

The most difficult group is the one consisting of plants which flower in early summer on shoots arising from the wood of the previous year, with another flush in late summer and autumn on wood produced in the current year. Notable among this group are 'The President', 'Duchess of Edinburgh', and *C. × jackmanii*.

**Pruning** To achieve the best of both worlds, you must cut back some of the stems from last year which have just flowered and they will set about providing growth which will carry flowers in early summer next year. The remainder will be left until the next early spring and then be cut to the lowest buds, to provide growths for flowering in the next late summer and autumn. The problem is that you may achieve a mediocre result in both early and late summer. The least troublesome conclusion is to leave all pruning until late winter.

Of the 'late flowering' group, some flower as early

Clematis 'Comtesse de Bouchard' is vigorous but not
tall. It begins to flower in early summer, the colour
being 'pinky-mauve' according to Christopher Lloyd,
with each flower from 10-15cm (4-6in) across, later
becoming smaller, always abundant

as midsummer, including 'Perle d'Azur', followed by
'Royal Velours', *C. orientalis*, *C.* × *jackmanii* and
*C. viticella*.
**Pruning** All these should be cut down to 30cm (12in),
or even less, in late winter. To encourage earlier flow-
ering, a few stems may be cut to 45cm (18in).

The third group starts with *C. cirrhosa balearica*,
an evergreen often in flower by late winter. *C. alpina*
starts to flower in early spring and includes 'Frances
Rivis', deep blue, and 'Pamela Jackman', azure. The
evergreen *C. armandii*, flowering mid-spring, benefits
from a wall on its north side. It has big leaves, brownish when young, and white flowers with good scent.
This group also includes *C. montana*, very vigorous,
as are its cultivars, except 'Picton's Variety'. 'Elizabeth'
(pink flowers with a good scent) is desirable.
**Pruning** Strictly speaking this group can be left
unpruned altogether, but all of these plants benefit
from all growth being pruned back by half when flowering has finished, after which they can set about
producing new growth to flower next year.

## CLERODENDRUM TRICHOTOMUM (*Verbenaceae*) (D)

This is far and away the best of this genus and *C. t.*
var. *fargesii* is only marginally more hardy. The type
is hardy enough and undemanding, up to 6m (20ft)
high with fragrant white flowers enclosed in maroon
calyces in late summer, followed by blue fruits which
eventually turn black.
**Pruning** Flowering is improved by cutting back the
wood of the previous year to the last pair of buds in
spring. It is important that ground for 1.8–3m (6–10ft)
around the tree should not be cultivated or dis-
turbed in any way, as any damage to roots near the
surface leads to a forest of suckers which may be
impossible to control.

## CLETHRA (*Clethraceae*) (D, E)

All plants in this genus, whether evergreen or deciduous, need acid soil, pH 5–6, and are not worth
attempting without it. The evergreen species are tender, but the deciduous types described are much
hardier.
*C. alnifolia* is a fully hardy, deciduous, bushy or suckering shrub reaching 2.4m (8ft). It produces fragrant
white flowers in late summer, and the cultivar
'Paniculata' is recommended.
*C. barbinervis* is rather less hardy but has very
pretty white flowers in late summer and early autumn
on an elegant upright bush with good autumn leaf
colour, reaching 3m (10ft).
*C. delavayi* reaches 4.6m (15ft) and is considered the
finest of all, with clusters of pink buds opening to fragrant white flowers in midsummer, but it is of doubtful
hardiness.
**Pruning** No regular pruning required. *C. alnifolia*
has a tendency to develop growths from the base
which means that, in the winter, older shoots can be
removed at ground level along with some of the
suckers. The other species shoot less freely from the
base, but some renewal pruning can be carried out
in winter.

## COLLETIA ARMATA (*Rhamnaceae*) (D)

This sturdy shrub is, perhaps, of more botanical than
garden interest, but it is moderately hardy and
grows well in full sun, reaching some 3m (10ft). The
young branches are, in fact, flat triangular spines and
leaves are few, especially on old plants. The flowers
are white and tubular, each 3mm (⅛in) long, produced
in late autumn or early winter. This plant might, in
10 years, make an impenetrable hedge.
**Pruning** Pruning is only needed to remove dead wood
or old branches that are too heavy, preferably in spring,
and new growths will readily be produced.

COLUTEA ARBORESCENS (*Leguminosae*)
Common bladder senna (D)

A hardy shrub that will grow well in any soil that is not boggy. It grows rapidly to make quite a tidy shrub 3m (10ft) tall and the yellow pea-like flowers are borne freely for several months from midsummer, followed by the inflated pods, 7.5cm (3in) long and light brown. It self-seeds readily and can be trained to tree form, reaching 1.8–2.4m (6–8ft).

**Pruning** Simply a matter of cutting away weak growths in spring, nothing more. If you think the author has a soft spot for *C. arborescens*, you may be right.

CONVOLVULUS CNEORUM (*Convolvulaceae*) (E)

Although this most attractive species is only hardy in the south-west of Britain, it can be planted in less favoured areas against a south-facing wall. The beautiful funnel-shaped flowers are white tinged with pink, and the narrow pointed leaves are a silky silver-green. It makes a shrub 60–90cm (2–3ft) high.

**Pruning** Long, old growths should be completely removed in spring.

CORIARIA TERMINALIS var. XANTHOCARPA (*Coriariaceae*) (D)

Unlike the other members of the genus in cultivation, this arching sub-shrub up to 1.2m (4ft) is hardy at the Royal Botanic Gardens, Kew, and produces greenish flowers of both sexes on terminal racemes, followed by yellow decorative fruits.

**Pruning** Pruning consists of cutting back in spring any shoots which have been damaged by frost, and removing some of the older growths entirely. The coriarias have a dubious reputation for being poisonous to animals, perhaps man as well, except *C. terminalis* which seems to be harmless – but take precautions, in any case.

CORNUS (*Cornaceae*) Cornel, dogwood (D)

A very large genus of shrubs and trees with variable characteristics. There is only room here to list the more important members.

*C. alba* produces stems which become a fine red in autumn and through winter. The cultivar 'Elegantissima' has leaves with a margin of creamy white, the centre grey-green, the stems in winter red. Cultivar 'Sibirica' is less vigorous than the type, and has bright red stems. 'Spaethii' has red bark and mid-green leaves which develop irregular areas of yellow which can occupy the greater part of the leaf area, and only start to fade as the leaves become ready to fall. To add to this the foliage is never scorched by sun and the plant also tolerates considerable shade.

*C. alternifolia* reaches 6m (20ft) and has alternate leaves, as does *C. controversa* (see below), 15m (50ft), the only other member of the genus in cultivation with this leaf pattern. *C. alternifolia* 'Argentea' is a favourite variegated shrub, usually growing slowly with tiered horizontal branches and reaching 2.5–3m (8–10ft) high. The leaves are small and have a creamy margin.

*C. capitata* (Bentham's cornel) Not a hardy tree but it can reach 11m (35ft) in sheltered areas. Pale yellow bracts surrounding small flowers are produced in early summer, followed by large red fruits.

*C. controversa* is a deciduous tree reaching 12–15m (40–50ft) in as many years. The branches are horizontal in tiers, the leaves are alternate and the flowers are white, in cymes about 13cm (5in) across. It does well in average soil, as does the cultivar 'Variegata', which has lanceolate leaves with a yellowish-white border of irregular outline. These trees may lose their leaves in a spring frost but manage to produce a second series in a short time.

*C. florida* (flowering dogwood) makes a small tree to 6m (20ft) high in Britain, but can be damaged by spring frost probably because of poor ripening of the wood in autumn.

*C. kousa* grows well in good soil, where it can reach 7m (23ft), and, like *C. florida*, owes its beauty to the four bracts that surround the otherwise inconspicuous inflorescence. The variety *chinensis*, not botanically distinct, is more vigorous and has large flowers. In both cases the branches are almost horizontal but the outline of the tree is upright and does not demand a great deal of space.

*C. mas* (cornelian cherry) is not difficult to grow and has an abundant display of yellow flowers in late winter on the leafless stems. The fruit is bright red but not regularly borne. This plant, whether tree or shrub, can reach 4.6m (15ft), needs plenty of room and ideally should have an evergreen background, of holly perhaps.

*C. nuttallii* (Pacific dogwood) is not successful in most of Britain, and only at its best on the Atlantic coast where it can reach 12m (40ft). It flowers when quite young but is reported to deteriorate without warning and die for no apparent reason. The flowers in late spring are small, purple, and surrounded by a whorl of bracts which are white, sometimes pink-flushed. In Cornwall, at Lanhydrock, it is unforgettable when flowering in May.

**Pruning** *C. alba*, when first planted, should be left unpruned for a whole season. In the following spring, when growth is apparent, it is cut almost to ground level. Shoots several feet high will follow and the pruning is repeated each year thereafter. If good feeding is applied regularly in late spring the process can be continued for years. The pruning of the cultivars is exactly that of *C. alba* itself.

A decision has to be taken with *C. mas* at an early stage whether to train it as a tree or allow its tendency to branch low down. If it does make a tree it is still desirable to retain the lower branches to some extent. The other species need no regular pruning.

### COROKIA COTONEASTER (*Cornaceae*) (E)

A tender shrub that will do well with the protection of a south-facing wall in most parts of Britain in any light soil. It should be planted at least 60cm (2ft) from the wall to allow for its natural rounded habit, and can reach 2.4m (8ft). The branches are twisted, covered with a white felt at first, later becoming almost black. The leaves are spoon-shaped and the flowers bright yellow in late spring.

**Pruning** No regular pruning required except for training. A problem with pruning is that the leaves are so sparse that it is difficult to tell live from dead tissue. Remember the pruners' rule: 'When in doubt, do nothing', although it should break readily from old wood if frosted or cut back.

### CORONILLA VALENTINA GLAUCA (*Leguminosae*) (E)

A bushy evergreen shrub to 1.2m (4ft) that needs shelter and a sunny position as it is liable to injury in any period of frost. It has blue-grey leaves and fragrant yellow pea-like flowers in spring and early summer.

**Pruning** Little regular pruning required. Damaged or failing growths can be cut back in spring as new growth appears.

### CORYLOPSIS (*Hamamelidaceae*) (D)

A genus of shrubs with fragrant yellow flowers appearing before the leaves in spring. Best in acid to neutral soil and in light shade.

*C. pauciflora* makes a dense shrub with long shoots and a neat surface over 1.8m (6ft) in diameter. Primrose-yellow flowers appear in early spring and last six weeks or more. If grown in full sun the leaves may be scorched.

*C. sinensis* var. *sinensis* (formerly *C. willmottiae*) is an elegant, vigorous shrub reaching 3.7m (12ft), with more spreading growth and lemon-yellow flowers.

**Pruning** No regular pruning required. If absolutely necessary, overlong shoots may be cut back, preferably straight after flowering.

### CORYLUS (*Corylaceae*) (D)

Large shrubs or small trees, all hardy, all thriving in good loam and chalk-tolerant. Attractive catkins are borne in late winter and spring.

*C. avellana* (hazel or cobnut) is a shrub or tree to 6m (20ft) but normally forms a thicket maintained by sucker growth if it is not cut down to make peasticks, walking-sticks or dowsing rods.

*C. colurna* (Turkish hazel) is an exceptionally graceful tree when young but when mature becomes less so, at least in Britain. It reaches 15m (50ft).

*C. maxima* (filbert) is little different from *C. avellana*, although stronger growing. The cultivar 'Purpurea' is well worth having if you like purple-leaved trees.

**Pruning** If *C. avellana* becomes ungainly it may be cut entirely to the ground in winter and will quickly renew itself. At the nursery stage *C. colurna* easily forms a leader and the lateral branches distribute themselves evenly. No pruning is needed, although suckers should be removed. The mature growths of *C. maxima* should be retained, and weak growths cut out in winter to encourage vigour.

### COTINUS COGGYGRIA (*Anacardiaceae*)
### Smoke bush, Venetian sumach (D)

This rounded bush, reaching 4.6m (15ft), should not be planted in rich soil as this inhibits its flowering, although it is an ideal plant for a large mixed border. The orbicular leaves are of a pleasant green turning yellow, less often red, in autumn. The inflorescences, 15–20cm (6–8in) long, develop in midsummer and last till autumn; they are light brown at first, finally turning grey. The cultivar, 'Foliis Purpureis' is also known as the Rubrifolius group and includes several forms with purple leaves, one of the best defined being 'Notcutt's Variety'.

**Pruning** All these plants can be pruned in one of two ways:

**1.** To encourage flowering, the shrub is allowed to build up a strong branch system from ground level. Once this has grown to 1.2–1.5m (4–5ft) there is no further pruning except removing or shortening straggly growths in early spring.

**2.** To encourage a display of foliage, the framework can be confined to two or three main stems from ground level. These are allowed to branch until the shrub is 60–90cm (2–3ft) high, after which the young wood of each is reduced to the two lowest buds in spring.

### COTONEASTER (*Rosaceae*) (D, E)

A large genus of flowering shrubs mostly with a pleasant character of growth and foliage; also fruits, in some. They do well in almost any soil if not waterlogged and are easily propagated.

*C. bullatus* is a graceful deciduous shrub with open, bushy habit reaching 4.6m (15ft) with good corrugated leaves, little flower beauty but clusters of strong

red fruits which are attractive to birds.

*C. conspicuus* is a prostrate evergreen shrub, only 30cm (12in) high but with a spread of 1.8–3m (6–10ft). It is excellent in flower and fruit.

*C. horizontalis* is an excellent deciduous plant, bearing its fishbone-like stems low in open ground but standing quite vertical, up to 2.4m (8ft) without support against a wall. This is useful if any work has to be carried out on the wall, as the shrub can be pulled away and later replaced.

*C. lacteus* is an evergreen reaching 3m (10ft) high and especially striking when flowering (white) in mid-summer.

*C. nitidus* (formerly *C. distichus*) reaches 1.8m (6ft) and is notable for its abundant bright red fruits, which birds ignore. Although deciduous to semi-evergreen, it retains its leaves until spring.

*C. salicifolius* is an evergreen growing to 7.6m (25ft) and spreads widely, needing plenty of room. The bright red fruits are only 5mm (¼in) wide but numerous enough to be spectacular.

**Pruning** No regular pruning required. Although most species will grow strongly if cut back hard, it is important to retain the natural habit, so select plants of an appropriate size for the available space. If necessary, prune deciduous in late winter, evergreens in mid-spring.

**ABOVE** *Cornus alba* 'Spaethii' is grown for its unusual leaf variegation, green and yellow in various proportions – the leaves can be anything from wholly green to wholly yellow. These colours do not fade until the leaves are about to drop, and they are never scorched by the sun. Pruning is simple – cut the stems to ground level every spring and manure liberally
**RIGHT** One of the purple forms of smoke bush, *Cotinus coggygria* is set off here by the scarlet autumn leaves of *Acer palmatum*. See p45 for pruning alternatives

## CRATAEGUS (*Rosaceae*) Hawthorn (D)

A large genus of large shrubs or small trees. All are easily cultivated in good loam and tolerate lime. They are best raised from seed but are still grafted sometimes, especially the less common sort.

*C. crus galli* (cockspur thorn) is a small tree up to 10m (30ft) with a broad top, branches armed with thorns 7.5cm (3in) long, flowers white and profuse in early summer, and fruits, ripening in early autumn, persisting until spring. It is perfectly hardy.

*C. × lavallei* 'Carrierei' is a fine tree to 6m (20ft), with handsome leaves, white flowers in early summer and orange-red fruits up to 2.5cm (1in) wide, persisting through the winter.

*C. monogyna* (common hawthorn) remains the best plant for a 'working' hedge to contain stock and keep out humans (see p117). It can also be trained as a tree with a bare trunk to 1.2–1.5m (4–5ft) and a dense crown, covered in mid-spring with fragrant white flowers.

*C. oxyacantha* (may) is similar to the common hawthorn but not as effective as a hedge.

*C. pedicellata* is a tree to 6m (20ft) bearing white flowers in late spring, followed by scarlet fruits 15mm (¾in) long, ripe in early autumn.

*C. phaenopyrum* (Washington thorn) is a tree to 9m (30ft) with a rounded crown on a thin trunk. The shoots have thorns 7.5cm (3in) long, glossy leaves like a maple and abundant white flowers in mid-summer. The scarlet fruits persist until spring and the leaves turn scarlet and orange in autumn.

**Pruning** No regular pruning required. If you buy an unusual thorn keep a lookout for suckers at a grafting level, just above ground, and remove them promptly. The tree forms need very little attention after their early training. Removing laterals to produce a bare trunk is important if the tree is near a path or in a cultivated area, as the spines are sharp.

### CRINODENDRON HOOKERIANUM (*Elaeocarpaceae*) (E)

A flowering shrub which is too demanding for any but maritime-climate areas of Britain. Not only is it strictly lime-hating, but it must have some shade and is tender. However, if these requirements are met, it is dazzling. The lanceolate leaves are handsome and from the terminal leaf-axils the crimson corolla of the flowers hangs down.

**Pruning** No regular pruning required. Cutting out dead growths in winter is the only attention it needs.

### CRYPTOMERIA JAPONICA 'ELEGANS' (*Taxodiaceae*) (CO, E)

This forms a beautiful bushy tree, 4.6m (15ft) high, with soft juvenile foliage that is retained permanently. The glaucous summer colour changes in winter to a foxy red, then back to grey-blue in spring. This tree is apt to be ruined by heavy rain or snow and may be bent down to the ground. 'Nana' is truly dwarf, 0.9–1.2m (3–5ft), with crowded mid- to dark green foliage, very handsome at all times.

**Pruning** No regular pruning required. If damaged, the main trunk can be cut to within a few feet of the ground and may regenerate, but not to perfection.

### × CUPRESSOCYPARIS (*Cupressaceae*) (CO, E)

These bigeneric hybrids – *Cupressus* × *chamaecyparis* – have all arisen in cultivation. They are extremely and sometimes unfortunately vigorous.

× *C. leylandii* (Leyland cypress) will produce a good specimen 15–18m (50–60ft) high in 25 years. It is perfectly hardy and not affected by sea winds. Where space is adequate it makes a fine conventional conifer specimen, furnished to the base with good dark green foliage on upswept stems. Its capacity to grow anywhere vigorously has got it a bad name but it does not deserve this poor reputation.

**Pruning** The use of × *C. leylandii* for hedging (see p117) shows its reaction to drastic pruning, to which it responds admirably.

### CUPRESSUS (*Cupressaceae*) (E, CO)

A genus of mostly columnar or conical trees tolerant of a wide range of soils but prone to damage if transplanted from open ground. For this reason they are usually pot grown.

*Cupressus macrocarpa* (Monterey cypress) is a popular tree reaching 21m (70ft). It has a tendency to become bare in its lower part, especially when used as a hedge. As a tree it does admirably in the warmer areas, being somewhat tender when young. When mature it develops a spreading habit.

*C. sempervirens* (Italian cypress) has a distinctive fastigiate habit and gives a special character to the Italian landscape, especially in Tuscany. In Britain there are fine trees in the south and south-west but their survival and eventual growth to 15m (50ft) is unpredictable in most areas.

**Pruning** *Cupressus* spp. need no pruning except for removal of competing leads in early to mid-spring. They do not respond well to clipping but if necessary it must be done in late spring or summer.

### CYDONIA OBLONGA (*Rosaceae*) Common quince (D)

A low tree of character, usually to 4.6m (15ft), with branches which crowd together, often crossing. The leaves are dark green above, pale below and turn a good yellow in autumn. The flowers in late spring are white, each at the end of a twig. The fruit is golden and pear-shaped.

**Pruning** The quince tends to sucker and that needs watching. It is best grown as a standard with a 1.8m (6ft) stem and an open-centred crown, with any crossing branches removed – although considering the density of the crown and perhaps the need for a ladder, this can be daunting.

### CYTISUS (*Leguminosae*) Broom (D)

This genus of flowering shrubs ranges 0.3–3.7m (12in–12ft) or more in height, some of them also spreading widely.

*C. ardoinii* is only a few centimetres high, of neat habit with golden flowers.

*C. battandieri* is like no other broom, having a tree-like form when it is grown in the open. It is usually hardy. The leaves are covered in silky hairs, and the early-summer flowers pineapple-scented and golden-yellow.

*C. × burkwoodii* is a hybrid growing to 1.2m (4ft) high, with cherry-red flowers, the wings dark red, edged yellow. A robust shrub, in early summer flowering well in partial shade.

*C. × kewensis* is a low dense bush, suited to the rock garden, with creamy flowers in spring.

*C. multiflorus* grows to 3m (10ft) or more and carries white flowers along the previous year's wood in late spring.

*C. × praecox* is a group of hybrids of which the original clone is *C. × praecox* 'Warminster'. In habit it resembles *C. multiflorus* but the growth is more dense and the flowers, of creamy yellow, are very abundant in late spring.

*C. scoparius* (common broom) is at its best in thin sandy soil, as are most brooms, and under these conditions may live for several years without becoming untidy and will display yellow flowers in abundance for many weeks. Hybrids of this broom are legion and include cultivar 'Andreanus', with brownish crimson wing petals, yellow standard petals stained with the former colour; 'Burkwoodii', cerise and maroon; 'Cornish Cream', cream and yellow; and 'Johnson's Crimson', clear crimson.

**Pruning** *C. ardoinii* should not be pruned. The horizontal lower branches of *C. battandieri* tend to die back and, if they do, should be removed at once. Old wood and any wayward shoots can be cut away in spring. No pruning is required of *C. × kewensis*. It is not essential to prune *C. multiflorus* but if it is desired the operation should be carried out immediately after flowering. No pruning is required for *C. × praecox*.

Pruning for the bushy brooms is definitely valuable. They flower on the wood of the previous year and as soon as the pods start to develop the flowered wood is cut back by two-thirds, being careful to avoid cutting into the old wood (which has no young shoots). This saves the energy of the plant and prevents it from becoming leggy. It also lessens the incidence of black-fly aphid infestation, which involves the pods.

DABOECIA CANTABRICA(*Ericaceae*)
St Daboec's heath (E)

This sub-shrub reaches 90cm (3ft) with rose-purple flowers appearing intermittently from early summer until autumn. There are several cultivars and hybrids.
**Pruning** These plants benefit from pruning in early spring, cutting down the flower spikes and about half the growth of the previous year.

DANAE RACEMOSA (*Liliaceae*) Alexandrian laurel (E)

This is the only species of its genus, resembling *Ruscus* and like it having glossy green 'leaves' which are flattened branches – phylloclades – and which serve the leaves' function. It makes an elegant slow-growing shrub to 1.2m (4ft) and tolerates shade.
**Pruning** No regular pruning required, beyond the removal in spring of any ragged or unhealthy leaves.

DAPHNE (*Thymelaceae*) (D, E)

A wonderful genus whose only fault lies in the reluctance of some of the species to do well in spite of apparently correct culture. They like neutral or limy soil, retaining moisture but draining well, and most are sun-lovers (not an easy prescription to satisfy).

*D. bholua* is a deciduous plant up to 2.4m (8ft) which seems to improve with every introduction, at least in hardiness, though variations in flower colour are disturbing.

*D. × burkwoodii* (*D. caucasica* × *D. cneorum*) and the clone 'Somerset' are wonderful and almost identical deciduous shrubs, except that 'Somerset' is said to be rather the larger. Experience confirms that they are fully hardy and in full sun maintain a good rounded shape to a little over 90cm (3ft) for up to 10 years, covered with very fragrant pink flowers in late spring. Propagation from cuttings is very easy, and it is prudent to have a young plant to hand.

*D. cneorum* (garland flower) is an evergreen, free-flowering, prostrate shrub only 10cm (4in) high but with long leafy branches spreading 50cm (20in). It seems to have no special soil needs but is far from easy to cultivate and therefore, for amateurs at least, layering of some shoots is well worth while.

*D. mezereum* is an erect, slender, deciduous shrub to 1.2m (4ft) with fragrant purple-red flowers on wood of the previous year in late winter, before the leaves appear. Rather difficult to grow well.

*D. × neapolitana* is an evergreen with most of the virtues of *D. × burkwoodii* – an easy-to-grow, hardy and comparatively long-lived shrub to 90cm (3ft) with dark green leaves densely arranged, and fragrant purple flowers from early spring for several weeks.

*D. odora* is evergreen with a cultivar, 'Aureo-marginata', that is, surprisingly, more hardy than the type, and reaches 1.5m (5ft). More important, the flowers, though not very pretty, are extremely fragrant and appear in midwinter, lasting for two months.

*Cotoneaster horizontalis* is fan-shaped in habit and has glorious scarlet foliage and red berries in autumn

**D. pontica** is an evergreen shrub 0.9–1.2m (3–4ft) high and wide-spreading, with light green leaves making a dense surface. The greenish-yellow flowers are inconspicuous but fragrant and appear in mid-spring. This plant likes at least moderate shade.
**Pruning** No regular pruning required. Dead shoots should, of course, be removed but even this mars the outline for some time. In general, the advice to those who plan to prune daphnes is, 'Don't'.

### DAPHNIPHYLLUM MACROPODUM (*Daphniphyllaceae*) (E)
Hardy, and makes a stylish rounded shrub to 1.8–2.4m (6–8ft), with inconspicuous pale green flowers and black berries.
**Pruning** No regular pruning required. It would be an insult to the handsome foliage of this shrub to suggest pruning, but plants grown in shade that develop a loose untidy habit can be cut back hard in spring.

### DAVIDIA INVOLUCRATA (*Davidiaceae*)
Dove *or* handkerchief tree (D)
The showy spring and summer display of insignificant flowers surrounded by the large white bracts that inspire the common name of this tree is also present in the variety 'Vilmoriniana', which is probably more hardy and easier to establish than the type. It reaches about 9m (30ft) and will grow in any good soil, although it does best in full sun and shelter. In a dry summer the leaves on many of the branches fall early and may give the impression that the tree is dying, but in the next spring the shoots develop normally.
**Pruning** No regular pruning required. It readily develops a leader and the trunk can be cleared of branches up to 1.8m (6ft) during late summer.

### DECAISNEA FARGESII (*Lardizabalaceae*) (D)
An upright shrub reaching 6m (20ft), that produces young shoots from the base and does not branch freely; the young shoots are subject to late spring frost damage. The leaves are pinnate, 90cm (3ft) long, the flowers yellow in racemes followed by sausage-shaped dull blue fruits 7.5–10cm (3–4in) long. It likes a rich loamy soil.
**Pruning** No regular pruning required, although weak branch systems can be cut back to ground level provided replacement growths are present.

### DENDROMECON RIGIDA (*Papaveraceae*) (E)
A vigorous, upright shrub reaching 3m (10ft) with grey-green foliage, and large fragrant flowers rather

like bright yellow poppies. Likes a sandy loam and some lime, with full sun and is best grown against a south-facing wall as it is far from hardy. Plants are trained fanwise and new growths arising from the base are tied in. Flowers are produced on laterals.

**Pruning** Weak and dead wood is cut out in spring when growth commences.

### DESFONTAINEA SPINOSA (*Potaliaceae*) (E)

A difficult plant to grow, this acid-loving shrub needs shelter, some shade and above-average rainfall. It has been cultivated successfully on the west coast of Scotland and in Northern Ireland, but in England there are few plants of any great size. The leaves are very like those of the common holly and the drooping tubular flowers, borne from midsummer until late autumn, have a scarlet corolla, with five yellow lobes; the calyx is green.

**Pruning** No regular pruning required.

### DESMODIUM ELEGANS (formerly D. TILIIFOLIUM) (*Leguminosae*) (D)

An upright semi-woody shrub with mid-green leaves. Large racemes of pale lilac to pink flowers appear on the current season's growths in late summer, followed by flattened seed pods. It needs a south-facing wall and plenty of sun.

**Pruning** Shoots normally die back to ground level in winter and are cut back during spring. No regular pruning required during the growing season.

### DEUTZIA (*Philadelphaceae*) (D)

These hardy flowering shrubs like a rich soil, retentive of moisture, and are mostly lime-tolerant. They are nearly all winter-hardy but some are lured into growth by any warm spell in spring, with loss of all bloom for that year should the weather turn wintry again.

*D.* × *elegantissima* is one of the Lemoine hybrids, the typical form an erect shrub to 1.5m (5ft) with flowers rose-pink, in corymbs.

*D. longifolia* is a shrub 1.5m (5ft) high with flowers in panicles, purplish-rose, paler at the margins of the petals, in early summer. A good doer.

*D.* × *rosea* 'Carminea' reaches 90cm (3ft) high with flowers rose-pink, bell-shaped, in large panicles.

*D. scabra* and its cultivars have a special virtue. Flowering in early summer on one-year-old wood, they escape the effect of late frosts in most years. The flowers of the type, borne on erect panicles up to 15cm (6in) long, are pure white and very striking.

*D. setchuenensis* is a fine plant but the variety 'Corymbiflora' is finer. It grows to 1.8m (6ft), with graceful shoots arranged closely together. The leaves are oval-lanceolate with fine teeth. It flowers in early summer in corymbs 7.5–10cm (3–4in) across, making a splendid picture of pink-white which may last from six to eight weeks.

**Pruning** The stooling habit of these shrubs means that they respond well to regular pruning, which involves cutting back the flowered shoots to their origins as soon as the bloom fades, in order to allow the maximum period for ripening the wood for the next year's flowering. Apart from this, removal of old and failing branches at the same time is helpful. Be ready to wait for five to six years for a young plant to give of its best.

### DIERVILLA SESSILIFOLIA (*Caprifoliaceae*) (D)

A small stoloniferous shrub which somewhat resembles weigela. Reaching about 90cm (3ft) high, it has pointed oval green leaves often with a coppery tint when young. Yellow tubular flowers are borne in cymes from early summer for several weeks.

**Pruning** *Diervilla* should be pruned in spring, cutting back the shoots to about 30cm (12in). New growth comes from the base.

### DIOSPYROS (*Ebenaceae*) (D, E)

*D. kaki* (Chinese persimmon) A deciduous tree to 12m (40ft) high, with shining dark leaves and producing its fruit with fair regularity if trained against a wall, at least in milder areas. Even without fruit it is a handsome tree and easy to grow. It is vulnerable to spring frost when young but later becomes hardy.

*D. lotus* (dateplum) is a perfectly hardy, handsome deciduous tree and in Britain reaches 9m (30ft) or a little more, with dark lustrous leaves. Female plants produce fruits which are like tomatoes but yellowish and too bitter for eating.

*D. virginiana* (persimmon) is a fine deciduous tree to 18m (60ft), tender at first but perfectly hardy in a few years. The pale yellow fruit is much favoured in its native region. This tree should be trained to have a clean trunk of 1.8m (6ft) and the lower branches will hang almost to ground level.

**Pruning** No regular pruning required, but any growths that die back can be cut out in early summer.

### DIPELTA FLORIBUNDA (*Caprifoliaceae*) (D)

The most effective species of this genus of easy-to-grow and hardy shrubs, rather similar to weigela in appearance, and notable for the bracts which surround the flowers in a shield-like form. The peeling bark on the older stems is attractive. Reaching 3m (10ft), this plant bears fragrant, pale pink flowers in late spring and early summer.

**Pruning** Die-back can occur at the centre of the

plant due to lack of light, and affected branches should be removed promptly. Immediately after flowering, some old branches can be cut back as new growths are readily produced from ground level.

### DISANTHUS CERCIDIFOLIUS (*Hamamelidaceae*) (D)

This lime-hating shrub reaches 2.4m (8ft) high and has insignificant dark red flowers in autumn, but leaves like those of the Judas tree (*Cercis siliquastrum*) giving one of the best autumn displays, mainly red and purple. It does well in woodland conditions but should be given ample space to allow the lower branches to droop to ground level.

**Pruning** No regular pruning required.

### DORYCNIUM HIRSUTUM (*Leguminosae*) (D)

A sub-shrub that forms a woody base and eventually becomes quite hardy if grown in a sunny position in light soil. It is a magnificent plant with grey hairy leaves, white flowers tinged pink, and reddish fruit pods, the whole a perfect colour composition not above 30cm (12in) high.

**Pruning** In spring the stems of the previous year are cut back to the younger basal shoots.

### DRIMYS (*Winteraceae*) (E)

Although frost-hardy, these shrubs benefit from the shelter of a south- or west-facing wall in cold areas, and moisture-retentive soil.

*D. lanceolata* (mountain pepper) is a dense upright shrub reaching 3.7m (12ft), with the young stems and petioles crimson for a year or more. The leaves are aromatic and peppery, and cream star-shaped flowers are produced in late spring.

*D. winteri* is a large shrub or tree of upright habit, capable of reaching 16m (50ft). The bark is aromatic, the leaves 20cm (8in) long, dark green above, glaucous beneath, the flowers fragrant, ivory white. The form *D. w.* var. *chilensis* (formerly *D. w. latifolia*) is hardier. It should be planted near to but not less than 90cm (3ft) from a wall and no training is required. A truly dwarf form, *D. w.* var. *andina*, is available and reaches no more than 90cm (3ft) high.

**Pruning** No regular pruning required. Shoots damaged during winter and old branches that restrict development of new growth from the base should be cut back as growth commences in spring.

### DRYAS OCTOPETALA (*Rosaceae*)
### Mountain avens (E)

A prostrate evergreen which grows to 7.5cm (3in) high with woody stems spreading to 60cm (2ft). White yellow-centred flowers appear in late spring and early summer, followed by fluffy seedheads.

**Pruning** No regular pruning required.

### ECCREMOCARPUS SCABER (*Bignoniaceae*) (CL, D)

A climbing sub-shrub, semi-woody and almost evergreen under sheltered conditions with light green, doubly pinnate leaves. The petioles end in branching tendrils which twist round any object they encounter. It flowers from early summer, orange or red or in between, and tolerates poor soil, thriving at the foot of a yew hedge, for example, on which it will climb to 3.7m (12ft), making seed freely and self-seeding. It is perennial and survives for several years in southern England. The seed pods are subject to invasion by a pest – the light-fingered visitor.

**Pruning** No regular pruning required. The stems produced from the woody base will be damaged even by a mild frost and can be cut back, hard if necessary, to living growth in spring.

### EDGEWORTHIA CHRYSANTHA (*Thymelaeaceae*) (D)

A shrub to 1.8m (6ft), the young shoots bearing silver, later glabrous olive, alternate leaves. The inflorescences form in autumn but do not expand until late winter in a terminal cluster of fragrant yellow tubular flowers.

**Pruning** Weak, older stems should be removed in later summer and will be replaced by new shoots that appear at the base of the plant.

### EHRETIA (*Ehretiaceae*) (D, E)

A mostly tropical genus of trees and shrubs. The cultivated species grow well in Britain in any fertile well-drained soil, including chalk. Mature growths are perfectly hardy but young and unripe shoots need protection in winter.

*A. acuminata obovata* (formerly *E. thyrsiflora*) is deciduous and hardy when adult. It reaches 9m (30ft) high and is a tree rather than a shrub. The leaves are large, oval, up to 18cm (7in) long, 7.5cm (3in) wide. The flowers are fragrant and white, borne in midsummer. Mature trees have an impressively corrugated bark.

*E. dicksonii* is a deciduous tree to 12m (40ft), vigorous with downy shoots. The large hairy leaves, up to 20cm (8in) long, are striking; the white flowers in late spring, less so. It is 7.6m (25ft) high at Tintinhull, Somerset, and has not suffered any damage from high winds though exposed.

**Pruning** No regular pruning required. Frost-damaged wood should be cut out in early summer, and is readily replaced by new growth.

ELAEAGNUS (*Elaeagnaceae*) Oleaster (D, E)
These useful, fast-growing shrubs are excellent for an exposed position, and do particularly well on a light, sandy soil; those with silvery leaves show their colour less well on a heavy one. The evergreen types can be grown as an informal hedge or windbreak.

*E. angustifolia* (Russian olive) makes a deciduous tree up to 6m (20ft) and produces fragrant but diminutive flowers from late spring to early summer. At this time it can be mistaken for *Pyrus salicifolia* because of the intensely silvery colour of the leaves but in midsummer they deteriorate and present a drab appearance.

*E. commutata* (silver berry) is a deciduous American native which has more conspicuous flowers and makes a shrub about 3m (10ft) high.

*E. macrophylla* is a strong-growing, rounded evergreen shrub with leaves silvery on both surfaces in spring, fading later. The fragrant flowers appear in autumn.

*E. × ebbingei* (*E. macrophylla × E. pungens*) is a bushy, dense evergreen up to 4.6m (15ft) with glossy dark green leaves with silver undersides and fragrant white flowers in mid- to late autumn. It has several cultivars with variegated leaves.

*E. multiflora* is a deciduous shrub to 3m (10ft) notable for its unusual and beautiful fruits, described as ox-blood in colour. Alas, this picture is short-lived if you have an active bird population around.

*E. pungens* is an evergreen most commonly grown as the cultivar 'Maculata'. The large dark green leaves have a deep yellow central area of varying size and shape, creating a strident effect, and it is a shrub that has to be placed with great care in the garden.

*E. umbellata* is a deciduous shrub reaching 9m (30ft) high. The flowers, in late spring, are larger than most in the genus.

**Pruning** No regular pruning required, but the shape and spread can be controlled if necessary. With *E. angustifolia* there is often considerable die-back, but with this comes new growth at a lower level and once this appears unhealthy branches can be removed. The unripe new growth will survive an average winter. On variegated forms, particularly *E. pungens* 'Maculata', shoots showing signs of reversion, with plain foliage, are bound to appear sooner or later. These should be cut off at once and a close watch kept for any recurrence. Generally, eleagnus respond well to hard pruning and shoot obligingly, even from old wood.

EMBOTHRIUM COCCINEUM (*Proteaceae*) Firebush (S/E)
A tall shrub or small tree to 10m (33ft) suitable for sheltered areas with plenty of light in lime-free soil.

In mid- to late spring it earns its common name with a dazzling display of orange-scarlet flowers. The Lanceolatum group consists of plants that are less evergreen but hardier.

**Pruning** No regular pruning required, and there is no need to train a single lead.

EMPETRUM NIGRUM (*Empetraceae*) Crowberry (E)
A dwarf carpeting shrub, 15–45cm (6–18in) tall. It must have lime-free soil and moisture. The tiny pink-purple flowers appear in summer.

**Pruning** As the plant ages, bare stems appear in the middle. Eventually it is necessary to replace with young specimens, but this can be delayed by regular trimming back in spring.

ENKIANTHUS CAMPANULATUS (*Ericaceae*) (D)
Easily outstanding among the species of the genus, this is a shrub to 3.7m (12ft) high which dislikes lime but tolerates a neutral soil. The leaves, which tend to be in a cluster, give a fine autumn display of orange and red. The flowers are yellow-veined and edged with crimson, borne in racemes in spring.

**Pruning** No regular pruning required but if for any reason stems do have to be cut back they will 'break' readily. New growth arises from the base in any case.

ERICA (*Ericaceae*) Heath (E)
The heaths form a large genus of flowering, mostly lime-hating shrubs ranging from miniatures of just 15–30cm (6–12in) to small trees reaching 6m (20ft) in sheltered areas. The enormous number of cultivars now available can provide a year-round display of flower and foliage. They are pruned according to habit and season of flowering, as follows:

**1. Summer-flowering** (*E. ciliaris, E. cinerea, E. vagans*, etc) Prune each spring, making sure to avoid cutting into old wood and therefore not going much below the flowered spikes, which should have been left on through the winter as they are decorative. As far as possible secateurs should be used, but if a large area

PAGE 54
*Deutzia setchuenensis* var. *corymbiflora* is very floriferous and valuable as a flowering shrub in midsummer. Prune back the flowered branches
PAGE 55
*Drimys winteri* is one of the most handsome evergreen shrubs for a sheltered corner. The fragrant flowers, opening in early summer, are ivory white. Winter-damaged and old shoots can be cut back in spring

shears can be substituted so long as you make some variation in the angle at which the blades are directed, in the hope of preserving a natural appearance. As the plants grow older take cuttings, and be ready to substitute them as signs of senility appear in the original stock.

**2. Winter-flowering** (*E. carnea, E. × darleyensis,* etc). Some authorities prune every second or third year or even do not prune at all. Experience suggests that cutting back immediately after flowering prolongs the healthy life of the shrub, but be sure not to leave it any later in the season, since new growth may already have begun. Very vigorous forms of *E. carnea* such as 'Springwood Pink' or 'Springwood White' may be cut back at this time to avoid collision with neighbours.

**3. Tree heaths** (**E. arborea, E. canaliculata, E. lusitanica,** etc), are less hardy, do well in mild maritime areas and flower abundantly but elsewhere need protection. *E. terminalis* is hardy, flowers throughout the summer and tolerates neutral soil. The flowers are rose-pink and the foliage rather dark green. It is widely available. These do not require regular pruning, but are likely to be cut back by frost.

ERIOBOTRYA JAPONICA (*Rosaceae*)
Loquat (E)

Makes a small tree or bushy shrub up to 8m (26ft) given the protection of a wall. It produces fragrant white flowers in large clusters through winter and may bear edible pear-shaped fruit, but this rarely ripens except in the mildest areas. The foliage is attractive, the glossy corrugated green leaves sometimes 30cm (12in) long.
**Pruning** No regular pruning required. Shoots are produced freely from the base and these will replace the oldest wood which can be cut out in spring.

ESCALLONIA (*Escalloniaceae*) (mostly E)

Summer-flowering shrubs, tolerant of coastal conditions but not always hardy. They thrive in any soil and are equally useful as free-standing shrubs or as informal hedges.
*E.* 'Langleyensis' (*E. virgata × E. rubra*) is a hardy arching shrub up to 2.4m (8ft) with rose-pink flowers. It has given rise to the notable hybrids 'Apple Blossom' (slow-growing with pink and white flowers) and 'Donard Seedling' (vigorous with white flowers).
*E.* × 'Iveyi' This plant is of uncertain parentage and has been damaged even against a wall, especially by late frosts, but quickly recovers. It reaches 3m (10ft), is beautiful in leaf and has large racemes of white flowers in autumn.
*E. virgata* Deciduous, bone-hardy, reaching 2.4m (8ft)

and bearing white flowers profusely in early summer.
**Pruning** No regular pruning required, but the occasional removal of a long branch spoiling the shape of the whole is quite acceptable, provided it is carried out as soon as the flowers drop. Plants which are cut to the ground by frost must not too readily be assumed to be dead; they may regenerate in late spring.

EUCALYPTUS (*Myrtaceae*) Gumtree (E)

A most complex genus which justifies confining attention to the two hardy members which can be planted without much risk in colder areas. Eucalyptus should be planted out from pots as soon as possible as they will suffer if the roots are damaged or restricted. They must be staked at first but later should not need any support.
*E. gunnii* (cider gum) has produced trees of 21–30m (70–100ft), but all in mild or maritime regions. It is hardy except in really severe winters but is often damaged by prolonged cold wind. It will grow in most soils but chalk is best avoided.
*E. parvifolia* (small-leaved gum) is about equally hardy and makes an elegant tree 10m (30ft) or more high with a dense crown.
**Pruning** These amenable trees can be pruned annually or every other year in spring to form multi-stemmed shrubs with juvenile foliage, or a single stem can be allowed to develop to form a standard. Should frost damage occur the young plant can be cut back to 30cm (12in) and should continue growth.

EUCOMMIA ULMOIDES (*Eucommiaceae*) (D)

This really does look like an elm, and is absolutely hardy and vigorous in good soil, reaching 18m (60ft). Uniquely for temperate climates, it produces rubber, though not of commercial quality. If a leaf is torn in two, strings of rubber can be seen.
**Pruning** It should be trained to a clean stem up to 1.8m (6ft) as the crown develops quickly once laterals are allowed to grow.

EUCRYPHIA (*Eucryphiaceae*) (D, E)

A genus of very ornamental shrubs with white flowers on mature specimens in summer. All eucryphias need sun but also some shelter; not always an easy combination to find.
*E. glutinosa* is a hardy deciduous species up to 9m (30ft) with large fragrant flowers and attractive autumn foliage colour. It seems to be lime-hating.
*E. cordifolia* is lime-tolerant but a rather tender evergreen. The hybrids are more satisfactory, especially:
*E.* × *intermedia* (*E. glutinosa × E. lucida*), an evergreen tree 2.4–5.5m (8–18ft) high.
*E.* × *nymansensis* (*E. glutinosa × E. cordifolia*) is

evergreen and has given rise to the selected clones 'Nymans A' and 'Nymans B'. The former, as 'Nymansay', has proved most successful and is hardy in mild maritime areas.

**Pruning** No regular pruning required.

### EUONYMUS (*Celastraceae*) Spindle tree (D, E)

Shrubs and creepers that thrive on a wide range of soils, including chalk.

*E. alatus* is a bushy deciduous shrub up to 2.4m (8ft), valued for its scarlet leaves in autumn.

*E. europaeus* is a deciduous shrub or small tree to 2.7m (9ft), with good autumn foliage colour and scarlet fruits with orange seeds in autumn.

*E. fortunei* is a very hardy trailing evergreen, useful as ground cover but when reaching an upright surface climbing by aerial roots in the same manner as ivy up to 4.6m (15ft). There are numerous variegated cultivars.

*E. japonicus* is an evergreen 3.7m (12ft) high, much used for hedging in seaside resorts (see p117).

**Pruning** No regular pruning required. The need for pruning in these and other species is only for shaping or size restriction and fairly obvious. The deciduous forms are often attacked by blackfly, which may be hard to control and may involve some cutting back.

### EUPATORIUM LIGUSTRINUM (*Compositae*) (E)

Usually grown as a pot plant in summer. It has survived outdoors in maritime sites and is worth a risk as it is a very shapely plant 1.8–3.7m (6–12ft) high and bears fragrant white flowers in late summer.

**Pruning** No regular pruning required. If it needs pruning something is amiss.

### EURYOPS ACRAEUS (*Compositae*) (E)

A truly evergreen shrub, forming a mound of silver-grey foliage up to 90cm (3ft) high with bright yellow flowers. It needs sun and a well-drained soil and has proved hardy in mild areas.

**Pruning** No regular pruning required.

### EXOCHORDA (*Rosaceae*) (D)

Hardy shrubs with profusely borne racemes of pure white flowers. All like good soil.

*A. racemosa* resents chalk and reaches 3m (10ft) or more.

*E. macrantha* 'The Bride' is the most popular cultivar, more free-flowering and up to 2.7m (9ft).

**Pruning** They are liable to produce sucker growths and these should be removed in winter until a clean leg of 30cm (12in) has been formed. After flowering any unwanted shoots can be cut away or rubbed off.

### FABIANA IMBRICATA (*Solanaceae*) (E)

The only species of this heath-like genus of shrubs in general cultivation, it produces a mass of tubular white flowers in early to midsummer. It reaches 2.4m (8ft), and likes a sandy, neutral to acid soil but is only successful in milder areas.

*F. i. f. violacea* is considered superior in all ways to the type, the branches projecting almost at right angles and making the shrub as wide as it is tall. As the name implies, the flowers are violet-purple.

**Pruning** One main leader should be maintained. If any laterals are damaged they can be removed straight after flowering and regeneration quickly begins, even from old wood.

### FAGUS (*Fagaceae*) (D)

Although it contains only some 10 species, and only a few of these in common cultivation, this genus includes some of the finest trees for specimen, plantation or hedge planting (see p117).

*F. sylvatica* (common beech) is a native of southern Britain and one of the nation's best-loved trees. It can reach 30m (100ft).

*F. grandiflora* (American beech) is not a success in Britain but can reach 9m (30ft). Perhaps lack of hot sun is a factor in its dislike of migration.

*F. engleriana* is a most charming specimen not exceeding 18m (60ft). The foliage, especially when young, has a very attractive light green colour.

**Pruning** No regular pruning required. When mature the lower branches of *F. sylvatica* die off and should be removed so that a healthy wound results. In maturity there is a tendency for large limbs to fall suddenly, leaving an ugly tear on the trunk. This is difficult to predict and, if there is a danger to the public, felling is the only solution when in doubt. In addition there are several fungus infections which may affect the root system and make the tree unsafe. The numerous forms and cultivars present the same problems as *F. sylvatica*. *F. engleriana* tends to branch early and that cannot be rectified.

### FALLOPIA BALDSCHUANICA
### (formerly POLYGONUM BALDSCHUANICUM)
### (*Polygonaceae*) (CL, D)

A very vigorous climber, hoisting itself by twining. The leaves are ovate, pale green, flowers white tinged pink, in crowded panicles from late summer and through the autumn. Its twining habit makes it more suitable for covering an unsightly object or an old tree than for training against a wall, on which it will look untidy and soon develop dead wood. It would also be effective growing up a bank.

**Pruning** No regular pruning required. If necessary,

the spread can be restricted during winter but it is better not to plant this vigorous climber in a confined place. Dead wood always builds up but is difficult to remove without damaging the living.

### × FATSHEDERA LIZEI (*Araliaceae*) (E)

This is an intergeneric hybrid of *Fatsia japonica* 'Moseri' × *Hedera hibernica*. It is a hardy shrub, enduring shade well, often grown against a wall and showing a tendency to climb, reaching 1.2–2.4m (4–8ft). The variegated form has very striking green and yellow leaves.

**Pruning** No regular pruning required. In a confined space pruning in early to mid-spring to direct growth is effective.

### FATSIA JAPONICA (*Araliaceae*) (E)

Usually a wide-spreading shrub reaching 6m (20ft) if trained up a wall. It has lobed, dark green leaves at least 30cm (12in) across and in autumn branching panicles of white flowers make a striking picture.

**Pruning** No regular pruning required, but size can be restricted by cutting straggly branches back to ground level in spring.

### FICUS CARICA (*Moraceae*) Common fig (D)

This attractive shrub with large lobed leaves will reach about 2.4m (8ft) if trained against a wall, which it certainly needs if it is to produce fruit, and 3.7m (12ft) if grown as a free-standing shrub in a sheltered position. Garden plants are always females, which can develop fruits without the help of a male.

**Pruning** When cut to the ground by frost it revives in the spring. If the shrub becomes untidy, as it usually does, it can safely be cut back to the ground in autumn or winter (see also pp174–7).

### FITZROYA CUPRESSOIDES (*Cupressaceae*) (CO, E)

A tree which grows slowly in northern temperate regions, where it is more often a shrub. Few reach 15m (50ft) even after 80–100 years. It is a handsome, bushy tree with leaves in whorls of three. It is quite hardy in the south and south-west of Britain and is easily propagated by cuttings taken in late summer.

**Pruning** Young trees 30cm (12in) high begin to form competing leaders, one of which should be selected and tied to a stake until well established, competitors being reduced to one.

### FORSYTHIA (*Oleaceae*) (D)

A widely grown genus of hardy flowering shrubs which tolerate lime. The yellow flowers are borne in early spring before the leaves appear.

This young tree of *Fraxinus pennsylvanica* was chewed by rams when the trunk was 1.2m (4ft) high. A group of new stems emerged in the following spring. The central, and longest, stem was selected, and all the others were cut away. The rams were also disposed of. The photograph shows the tree flourishing after four years

*F. × intermedia* 'Spectabilis' is a vigorous shrub, 2.4m (8ft) tall, with a profusion of strong yellow flowers and is understandably the most popular member of the genus.

*F. suspensa* bears smaller, paler yellow flowers and is best grown against a wall where its arching main branches can reach 4.5–6m (15–20ft), the slender laterals being allowed to hang down.

**Pruning** In essence, pruning is the same for all types of forsythia. Most produce shoots from ground level readily and these are the replacements for the oldest stems, which are removed immediately after flowering. *F. × intermedia* is likely to produce vigorous growth after pruning and not much flower until another year is past. Older branches of *F. suspensa* can be cut out after flowering and younger laterals trained in as replacements.

### FOTHERGILLA MAJOR (*Hamamelidaceae*) (D)

A hardy spring-flowering shrub to 2.4m (8ft), which prefers a sandy soil but dislikes lime. The spikes of white fragrant flowers are produced before the leaves, which turn yellow in autumn, then orange and finally red.

**Pruning** No regular pruning required. The growths which occur at the base should not all be removed as

*Fothergilla major*

they may provide a replacement if a mature branch dies. Any dead wood should be removed to the base in winter, taking care not to damage any of the other crowded growths.

### FRAXINUS (*Oleaceae*) Ash (D)

A genus of over 30 trees and a few shrubs. Most of the trees are shapely and have good pinnate leaves. They are hardy, tolerant of most soil types and fast-growing.

*F. americana* (white ash) reaches 25m (82ft) and is one of the best American trees brought to Britain, notable for its handsome outline and the quality of its timber.

*F. excelsior* (common ash) is a British native which at its best is a really noble tree of up to 30m (100ft). This is most likely to be achieved in a deep moist soil, often clay, and not excluding lime. Its timber is exceptionally tough and durable. Though this ash is hardy enough, it sometimes loses its first growth of leaves from a late frost. However, the foliage is quickly replaced.

*F. ornus* (manna ash) is a relatively small tree, reaching 15m (50ft). It is easily grown and within a few years produces off-white flowers in spring, rather malodorous but pretty.

*F. pennsylvanica* is less tall than *F. americana* but even more handsome in Britain.

**Pruning** No regular pruning required. A single lead should be maintained for as long as possible to prevent a head being formed too early. The lower shoots of *F. ornus* should be removed gradually to give a clean stem as the branches tend to droop. The crown is dense but should not be thinned.

### FREMONTODENDRON CALIFORNICUM (*Sterculiaceae*) (E, S/E)

Makes a shrub or small tree, up to 6m (20ft) when grown against a south- or west-facing wall. It does best in light, well-drained soil and tolerates chalk. The cup-shaped flowers are golden-yellow on leafy spurs. It is not hardy except in the mild areas and should be pot-grown until planted in its permanent site as it hates disturbance at the root. It should be staked until established.

**Pruning** No regular pruning required, but shoots damaged during winter can be removed in mid-spring.

### FUCHSIA (*Onagraceae*) (D)

Very popular shrubs producing pendulous flowers during summer and early autumn. They are best represented in gardens by hybrids, mostly derived from *F. magellanica*, up to 3m (10ft) in favoured areas where they are sometimes grown as a hedge. The oldest of the hybrids is 'Corallina', with reddish-purple flowers. 'Madame Cornelissen' and 'Mrs Popple' are both levelled to the ground in winter but revive in spring. 'Riccartonii' is almost hardy, quite so in the mild regions and especially in the west of Ireland, where it naturalizes.

**Pruning** In cold areas old growth on hardy species and hybrids should be cut back in early to mid-spring, having served as a marker and possibly provided some protection to new shoots. In sheltered areas a framework of branches can be built up over the years and laterals pruned back in spring.

### GARRYA ELLIPTICA (*Garyaceae*) (E)

A shrub with leathery dark green leaves and pendent catkins, borne from mid-winter until spring, which are showier on male plants, up to 15cm (6in) long in cold areas, nearer 30cm (12in) in warmer places. The cultivar 'James Roof' seems a superior plant with much longer flowering catkins.

*Garrya elliptica*

**Pruning** No regular pruning required. Straggly growths should be shortened after the catkins fade but before new growth starts.

### GAULTHERIA (*Ericaceae*) (E)

Spring to summer-flowering shrubs, ideal for ground cover on an acid soil provided there is adequate moisture, and a sheltered position with some shade. All are hardy. The following are the most favoured.

*G. cuneata* reaches 30cm (12in) with white flowers, early summer. Fruits white.

*G. miqueliana* reaches 30cm (12in) with white flowers. The fruits are white or pink.

*G. procumbens* is only 7.5–15cm (3–6in) with pinkish-white flowers. The fruits are bright red.

*G. shallon* grows to 1.2–1.8m (4–6ft) and is vigorous with pink-white flowers in spring and summer. Fruits dark purple.

**Pruning** No regular pruning required. In the unlikely event of the spread of this shrub having to be restricted, it can be pruned back in spring or summer.

## GENISTA (*Leguminosae*) Broom (D)

A large genus of almost leafless shrubs and trees, the green stems fulfilling the function of leaves. Some are dwarf and, at the other extreme, some are 6m (20ft) or over.

*G. aetnensis* is more a tree than a shrub, up to 6m (20ft). Wonderful in summer when the fragrant golden-yellow flowers appear in profusion, it is still handsome with its bright stems at other times.

*G. hispanica* (Spanish gorse) is a small shrub not much more than 30cm (12in) high, and rounded. It likes a light soil, not rich, and a sunny position. In early summer it covers itself in golden-yellow blossom.

*G. lydia* has an arching habit and reaches some 60–90cm (2–3ft). The bright yellow flowers are freely borne in early summer.

*G. pilosa* reaches only 45cm (18in) and makes dense ground cover, useful for sunny slopes.

*G. tenera* is another large species, reaching 3.3m (11ft), very regular in outline and flowering in summer. It is difficult to get but *G. cinerea* creates a similar effect.

**Pruning** No regular pruning required. Young plants can be encouraged to develop a bushy habit by pinching out the growing tips after flowering. *G. aetnensis* should be staked in the nursery stage and pruned to a 0.9–1.2m (3–4ft) leg to create the desired shape. *G. hispanica* can develop dead wood if overfed, but this can be cut out and healthy stems pegged into the soil, which should be enriched with leaf mould, to fill the gap. *G. lydia* suffers in the same way but cannot be pruned effectively.

## GINKGO BILOBA (*Ginkgoaceae*) Maidenhair tree (D)

This hardy deciduous tree is the only member of an ancient genus, apparently growing some 160 million years ago. It is related to conifers, although it has no cones, and has very distinctive and beautiful fan-shaped entire leaves with fine yellow autumn colours.

Although tolerant of most soils, it grows slowly – very slowly if the earth is not rich and loamy – but can theoretically reach 25m (82ft) or more.

**Pruning** After it has been raised from imported seed and planted out it is vital to maintain an upright leader. If neglected the growth can be quite irregular and very difficult to straighten. A bamboo stake does help and the tree does respond to pruning by growing, but attention to rival leaders has to be kept up, perhaps for years. It's worth it.

## GLEDITSIA TRIACANTHUS (*Leguminosae*) (D)

This is the most widely grown of this genus of deciduous, spiny pod-bearing trees, tender when young but improving later. Fond of good soil and plenty of sun, it is usually grown as a specimen tree. The fern-like leaves turn yellow in autumn, and the spines are smaller on plants grown in shady places than on those grown in sunlight. In addition the fruits are in pods over 30cm (12in) long, which rattle in the wind.

*G. t. inermis* is said to be free from spines altogether and the cultivar 'Sunburst', also unarmed, has leaves golden in spring, becoming green later.

**Pruning** No regular pruning required. These plants make a leader readily and need pruning only for cosmetic reasons or to remove dead wood. Prune in autumn or early winter to avoid bleeding. They deserve to be more widely planted.

## GREVILLEA ROSMARINIFOLIA (*Proteaceae*) (E)

Only reliably hardy in the mildest places, and even then requiring the shelter of a south- or west-facing wall, this handsome rounded shrub reaches 1.8m (6ft) and produces racemes of tubular crimson flowers in summer.

**Pruning** Straggly or winter-damaged shoots can be pruned in spring.

## GRINDELIA CHILOENSIS (*Compositae*) (E)

A sub-shrub that can, in sheltered areas, develop a woody framework of 60–90cm (2–3ft) high. It belies its reputation for tenderness and is hardy in the southern half of England, but it needs full sun and good drainage. The large daisy-like flowers are rich yellow through the summer.

**Pruning** Dead growth can be removed in spring and new growth will soon appear.

## GRISELINIA (*Cornaceae*) (E)

Two species of these foliage shrubs with insignificant flowers are in common cultivation in Britain.

*G. littoralis* is not hardy except in mild regions, although it tolerates chalk and stands up well to Atlantic wind. It hardly seems to possess sufficient charm for a specimen shrub, although the apple-green leaves are pleasant and its fast-growing, dense habit makes it an excellent windbreak or hedge for maritime areas, where it is commonly used for hedging (see p118). *G. lucida* is less hardy but has larger leaves.

**Pruning** No regular pruning required. Straggly shoots can be trimmed back in mid-spring or late summer.

### GYMNOCLADUS DIOICA (*Leguminosae*) Kentucky coffee tree (D)

An attractive hardy tree that likes a rich soil but grows very slowly to 18m (60ft) and seldom produces its small, white, star-shaped flowers when grown in Britain. The large leaves are pink when young, turning green then yellow before they fall.

**Pruning** No regular pruning required. A single lead should be maintained for as long as possible, then the trunk can be cleared to 1.8m (6ft) or a little more. Prune in midsummer to avoid bleeding, which occurs in late winter and early spring.

### HALESIA (*Styracaceae*) Snowdrop tree (D)

A genus of shrubs or small trees with lovely flowers reminiscent of snowdrops borne on naked branches in late spring. All the species seen in Britain like a soil which drains well but does not dry out (not easy to supply). They also hate lime.

*H. tetraptera* (formerly *H. carolina*) makes a beautiful spreading tree to 6m (20ft) and produces flowers in late spring, in white clusters on the wood of the previous year.

*H. monticola* quickly forms a tree 12m (40ft) or more in height and flowers when still quite young. The variety *H. m.* var. *vestita* is not significantly different.

**Pruning** No regular pruning required. *H. tetraptera* branches freely from the base and is best kept as a bush. The natural habit is for it to be thickly branched and no thinning-out is required. It can be cut back after flowering to restrict its size. *H. monticola* should be grown with a single leader, with any rivals removed. The trailing branches should not be thinned.

### × HALIMIOCISTUS (*Cistaceae*) (E)

An intergeneric hybrid of *Cistus × Halimium* that requires full sun, shelter and well-drained soil.

× *H. wintonensis* reaches 60cm (2ft), has grey foliage and white, maroon-banded, yellow-centred flowers in late spring and early summer.

× *H.* 'Ingwersenii' is a pretty, hardy shrub on a similar scale with pure white flowers from spring into summer.

× *H. sahucii* reaches about 45cm (18in), with white flowers in early summer.

**Pruning** Like *Cistus*, none of these hybrids responds well to pruning but dead wood and flowerheads can be cut back in spring.

### HALIMIUM (*Cistaceae*) (E)

A small genus of shrubs with showy flowers, well suited to coastal gardens.

*H. lasianthum* is a spreading shrub rarely more than 30cm (12in) high. The flowers are yellow with a purple blotch near the base.

*H. ocymoides* may reach 60–90cm (2–3ft) high with downy shoots and panicles of yellow flowers, each with a purple blotch at the base. It seems hardy and long-lived.

**Pruning** Generally, this genus does not respond well to pruning. *H. lasianthum* can be discreetly pruned in spring to restrict its spread. *H. ocymoides* does not need pruning if given enough room.

### HALIMODENDRON HALODENDRON (*Leguminosae*) Salt tree (D)

A shrub 1.2–1.8m (4–6ft) high with a spreading habit and spiny branches. The pea-like, pale purple flowers are borne in early summer and the foliage is grey.

**Pruning** No regular pruning required. It has in the past been grafted on *Caragana arborescens* or *Laburnum* and if so a watch should be kept for suckers, which should be removed promptly.

### HAMAMELIS (*Hamamelidaceae*) Witch hazel (D)

The fragrant, frost-resistant flowers of these shrubs have very narrow petals up to 2.5m (1in) long. They like a good average soil, preferably neutral.

*H. mollis* (Chinese witch hazel) reaches 3.7m (12ft) and has spreading branches. The yellow midwinter flowers are borne on bare branches.

*H. × intermedia* 'Pallida' reaches 3m (10ft) and has flowers of a soft sulphur yellow in midwinter.

*H. virginiana* may make a small tree, more often a low spreading bush to 3.7m (12ft). The small golden-yellow flowers appear in late summer and continue until late autumn, but are obscured by the leaves, which fall rather late.

**Pruning** No regular pruning required. Pruning should be restricted to limiting unwanted spread, and be carried out between flowering and the appearance of the leaves. It may be worth training a leader of *H. mollis* to raise the plant to 1.8m (6ft) high, so that the midwinter flowers and their scent can be enjoyed.

## HEBE (*Scrophulariaceae*) (E)

In this genus of shrubs with attractive foliage and often dense spikes of flowers, intermediate forms abound, probably hybrids, and that makes identification difficult. The various forms vary in height between 60cm (24in) and 2.4m (8ft) and the flower colours range from white through pink and lilac to deep violet-purple. Variable in hardiness, they are easy to grow and do best in light sandy soil, tolerating chalk. Many of the large-leaved species, such as *H. speciosa*, are tender and are cut back severely in a frost of any magnitude.

**Pruning** No regular pruning required. Specimens damaged by frost should be left untouched until spring when new growth appears (if the plant has survived) and then pruned. Spring pruning also benefits those which are untidy. The very desirable *H. hulkeana* seems to benefit from removal of the spent flowers, as the fruits are large and drain the plant's vitality.

## HEDERA (*Araliaceae*) Ivy (CL, E)

All ivies climb by means of aerial roots, which attach themselves firmly to any surface while the leaves arrange themselves in one plane. Eventually the plant produces bushy growths and flowers, but ceases forming aerial roots.

*H. canariensis* can climb to 6m (20ft) and is now

*Hedera colchica* makes a fine covering for a wall with its large, dark green leaves. It is one of the best ivies and makes an ideal backdrop for other, more showy plants

mainly represented by the cultivar 'Gloire de Marengo', with large leaves margined with creamy white and irregular splashes of green along the main veins. It is often used as a house plant, but is reasonably hardy.

*H. colchica* (Persian ivy) has large, handsome, dark green leaves to 15–18cm (6–7in) long, reaches 10m (30ft) high and makes a good dense cover for a wall. *H. colchica* 'Sulphur Heart' has leaves with an irregular central splash of yellow merging into pale and finally deep green.

*H. helix* (common ivy) is the toughest and hardiest of the ivies, a plant which will grow well where few others will – a virtue in rough parts of the garden – and to some extent against buildings or trees, where it will attain 10m (30ft). However, it is a considerable nuisance in a hedge bottom or among valued trees. The cultivars are legion, among them 'Conglomerata', suitable for a rock garden at 90cm (3ft) in height and spread, with erect stems and leaves with a wavy margin. It needs some support. 'Sagittifolia' has five-lobed leaves, the central one large and triangular. It grows slowly to 1.2m (4ft) high.

*H. hibernica* (Irish ivy) has bright green leaves, turning to copper in winter. It is useful for ground cover, rooting readily and spreading or climbing to 6m (20ft).
**Pruning** This usually consists of clipping over the surface of the plant in late spring, although it leaves a bare stem for three or four weeks. An alternative is to pull off the growth, having hooked it from the wall, leaving a few feet of the plant only from ground level. Avoid this if there is old mortar but with ivy up a tree it is the best system.

### HEDYSARUM MULTIJUGUM (*Leguminosae*) (D)
In this mostly herbaceous genus, *H. multijugum* is a shrub growing up to 1.5m (5ft) high with sparse growth. The pea-like flowers are magenta and produced in summer.
**Pruning** Long branches may be cut back in spring but may also be pegged down at that time to make replacements.

### HELIANTHEMUM (*Cistaceae*) Sun rose (E)
These attractive, spring- to autumn-flowering shrubs will grow in any soil, including limestone, but they must have full sun. Their low spreading or hummock-forming habit makes them ideal for rock gardens and dry slopes. They vary in height from 10–30cm (4–12in) and the flower colour ranges from white through yellow, orange and pink to carmine.
**Pruning** They benefit from light pruning with secateurs as flowers fade.

### HELICHRYSUM SPLENDIDUM (*Compositae*) (E)
This dense, bushy shrub will grow to 90cm (3ft) high and more across. The shoots and foliage are silvery-white, and the flowers, usually removed, are bright yellow.
**Pruning** This plant is best pruned hard in spring and trimmed lightly in summer to keep the foliage display looking its best.

### HIBISCUS SYRIACUS (*Malvaceae*) (D)
Not a graceful shrub, with its upright branches often crowded together, but it has the virtue of producing its large, trumpet-shaped flowers in late summer. It is hardy except in the north, reaching 3m (10ft), and grows in an average soil but must not be shaded. Of the numerous varieties the single-flowered are more elegant, in colours ranging from white through pink to dark purple-blue.
**Pruning** No regular pruning required. Dead or diseased wood can be cut out in spring or summer. For a formal effect, even a hedge, cutting back in spring is appropriate.

### HIPPOPHAE RHAMNOIDES (*Elaeagnaceae*) (D)
This arching shrub or small tree is native to Britain in maritime areas but grows perfectly well inland in average soil, reaching 6m (20ft). The features are the silvery leaves and the orange berries, ripe in autumn and persisting for months.

*Hippophae rhamnoides*

**Pruning** No regular pruning required. Dead wood can be cut out in summer.

### HOHERIA (*Malvaceae*) (D, E, S/E)
A genus of trees with attractive flowers. In cold areas they are best grown against a sunny sheltered wall.
*H. glabrata* is a small deciduous tree to 6m (20ft) with grey leaves and clusters of fine white flowers in summer. It is hardy except in severe winters.
*H. lyallii* is very similar.
*H. populnea* is a tender evergreen with attractive pale flaky bark, reaching 10m (30ft) with white flowers in autumn.
*H.* 'Glory of Amlwch' is a semi-evergreen hybrid reaching 7m (23ft). The white summer flowers are particularly large, but it is tender when young.
**Pruning** *H. lyalli* benefits from having a proportion of the oldest wood cut out in spring. The evergreen types can be carefully pruned in spring to restrict size if necessary. Coral spot is a problem in damp situations.

### HOLBOELLIA CORIACEA (*Lardizabalaceae*) (CL, E)
A vigorous climber scrambling to 5.5m (18ft) and suitable for growing up a wall or tree. The leaves have three glossy green leaflets and flowers are produced in mid-spring, the male purple in terminal clusters, the female green-white in axillary clusters. The fruit is a pod 7.5cm (3in) long.
**Pruning** In spring, the weaker growths may be cut and in summer, long growths should be shortened.

## HOLODISCUS DISCOLOR (*Rosaceae*) (D)

This forms a vigorous arching shrub up to 3.7m (12ft), with lobed leaves and panicles of creamy flowers in summer. It needs good soil and an isolated but not shady position. The flowering period is regrettably short. Young canes are produced from the base.

**Pruning** The oldest stems may be removed each year after flowering. Some must be left but are cut back to a point at which young shoots are growing.

## HYDRANGEA (*Hydrangeaceae*) (CL, D, E) (D)

This genus of mainly deciduous shrubs and climbers is grown largely for the domed or flattened flowerheads, usually made up of tiny inconspicuous fertile flowers surrounded by larger, more showy sterile flowers. All the species like a rich soil; some tolerate chalk, and some shade.

*H. arborescens* can reach 3m (10ft) with loose growth. It has fertile flowers of dull white but is far surpassed by *H. a.* 'Grandiflora', a splendid plant whose stems bend under the weight of the flowerhead, a fault which is easily corrected by installing at an early stage a circular support such as is used for paeonies. It has pure white flowers (large, sterile) through summer and is hardy.

*H. aspera sargentiana* is a noble plant when seen at its best, reaching 2.4m (8ft) high. The leaves are large, up to 25cm (10in) long and 15cm (6in) wide, with a hairy covering like velvet on the upper surface. The sterile flowers are white on the outer side; the fertile ones are beautiful rosy-lilac. It is subject to damage from spring frosts but recovers quickly, though a year's flower may be lost. The woody framework is absolutely hardy.

*H. a. villosa* reaches up to 3m (10ft) and wider across. This plant is most desirable, with rosy-tinted white outer flowers and bluish-purple ones at the centre of the head. It is somewhat tender and apt to lose its flower buds in a spring frost.

*H. macrophylla* is a parent of the dozens of garden plants, possibly hybrids, that are divided for convenience into Hortensias and Lacecaps.

Hortensias have flowerheads which are globose corymbs: white, pink, red, blue or a combination. Hortensias, also known as mop-headed hydrangeas, commonly reach 1.8m (6ft), but in mild areas they can grow as tall as 3m (10ft).

Lacecaps have large flattened corymbs of fertile flowers surrounded by coloured ray-florets. They are mostly vigorous and of a similar size to the Hortensias. They include 'Blue Wave' and 'Mariesii', whose flowers are blue only in acid soils, otherwise pink or lilac.

HYDRANGEA MACROPHYLLA

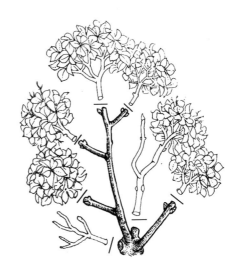

**Flower heads of the previous season are left on the shrub until spring and are then cut away, together with any failing stems. Basal growth of new stems does not always form readily, and manuring is advisable at this time**

**The result: good flowering, and new growth for next season**

ABOVE *Hydrangea arborescens* 'Grandiflora' is a cultivar from Ohio, markedly superior to the type. Pure white flowers appear from midsummer for many weeks. The plant needs support as its stems extend

LEFT An informal hedge of *Hibiscus syriacus* 'Blue Bird' ('Oiseau Bleu') needs full exposure to sun and a fertile soil. It grows slowly and is hardy, but only flowers freely in mild areas, and never as well as in its native France. When a framework has been formed by cutting stems to half their length each spring, the pruning will then cut back all growths to three or four buds from their origin, again in spring

*H. paniculata* 'Grandiflora' grows to 6m (20ft) high and has flowers white to pink, all sterile, in a pyramid. It requires good loamy soil and a mulch of manure once growth has started.

*H. petiolaris* is a deciduous climber that will reach 18m (60ft) up a tree by means of aerial roots and does well on a north-facing wall. It can also be used as a sort of ground cover, for example on a mound 90cm (3ft) high, which it will soon smother. The leaves are ovate and dark green. Corymbs up to 25cm (10in) across expand in early summer, with white sterile flowers at the margin and small, dull white flowers filling the centre.

*H. quercifolia* (oak-leaved hydrangea) reaches up to 1.8m (6ft) when grown in the shelter of a cool shady wall. The white flower panicles are erect through summer and numerous in these conditions.

*H. serratifolia* is a vigorous evergreen climber with tough, obovate leaves reaching 20m (60ft) or more. It is best grown against a sunny sheltered wall as it is barely hardy. Small white flowers are borne in crowded panicles in late summer.

**Pruning** *H. arborescens* and *H. paniculata* flower on the ends of current season's wood. The flowering stems are cut back to two to four buds in early spring. *H. aspera* and *H. quercifolia* should be encouraged to build up a permanent framework and need little pruning, but weak growths can be cut back in spring.

The flowering stems of Hortensias are cut back to 5cm (2in) from the old wood once the flowers are spent. In cold areas delay this until the following spring. The pruning of lacecaps is delayed until the point in spring when buds are developing well. It is thought that the dead flowerheads provide some frost protection through the winter. In spring cut back to a healthy bud and remove any shoots that look weak. In fact, if hydrangeas are treated well with regular manuring, weak and worn-out shoots are not very common, and it is often possible to do no more than remove dead flowerstalks.

When *H. petiolaris is* grown on a wall, extension growths which are not needed are cut back as they emerge in summer. Some of the spurs are cut to two or three buds in spring each year. As ground cover it needs only light pruning to restrict erratic growth. *H. serratifolia* does not require regular pruning but it can be restricted by cutting back in spring, only one-third of the plant each year.

### HYPERICUM (*Hypericaceae*) (D, E, S/E)

These shrubs and sub-shrubs are valued especially for flowering in late summer and autumn, but their foliage is healthy and a good green for many months. They like good soil, most tolerating chalk, and are hardy.

*H. calycinum* (rose of Sharon) is an excellent evergreen sub-shrub for ground cover in shade and produces beautiful golden-yellow flowers for most of the summer.

*H. kouytchense* is semi-evergreen, reaching 90cm (3ft), with good golden-yellow flowers followed by red fruits. Two notable hybrids are *H.* 'Hidcote', quite hardy, and *H.* 'Rowallane', both reaching 1.8m (6ft) in sheltered areas and having particularly large flowers. The latter is not fully hardy, but if frosted will usually recover and flower later in the year.

**Pruning** Pruning for *H. calycinum* is simple, consisting of cutting the whole plant almost to ground level. The more shrubby types can be pruned in spring, removing the dead ends of the shoots and shortening the living portion by a few centimetres to produce a sizeable shrub – or alternatively, and less desirably, cut right back.

### HYSSOPUS OFFICINALIS (*Labiatae*) (S/E)

A dense upright shrub to 45cm (18in) with bright green narrow aromatic leaves, and small, densely clustered dark blue flowers. It is also available in pink and white forms.

**Pruning** Cut back in early spring, hard if grown as a shrub, lightly if grown as a hedge.

### IDESIA POLYCARPA (*Flacourtiaceae*) (D)

This summer-flowering tree grows well in neutral or acid soil, readily forming a straight trunk, and will reach 12m (40ft). The horizontal branches grow in tiers and are long enough to shade neighbouring areas of the garden. The flowers are tiny but large bunches of red berries may appear in exceptionally hot years.

**Pruning** No regular pruning required. Given sufficient space, this forms a shapely tree. The lower branches can be removed if they cast too much shade.

### ILEX (*Aquifoliaceae*) Holly (D, E)

All species of these shrubs and trees like a moist, loamy soil, but often the common ones do not get it. They have alternate, glossy, more or less spiny leaves, flowers of little account except to bees, and the fruit is not a berry but a drupe (with a skin and a fleshy layer that acts as a store and protects the seed).

*I.* × *altaclerensis* is a group of vigorous evergreen hybrids including 'Camelliifolia', up to 14m (46ft), 'Golden King', golden-variegated up to 6m (20ft), and 'Hodginsii', up to 14m (46ft) and formerly much planted in industrial areas because of its tolerance of a polluted atmosphere.

*I. aquifolium* (common holly) is so common that its virtues are often overlooked. It can make an evergreen tree to 15m (50ft), a specimen shrub or a splendid hedge (see p118). After centuries of cultivation it has accumulated a vast collection of varieties and cultivars, of which one of the best is 'J. C. Van Tol', up to 6m (20ft).

*I. verticillata* Of the deciduous hollies, this does best in Britain, with scarlet berries maturing before the leaves fall then lasting well on the bare branches. It has a suckering habit and grows up to 1.8m (6ft).

**Pruning** No regular pruning required. This adaptable plant responds well to formal training or more natural treatment. In the former case, it should be trimmed in mid-spring, when wounds will soon be hidden by new growth; in the latter case, straggly growths can be cut back individually in mid- to late summer using secateurs to maintain the general outline.

### ILLICIUM (*Illiciaceae*) (E)

These shade-loving evergreens have unusual star-shaped flowers and attractive aromatic foliage. They require neutral to acid soil.

*I. anisatum* is a conical shrub or small tree, hardy in milder regions where it may reach 6m (20ft). It prefers an acid soil and some shelter from high winds. The greenish-yellow flowers appear in spring.

*I. floridanum* is a bushy shrub reaching 1.8m (6ft) and is as hardy as the above species. The maroon-purple flowers appear in late spring.

**Pruning** Pruning is only necessary to control wayward growth, and is best carried out in autumn.

### INDIGOFERA (*Leguminosae*) (D)

These shrubs will lose all their shoots in winter if unprotected, but do survive. All they ask is a sunny position, and they seem to tolerate a moderately limy soil.

*I. amblyantha* is hardier than most and reaches some 1.8m (6ft). The pinnate leaves are pleasant and the flowers, in upright racemes, are rosy-pink and appear throughout the summer.

*I. potaninii* has a similar habit of growth and flowering.

**Pruning** Despite the winter damage, both species preserve a short woody branch system. Pruning in early spring removes the dead part of the shoots and 2.5–5cm (1–2in) of the new growth.

### ITEA ILICIFOLIA (*Escalloniaceae*) (E)

A holly-like plant on which the pendulous racemes of greenish-white flowers hang vertically, 30cm (12in) or more long and quite crowded.

**Pruning** The best crops of catkins develop on growth made the previous year, so once a framework of branches has developed some of the oldest shoots can be cut out after flowering.

### JASMINUM (*Oleaceae*) (CL, D, E)

Although the climbers are better known, there are several shrubby members of merit.

*J. beesianum* is a vigorous deciduous climber to 4.6m (15ft) with dark green leaves above, and flowers rose to carmine in early summer. The fruit is pea-like but black and shiny.

*J. humile* 'Revolutum' is an evergreen to 2.4m (8ft) with good leaflets and slightly fragrant, rather hard yellow flowers in midsummer. It is reasonably hardy in milder regions.

*J. mesnyi* is an evergreen climber, regarded by most experts as only suitable for the mildest areas. It is most often grown in a pot from spring until autumn and then put under cover for the winter.

*J. nudiflorum* (winter jasmine) is not a climber, but is usually trained against a wall where it produces many flowers of a bright yellow on bare stems during winter months. The best scheme of training is to use a fan system of bamboos, tying them to horizontal wires on the wall.

*J. officinale* is a deciduous climber up to 10m (30ft), and a classic plant of English gardens. It forms a self-supporting bush but can also be trained against a house wall without any support if pruned back every spring.

**Pruning** *J. beesianum* does not require regular pruning, but shoots may need thinning in spring every few years. Laterals from the leading shoots of *J. nudiflorum*, *J. humile* and *J. officinale* flower mainly on the previous year's wood and can have some shoots cut back immediately after flowering. New shoots should be tied in as they appear. Good feeding of these plants after pruning is important. *J. mesnyi* and *J. officinale* should have crowded, over-long and frosted shoots cut out in spring.

### JUGLANS (*Juglandaceae*) (D)

These hardy, fast-growing trees have attractive aromatic leaves and, in the species described here, edible nuts.

*J. nigra* (black walnut) is one of the greatest park trees, reaching 30m (100ft). It is very fine when quite young but is not easy to rear as it quickly forms a tap root and then resents interference.

*J. regia* (common walnut) reaches some 20m (60ft). If you have a spare acre, consider an orchard.

**Pruning** *J. nigra* does keep a leader well, and it is possible to remove lower branches to give a clear trunk to 4.6m (15ft), not forgetting that pruning should not be delayed after Christmas as bleeding does occur once the growing season begins.

When *J. regia* is young it is subject to frost damage and may lose the leader. A replacement must be trained and kept under observation, rivals being cut away as soon as possible. Bleeding is to be avoided here also.

### JUNIPERUS (*Cupressaceae*) (CO, E)

A large genus of trees and shrubs from prostrate alpines to tall columnar trees.

*J. communis* (common juniper) can claim one cultivar which is truly dwarf, even prostrate: 'Hornibrookii', collected in County Galway, Eire, where it spreads up to 90cm (3ft) over the rocks but only 10–13cm (4–5in) high.

*J. horizontalis* has produced the dwarf cultivar 'Bar Harbor', found wild in Maine, growing in crevices on the rocky coast. The leaves are glaucous, almost steel-blue, and it is similar in size to the above species.

*J. × media* The cultivar 'Pfitzerana' is the most favoured of all junipers, and understandably so. It is a shrub reaching rather more than 1.8m (6ft) high and spreading widely with a flat top. 'Pfitzerana Compacta', with mainly juvenile awl-shaped leaves, is smaller and more compact.

*J. recurva* var. *coxii* makes an elegant tree up to 6m (20ft), with drooping branchlets of sage-green foliage.

*J. sabina* 'Tamariscifolia' is a low shrub of less than 1.8m (6ft), with leaves mostly juvenile, awl-shaped. It is used for clothing dry banks and can extend for several metres.

*J. virginiana* is hardy and makes a slow-growing conical tree to 15m (50ft). It does well on chalk and needs sufficient space to develop. Into maturity it is well furnished with foliage almost to ground level.

**Pruning** No regular pruning required. They should be given sufficient space and light, otherwise they may die back unattractively.

*Itea ilicifolia* is a superb evergreen shrub, but needs some shelter and is not suitable for cold districts

### KALMIA (*Ericaceae*) (E)

These attractive flowering shrubs must have acid soil and moisture and are slow-growing even when given good conditions. Full sun is required for good flowering.

*K. angustifolia* (sheep laurel) is evergreen, grows to 90cm (3ft) high, and has a spreading habit. The flowers are deep rosy-red, appearing in late spring.

*K. latifolia* is an evergreen 3m (10ft) high and 4.6m (15ft) across. The flowers are white or blush to deep rose.

**Pruning** No regular pruning required if the plant is correctly sited. After a number of years the plants may become woody or straggly, in which case a few of the oldest shoots may be cut back in spring.

### KALOPANAX PICTUS (*Araliaceae*) (D)

A small tree resembling a maple. The branches carry stout prickles. The palmate leaves on young plants are over 30cm (12in) long, deeply five- or seven-lobed. An elegant tree, quite hardy.

**Pruning** No regular pruning required. Rival leads should be removed as the plant develops and the stem cleared to a height of 1.8m (6ft) or so.

### KERRIA JAPONICA (*Rosaceae*) (D)

A hardy deciduous shrub to 2.4m (8ft) in woodland conditions. The leaves are light green, and golden-yellow flowers are borne singly on short leafy twigs in mid- to late spring. The green stems look well in winter. The cultivar 'Pleniflora' is much more common and much less attractive.

**Pruning** In both types suckers abound, and lead to a thicket if not controlled by removing some and cutting some of the old shoots to the ground. This is best done after the flowers fade.

### KOELREUTERIA PANICULATA (*Sapindaceae*)
### Pride of India (D)

A hardy tree occasionally up to 18m (60ft), although usually smaller, with attractive pinnate leaves of light green. The midsummer flowers are borne in panicles up to 30cm (12in) long, bright yellow, followed by brown capsules containing seeds like a pea. The leaves have good yellow autumn colour but are subject to coral spot.

**Pruning** No regular pruning required, except in the early years in order to maintain a central leader.

### KOLKWITZIA AMABILIS (*Caprifoliaceae*) (D)

A large shrub up to 3.7m (12ft) high, growing well in average soil and tolerating chalk well. It needs sun. The leaves are nondescript but the abelia-like soft pink flowers in late spring, more definite in the clones 'Rosea' and 'Pink Cloud', are splendid.

**Pruning** Advice on pruning ranges from 'can be left to develop naturally' to 'prune after flowering, cutting back to new young growth'. No doubt in the early years pruning is not essential, but eventually the plant's performance deteriorates and it becomes necessary to cut out whole lengths of old wood on which there are no new shoots, which suggests that good feeding every year might have saved the day. When this valuable plant is in its prime its performance for six weeks or even more in early summer merits a deal of thought and effort.

### × LABURNOCYTISUS ADAMII (*Leguminosae*) (D)

A graft hybrid between *Laburnum* and *Cytisus*, this small tree is of botanical interest, with some branches bearing laburnum-type flowers, others the cytisus-type and still others an intermediate, copper-pink flower. It is usually grown as a standard.

**Pruning** No regular pruning required, but suckers must be removed immediately.

### LABURNUM (*Leguminosae*) (D)

These small, fast-growing trees grow well in any soil not waterlogged, but do not often exceed 7.6m (25ft).

*L. anagyroides* reaches 7m (23ft) with grey-green leaves and short hanging clusters of yellow, pea-like flowers in spring and early summer.

*L. alpinum* (Scotch laburnum) reaches 6m (20ft). In summer it has dark green leaves and golden-yellow flowers borne on pendulous racemes of 0.3m (12in) or more.

**Pruning** These specimens are easily trained to a tree form with a 1.8m (6ft) leg and after that need little pruning. The branches are quite often misdirected and those which are crossing and rubbing should be removed entire. *L. anagyroides* may be spur-pruned, cutting back the young growth to two buds in early winter, and this is the method used for covering arches, pergolas or tunnels.

### LARIX DECIDUA (*Pinaceae*)
### European larch (CO, D)

This is the most satisfactory if not the most beautiful larch. It starts with a conical shape, later with branches drooping. The leaves are light green, especially on emerging in spring.

**Pruning** No regular pruning required. It is best as a single specimen with ample space to develop its shoots, otherwise the lower branches die off and cannot be replaced. Shortening the branches does not help.

### LAURUS NOBILIS (*Lauraceae*) Bay laurel (E)

This bushy, conical tree is tender in inland areas, often scorched by frost, and in such places is cut to the ground every few years, but always revives and gets away quickly. In maritime sites it stands the weather well, and can even reach 12m (40ft) in ideal conditions. The fragrant leaves are tough, dark shining green and make a fine bush, tree or hedge. The flowers are inconspicuous.

**Pruning** Although it can be left to its natural habit, the bay responds well to pruning in spring and can be trimmed to shape in summer. It is often grown in tubs, where it requires little attention apart from reducing the new growth to shape with secateurs every few weeks in summer.

### LAVANDULA (*Labiatae*) (E)

This popular genus of fully to half-hardy shrubs is grown both for the aromatic foliage and the attractive flower spikes. All species require a sunny, well-drained site.

*L. angustifolia* is a sub-shrub growing to 90cm (3ft) with purple flowers from summer to autumn. Among the more popular forms are 'Hidcote' and 'Munstead', both around 75cm (2½ft).

*L. stoechas* (French lavender) reaches 60cm (2ft) high and the same across. It has grey-green leaves and dark purple flowers in spikes 5cm (2in) long, with a tuft of purple bracts on each spike. A very attractive, but less hardy, plant.

**Pruning** All lavenders need pruning each spring, cutting off the flowers of last year and the young growth to near the base. Eventually it will not be possible to overcome lavender's tendency to sprawl and die back, so replacement cuttings should be made ready.

### LAVATERA (*Malvaceae*) (D)

These showy, vigorous flowering shrubs do well in poor soil, given a sunny site.

*L. maritima* is the best species, but is unfortunately tender. The flowers are pale lilac with purple veins and a crimson blotch at the base of the petal. It will reach 1.5–1.8m (5–6ft) in maritime places or against a sunny wall.

*L. olbia* 'Rosea' is a favourite plant, vigorous and also reaching 1.5–1.8m (5–6ft). The flowers are profuse and reddish-pink from midsummer until autumn. The cultivar 'Barnsley', which has white flowers with a pink eye, is now even more favoured. Both are hardy for practical purposes, but rather short-lived.

**Pruning** All lavateras should be cut back in spring to 15cm (6in) from the ground.

## LEDUM (*Ericaceae*) (E)

These shrubs have aromatic foliage as well as small white flowers. They are definitely calcifuge and like damp soil.

*L. glandulosum* grows to 90cm (3ft) high, occasionally more. The white, rather unexciting flowers appear in late spring.

*L. groenlandicum* is very hardy, reaches 75cm (2½ft) and has better white flowers.

**Pruning** Neither needs pruning except to control spread, but dead-heading probably helps to preserve the vigour of the shrub since it prevents seeding.

## LEIOPHYLLUM BUXIFOLIUM (*Ericaceae*) (E)

A neat shrub with small leaves on short stalks and pink flower buds opening white.

**Pruning** The pruning requirements are as for *Ledum*.

## LEPTOSPERMUM (*Myrtaceae*) (E)

These small trees or shrubs are not fully hardy except in the warmest areas, where they may reach 3.7m (12ft). They can grow well in maritime areas provided they are sheltered.

*L. grandiflorum* (formerly *L. rodwayanum*) has white flowers and is comparatively hardy; *L. lanigerum* is of similar hardiness and also has white flowers. It has lived for years at Tintinhull near the southern side of a wall.

*L. scoparium* is the best-known species and is spectacular at Tresco Abbey in the Scilly Isles. At Kew, against a wall, it is killed in severe winters. There are cultivars of great merit, notably 'Nichollsii' (crimson) and 'Ruby Glow' (deep red and double).

**Pruning** Leptospermums do not break readily if cuts are made into old wood. If necessary, young growth can be cut back in late spring to create a bushy habit. If grown with wall protection, don't train them on the wall.

## LESPEDEZA THUNBERGII (*Leguminosae*)
### Bush clover (D)

This fine shrub has grooved stems of 1.2–2.4m (4–8ft) rising from a woody rootstock and then dying back in the winter. A fresh set arises in the late spring making a mass of stems which, in autumn, bear large panicles of purple pea flowers. Some protection from frost in winter is wise.

**Pruning** In spring the old growths are cut to the ground.

## LEUCOTHOE FONTANESIANA (*Ericaceae*) (E)

This hardy shade-loving shrub reaches 1.8m (6ft) and needs a lime-free, rich soil. It has tapering leaves and white flowers in late spring which, unfortunately, are borne on the lower side of the branches and one needs Miss Jekyll's two men with a rope (see p81) to bring them all into view.

**Pruning** Any pruning of an unhealthy stem should remove it at ground level. New growths form from the base and flower in the first year, so pruning can be completed in early spring.

## LEYCESTERIA FORMOSA (*Caprifoliaceae*) (D)

This frost-hardy, half-woody shrub is stool-like in its growth. In one season hollow stems rise to 1.5m (5ft) or more, and flower in summer with claret-coloured bracts and a purplish corolla. It likes rich soil and a sunny site.

**Pruning** It really has to be pruned; if left alone it quickly becomes a mass of weak and dying growths. Thinning these out is seldom enough. Better to cut down all growth to 10cm (4in) from the ground in early spring. In this case it is even more than usually necessary to apply a heavy mulch in spring and water in summer. Whether it is worth it is a matter for individual taste.

## LIGUSTRUM (*Oleaceae*) (D, E, S/E)

*L. japonicum* has evergreen, glossy and almost black leaves 10cm (4in) long and can reach 3m (10ft). White flowers are borne in 20cm (8in) panicles in midsummer. It needs some shelter.

*L. lucidum* makes a sizeable evergreen tree, sometimes 12m (40ft), with glossy dark green leaves. The flowers are white in erect panicles 15cm (6in) or more high.

*L. ovalifolium* is seen most often as the cultivar 'Aureum' (golden privet). It has been very widely used in town planting and only fashion has reduced it, as it will brighten places in which hardly anything else will grow. The leaves are green in the centre with a border of golden-yellow. It is semi-evergreen or, in the worst soil conditions, deciduous. It can reach 3.7m (12ft) high and is useful as a hedge (see p125).

*L. quihoui* makes quite an elegant deciduous shrub with arching stems up to 2.4m (8ft) and fragrant white flowers in late autumn.

*L. sinense* is a hardy deciduous or semi-evergreen shrub up to 3.7m (12ft) with abundant panicles of white flowers followed by round, black-purple fruits persisting until New Year.

**Pruning** Most species respond to hard pruning with vigorous growth but are also attractive when allowed to grow with minimal intervention. They can simply be pruned back when necessary to retain the natural habit.

LINDERA OBTUSILOBA (*Lauraceae*) (D)

This bushy rounded shrub has a height and spread of up to 6m (20ft). The aromatic leaves are an interesting lobed shape, dark glossy green above, turning butter-yellow with a hint of pink in autumn, but not always in colder climates. Like all the genus it must have a lime-free soil.

**Pruning** No regular pruning required. Growths killed during winter should be removed in spring as growth commences.

LINNAEA BOREALIS (*Caprifoliaceae*)
Twin flower (E)

This sub-shrub must be included out of respect for Linnaeus, the eighteenth-century Swedish botanist who devised the binomial system of classification for plants that is still in use today. It is a creeper, only 2cm (¾in), and suitable for an informal rock garden. The flowers are produced in summer in pairs, pink or white.

**Pruning** No regular pruning required.

LINUM ARBOREUM (*Linaceae*) (E)

This neat but spreading shrub has height and spread of 30cm (12in) and golden flowers in summer. It needs a well-drained soil and full sun.

**Pruning** No regular pruning required. Cut back if invasive.

LIQUIDAMBAR (*Hamamelidaceae*) (D)

Trees with maple-like leaves, inconspicuous flowers and good autumn colour. Does not tolerate chalky soils.

*L. formosana* var. *monticola* reaches 12m (40ft) and seems to be almost hardy, with leaves which turn from purple to crimson then dull green, but are crimson again in autumn.

*L. styraciflua* (sweet gum) likes a good acid or neutral soil, though flourishing less in the latter. It makes a fine tree up to 25m (80ft) with a pyramidal crown. The leaves, like those of a maple, turn a striking crimson in autumn. The cultivar 'Worplesdon' has become popular.

**Pruning** *L. styraciflua* is best grown with a clear trunk up to 6m (20ft), and the lower branches should be removed as the tree grows taller.

LIRIODENDRON (*Magnoliaceae*) (D)

These fast-growing trees have large attractive leaves and summer flowers.

*L. chinense* is hardy and needs good deep soil to show at its best. It dislikes being transplanted and should be put in its permanent place early. At Kew it has reached 15m (50ft) in 70 years.

*L. tulipifera* (tulip tree) grows to a greater size than the above, up to 25m (82ft). The trunk is very fine and smooth. The leaves are usually cut off almost square at the apex, as on no other tree. The flowers in early summer do resemble a tulip in shape, the petals greenish-yellowish with an orange spot near the base, which is a pity.

**Pruning** *L. chinense* makes a good leader without much help. *L. tulipifera* may need some help, rival leaders being searched out regularly and removed. The trunk should be cleared to 4.5–6m (15–20ft) from the ground by gradual shortening and removal of laterals after three or four years.

LITHOCARPUS DENSIFLORUS (*Fagaceae*)
Bark oak (E)

This frost-hardy tree resembles an oak but is botanically related to *Castanea*. It is more or less hardy in the south of Britain and perfectly so at Kew, reaching 10m (30ft).

**Pruning** A leader must be kept going by removal of rivals, as the foliage is very heavy and small shoots are easily damaged by storms. This tree is not readily available.

LONICERA (*Caprifoliaceae*) (CL, D, E, S/E)

These hardy plants tolerate most soils. The climbers are nearly all worth growing but the bushy shrubs are disappointing. They are often damaged by spring frosts and lose their flowers, and therefore berries also.

*L.* × *americana* is a deciduous climber to 7m (23ft) with fragrant yellow, purple-tinged flowers in whorls during early summer. It is a very fine plant.

*L. brownii* is a deciduous climber to 3.7m (12ft) usually seen as 'Dropmore Scarlet' with orange and scarlet flowers. It is best on a wall.

*L. chaetocarpa* is deciduous and promising in form and foliage but the floral performance, eagerly awaited, comes to very little. It reaches 1.8–2.1m (6–7ft).

*L. giraldii* is an evergreen climber that makes a dense spreading mound to 1.2m (4ft) of hairy stems with a velvet surface of leaves. The purple flowers are small, but the leaves are enough to make it worthwhile.

*L. japonica* is an evergreen climber to 7m (23ft) with very fragrant flowers, white turning to yellow in the cultivar 'Halliana', perhaps the finest of all climbing honeysuckles.

*L. japonica* 'Aureoreticulata' is an evergreen or semi-evergreen climber often grown against a wall, where it will reach 10m (30ft).

*L. nitida* has tiny evergreen leaves and is much used

*Lavandula angustifolia* 'Jean Davis'. All lavenders benefit from being clipped back immediately after flowering is over. They are good edging plants, decorative and architectural

for hedging in the form 'Ernest Wilson' (see p125) and in the yellow-leaved form 'Baggesen's Gold' as a specimen also, when it will reach 1.5–1.8m (5–6ft). *L. periclymenum* (woodbine, honeysuckle) is a deciduous climber to 6m (20ft) with yellowish-white flowers, turning orange-brown after pollination, extremely fragrant especially in the early morning or evening, continuing from midsummer for two months. The cultivar 'Belgica' is more bushy; 'Serotina' is said to have a longer flowering period. *L. pileata* is a respectable, if unexciting, deciduous shrub reaching 1.5m (5ft) and remaining evergreen in a sheltered place. The young leaves are bright green, the flowers insignificant. Amethyst-coloured berries are infrequently produced. *L. sempervirens* is a splendid evergreen climber to 3.7m (12ft) with flowers of rich orange-scarlet in whorls throughout summer. *L. × tellmanniana* 'Superba' is a deciduous climber to 4.6m (15ft) with unscented flowers, 5cm (2in) long, yellow tipped with red in profuse clusters from early summer. The lower half should be shaded if possible by a shrub of modest size such as *Daphne burkwoodii*. *L. tragophylla* is a deciduous, shade-loving climber to 4.6m (15ft) with bright yellow flowers. **Pruning** Shoots of shrubby types which have flowered are cut back promptly and severely. Climbers can either be left unpruned to form a natural tangle or the oldest third of shoots can be cut back to ground level in spring, but this must be done from the outset before the shoots twine together.

## MAACKIA (*Leguminosae*) (D)

A genus of very hardy trees, growing well in any good soil in sun.
*M. amurensis* usually only forms a shrub in Britain, reaching 4.6m (15ft) very slowly; heavy feeding may help to produce a tree. The pinnate leaves resemble those of *Cladrastis* and the flowers in midsummer are dull white.
*M. chinensis* will make a tree up to 12m (40ft) on which the leaves are silvery and the flowers unimpressive.
**Pruning** Early pruning is directed to maintaining a leader, but beyond that no regular pruning required.

## MACLURA POMIFERA (*Moraceae*)
Osage orange (D)

A hardy tree to 15m (50ft) with spiny, spreading branches, long and dark green leaves, inconspicuous flowers and inedible round fruits, 5–10cm (2–4in) across. It is widely used as a hedge in the USA and Central Europe.
**Pruning** No regular pruning required.

## MAGNOLIA (*Magnoliaceae*) (D, S/E, E)

All magnolias are worthy of cultivation with the exception, for gardeners, of *M. acuminata*, a very grand tree with negligible flowers. The others range in size from about 3m (10ft) to 15m (50ft). The needs of these flowering trees and shrubs in the matter of soil, however, are not clearly established; some authorities maintain that over half the species will not tolerate alkaline or chalky conditions while others claim that the only difficulty in cultivating these trees is in establishing them after transplanting. There can be little doubt that the deciduous species *M. campbellii*, *M. dawsoniana*, *M. denudata*, *M. hypoleuca*, *M. liliiflora*, *M. salicifolia* and *M. sprengeri* cannot be made to thrive in chalky soils, although in some cases the British climate may be at fault. Fortunately British gardeners can grow the magnificent evergreen *M. grandiflora* with wall protection. The deciduous *M. kobus*, *M. × loebneri*, *M. × soulangiana*, *M. × lennei*, *M. stellata* and *M. wilsonii* all need rich soil, retentive of moisture, and most require some shade – as in woodland.
**Pruning** No regular pruning required. Most magnolias regenerate well even from old wood, and correction of faulty growth is straightforward. Any removal of stems more than 1cm ($\frac{1}{2}$in) in diameter is best left until the dormant period, from early autumn until midwinter. If it is left any later in the season than this there is likely to be bleeding, as growth will already have started. From long experience it is possible to say that painting wounds has no beneficial effect. If the cut is well made, neither infection nor die-back occur.

## × MAHOBERBERIS AQUISARGENTII (*Berberidaceae*) (E)

This shrub is an intergeneric hybrid of a *Mahonia* with a *Berberis* and reaches 1.5m (5ft) in 10 years. Some of the erect stems and leaves are like those of *Mahonia*, others are like those of *Berberis*, all shining dark green. The late spring flowers are yellow, but not freely borne.
**Pruning** As the stems differ in length some shortening of the longer ones in spring, usually the mahonia-like specimens, improves the shape.

MAHONIA (*Berberidaceae*) (E)

A genus of evergreen shrubs, closely related to *Berberis* but having simple pinnate foliage and no spines on the branches. They are mostly hardy, although there are some notable exceptions, and like a good, rich soil.

**M. aquifolium** (Oregon grape) is a small very hardy shrub which against a wall or hedge may rise to 90cm (3ft). It has glossy dark green leaves and yellow flowers in dense racemes in early spring, followed by black berries.

**M. 'Charity'** will attain 3m (10ft) and has beautiful yellow flowers in early winter. 'Buckland' and 'Lionel Fortescue' are a similar size with racemes freely branched and fragrant flowers opening in early winter.

**M. fremontii** will reach 1.8m (6ft), with blue-green leaves and flowers in small clusters, but is hardy only on a sunny sheltered wall.

**M. japonica** is a hardy and robust shrub to 1.8m (6ft) high with splendid pinnate leaves and fragrant flowers opening from autumn through winter to make it a very desirable plant.

**M. lomariifolia** is not fully hardy but in a sheltered, partially shaded spot it flowers well on long erect spikes in late autumn and winter and grows up to 3m (10ft).

**M. pinnata** will reach 3m (10ft) and makes a graceful shrub, flowering profusely in early spring.

**M. trifoliolata** var. *glauca* is upright to 1.8m (6ft) high and, if against a wall, makes branches which arch forward. It has good glaucous leaves, some nearly white, and flowers in spring.

**Pruning** No regular pruning required, though removal of flowered shoots to control spread can be performed without any ill effect once they fade. *M. aquifolium* responds well to pruning if that becomes necessary, when it is best done in spring.

MALUS (*Rosaceae*) (D)

A large genus of deciduous trees including *M. domestica*, now the domestic apple, and *M. sylvestris* (wild crab). *M. domestica*, uniform in its essential botanical characteristics, is considered to be a group of hybrids, some of great antiquity. Excluding *M. domestica*, the term 'crab apple' refers to plants derived from orchard apples crossed with 'Siberian' crabs. The following hybrids are valued especially for their fruits, though most have worthy flowers. They do not exceed 10m (30ft).

**M. 'Dartmouth'** Fruit crimson.

**M. 'Golden Hornet'** Fruit deep yellow.

**M. hillieri** Fruit yellow, worthy flowers.

**M. 'John Downie'** Fruit orange and scarlet, worthy flowers.

**M. 'Mahaleb'** Fruit yellow, worthy flowers.

**M. floribunda** is a dense-headed tree to 10m (30ft) high, more across. It flowers in spring with a great profusion of rose-coloured buds opening white with a pink blush.

**M. hupehensis** is a fine, well-shaped, hardy tree to 12m (40ft), with fragrant, white spring flowers tinged with pink in the bud, regrettably only for two weeks, followed by small fruits, becoming dark red.

**M. tschonskii**, is grown only for autumn leaf colour in hues of yellow, orange, purple and scarlet.

**Pruning** If a feathered plant with a good central leader is obtained, this may be trained either on a leg of 60–90cm (2–3ft) to produce a low-growing tree, even a bush; or on a leg of 1.8–2.4m (6–8ft), to form a wide branching tree. It is not necessary to prune the centre as a rule, allowing the natural development even if this is a little untidy. Look out for suckers on a grafted specimen (as many are).

MELIOSMA VEITCHIORUM (*Samiaceae*) (D)

A superb slow-growing tree 9–15m (30–50ft) high with erect branches. The leaves are up to 17cm (7in) long with red petioles. Panicles up to 45cm (18in) long by 30cm (12in) wide carry creamy white flowers in late spring, followed by violet fruits.

**Pruning** This should be trained with a single lead and planted with sufficient space. Frost damage may occur in spring and can be removed after the likelihood of further frost has passed.

MENZIESIA CILIICALYX (*Ericaceae*) (D)

A shrub to 90cm (3ft) high, rather similar to an azalea in appearance, with oval leaves and flowers ranging from cream to pale purple in clusters on shoots of the previous year, in late spring.

**Pruning** After flowering the shoots should be cut back when the blooms fade, in order to allow maximum time for the ripening of new wood and to save the energy needed to form seed.

METASEQUOIA GLYPTOSTROBOIDES (*Taxodiaceae*) Dawn redwood (CO, D)

A vigorous deciduous tree up to 20m (60ft) with shaggy grey bark, peeling eventually. The leaves are opposite in two ranks, blue-green above, light green below, on opposite branches. The tree is hardy apart from susceptibility to damage by late spring frosts, thriving in moist but well-drained soil.

**Pruning** It readily forms new leaders – too readily – but those that are superfluous make excellent cutting material if cut out in spring to summer. It has not been a success for hedging because hard pruning leads to abundant top growth.

MITRARIA COCCINEA (*Gesneraceae*) (E)
A low, spreading shrub with bright orange-scarlet tubular flowers in succession from late spring until summer's end.
**Pruning** No regular pruning required.

MOLTKIA (*Boraginaceae*) (S/E)
Sun-loving shrubs and sub-shrubs suitable for well-drained, neutral to acid soil.
*M. petrea*, although initially grown as a greenhouse plant, has proved itself able to survive in rock gardens with some extra care. It is a sub-shrub to 30cm (12in) with long narrow leaves and clusters of violet, funnel-shaped summer flowers. It has been largely replaced by *M. × intermedia*, a shrub 30cm (12in) high with blue flowers through summer.
**Pruning** This consists simply of tidying straggly shoots in spring.

MORUS (*Moraceae*) Mulberry See Fruit Trees & Bushes.

MYRICA GALE (*Myricaceae*) Sweet gale (D)
A dense shrub around 90cm (3ft) high with shoots and leaves that are fragrant when crushed. The flowers appear in short tawny catkins during early summer on wood of the previous year. An acid, moist soil is necessary.
**Pruning** Long growths become untidy and may be cut to the ground after flowering, when suckers will fill the gap.

MYRTUS (*Myrtaceae*) Myrtle (E)
A number of plants previously thought to be species of this genus have recently been reclassified but are included here for convenience.
*M. bullata* (now officially known as *Lophomyrtus bullata*) is a shrub 3–4.6m (10–15ft) high, hardy only in maritime regions, with sparse white flowers.
*M. chequen* (now *Luma chequen*) is a very leafy, not very hardy, shrub with white flowers usually found in wet places and reaching about 3.7m (12ft).
*M. communis* (common myrtle) remains in the genus, and has beautiful white, fragrant flowers in midsummer. Only hardy in the mildest areas, it is commonly grown against a wall, or rather 0.3–0.6m (1–2ft) from it, where it will attain 1.8m (6ft).
*M. lechlerana* (now *Amomyrtus luma*) is a bushy shrub which does well in the mild regions. It has creamy white flowers in late spring but is subject to damage by late frosts. A hedge, perhaps unique, is 7.6m (25ft) high at Trewithen in Cornwall.
*M. luma* (now *Luma apiculata*) is a bush to 6m (20ft) high, sometimes a tree. In mild parts it has

flourished and self-seeded. It is noted for its flaking cinnamon-coloured bark and white flowers in late summer and early autumn.
*M. ugni* (now *Ugni molinae*) forms a shrub less than 1.8m (6ft) high, with rounded, rose-tinted flowers in late spring. It is hardy in mild regions.
**Pruning** If it is intended to produce a tree, the normal process of training a leader and reducing side shoots progressively is required. These shrubs are mostly able to grow without support especially if near, but not touching, a wall. *M. communis* can be clipped over every year. Otherwise little pruning is practised, apart from shortening wayward shoots.

NANDINA DOMESTICA (*Berberidaceae*) (E)
A shrub 1.8m (6ft) high with erect unbranched stems. The large compound leaves have many leaflets and the flowers are small and white in large panicles in summer. It needs a rich soil, a sunny position and shelter, with which it is hardy except in the coldest areas. It is worth growing for its shoots and leaves, the flowers being of little account except in hot summers.
**Pruning** Bedraggled, weather-beaten stems can be cut away at ground level in spring. Shortening them is of no avail. If it is well fed strong growths arise from the base to replace them.

NEILLIA THIBETICA (*Roseaceae*) (D)
This is the best species, reaching 1.8m (6ft) high with erect stems, ovate pointed leaves and white flowers on branched racemes in late spring; an elegant picture. Young canes arise from the base if the plant is well nourished and suckers may arise from roots 30–60cm (1–2ft) from the main plant.
**Pruning** Some of the old wood can be removed each year, immediately after flowering, at the same time shortening the younger growths by a half.

NEOLITSEA SERICEA (*Lauraceae*) (E)
A small, conical tree reaching 6m (20ft), but only for the mildest areas. The large leaves, when young, are covered with brown hairs, later becoming dark green above and glaucous on the underside. The flowers, greenish yellow in clusters, appear in autumn.
**Pruning** No regular pruning required except to remove dead or unhealthy growths.

NICOTIANA GLAUCA (*Solanaceae*) (D, S/E)
One of the few woody tobacco plants. As seen at Tintinhull, Somerset, it is an erect branching shrub, 2.4–3m (8–10ft), often becoming tree-like with glaucous stems, glabrous as are the leaves on both

surfaces. The terminal panicles bear yellow flowers too diminutive to be in scale with the rest of the robust plant. They appear from early summer onwards. In hot summers, they self-seed to an embarrassing degree but are only hardy in mild winters.

**Pruning** Unwelcome branches can be removed straight after flowering without damage to the rest of the tree.

### NOTHOFAGUS *(Fagaceae)*
### Southern beeches (D, E)

The insignificant flowers of these fine trees are more than made up for by their foliage and habit.

*N. alpina* (formerly *N. procera*) is deciduous and certainly tender in the first few years, at least in some clones, but later becomes hardy and grows away to 23m (75ft). The leaves are narrowly oval, finely toothed and pale green.

*N. antarctica* is a deciduous tree usually less than 15m (50ft) high. It is perfectly hardy and grows well in the first few years but then slows down. The round leaves are dark green, set closely on the branches and sometimes fragrant. The habit of this tree is somewhat ungainly, even if the leader is carefully trained, and it is inclined to be blown over in violent storms.

*N. betuloides* is an evergreen tree slowly reaching 13m (45ft). In temperate regions of the northern hemisphere it is hardy though intolerant of cold winds.

*N. dombeyi* is a relatively fast-growing and hardy evergreen to 15m (50ft) or more. It usually makes good any loss of foliage in a severe winter and is the most satisfactory of the evergreen species in temperate climates of the northern hemisphere.

*N. obliqua* reaches 23m (75ft), is deciduous and has leaves that are dark green above, pale below. The wood is rather brittle and an exposed site should be avoided.

**Pruning** There are no specific pruning problems with this genus, but a single lead should be maintained and trees should be staked in the early stages.

### NOTOSPARTIUM CARMICHAELIAE
### *(Leguminosae)* Pink broom (D)

A leafless shrub to 1.8m (6ft), best grown in a pot with protection in winter, until woody growth is established when it can be planted out and is almost hardy. The slender arching branches are wreathed in summer with pink pea flowers.

**Pruning** Normally pruning only involves tidying up, but when a bush is old and weak the whole may be cut away to young stems which are usually present at the base of the plant.

*Malus floribunda* is probably a hybrid, and perhaps the most beautiful of all crabs in blossom. The flowers are red in bud, pink when open and very abundant

### NYSSA *(Nyssaceae)* (D)

Before planting either of these trees, it is important to bear in mind that their only outstanding feature is autumn colour, the flowers and fruit being of no aesthetic value.

*N. sinensis* is said to reach 15m (50ft) high, but in temperate climes is smaller, sometimes a shrub. The leaves are oval, narrow and 15cm (6in) long, dark green. Their autumn colour is red and yellow.

*N. sylvatica* is slow-growing and few are more than 15m (50ft) high. The leaves are variable in shape, size and colour, usually dull green. In autumn they turn red and yellow and are very handsome.

**Pruning** A good leader should be established early and the lower branches gradually shortened and eventually removed, to give a clear trunk to 1.8m (6ft) or more. The remaining branches can be allowed to develop a pendulous habit, which is natural and displays the autumn colour well.

### OEMLERIA CERASIFORMIS *(Rosaceae)* (D)

*O. cerasiformis* is a suckering shrub, formerly known as *Osmaronia cerasiformis*. It makes a thicket 2.4m (8ft) high and 3.7m (12ft) across with lanceolate, sea-green leaves. In spring the fragrant white flowers, in pendent racemes, are followed by brown, then purple, very bitter fruits. This is a very hardy plant and grows well in good soil, but dislikes chalk.

**Pruning** Before the thicket becomes really large it is possible to prune by cutting down the shoots which have flowered as soon as they have done so.

### OLEA EUROPAEA *(Oleaceae)* Olive (E)

In Italy the gnarled branches of this tree with their grey-green foliage are a leading feature of the landscape. In Britain it is cultivated only in the mildest areas. A well-known tree grows in the Chelsea Physic Garden, London and is over 6m (20ft) high in an open site. It occasionally bears fruit.

**Pruning** When grown in the open, a central lead should be trained. Winter damage can be cut back in spring when young growth breaks freely.

### OLEARIA *(Compositae)* Daisy bush (E)

Most of these shrubs are medium-sized, reaching 0.9–6m (3–20ft) high. They like a well-drained loamy soil and none object to chalk. Nearly all are propagated quite easily from cuttings and that is an encouragement to try them out.

*O. avicenniifolia* reaches 3m (10ft), with white flowers in corymbs in late summer. One of the hardiest. *O. cheesemanii* is also hardy as the last, and the flowers are more abundant.

*O.* × *haastii* is a fully hardy, rounded shrub up to 2.7m (9ft) high with leaves jostling on the branches, thick dark green above, white-felted beneath. White, fragrant flowers appear during mid- to late summer in corymbose clusters. This shrub stands Atlantic weather well and makes a good shrub under those conditions. It is propagated with the greatest of ease from cuttings taken in early autumn.

*O. macrodonta* is the right choice for the weekend gardener – almost hardy, robust, usually to 3m (10ft), but sometimes 6m (20ft) high. The leaves are sage-green above, white-felted below, with early summer flowers in branched clusters. In a sandy soil it presents a splendid picture and asks only for a modest weed-free area in return.

*O. phlogopappa*, 1.8m (6ft) height and spread, is exciting as represented by the 'Splendens' group, especially in its blue-flowered form. Unfortunately it is not hardy and if grown in the open should be propagated by a cutting in midsummer lest the worst should befall.

**Pruning** Pruning of olearias may be undertaken when new growth appears after winter damage, or in order to reduce any overgrown plants.

## ORIXA JAPONICA *(Rutaceae)* (D)

A graceful shrub 1.8m (6ft) high, spreading, with long branches. The scented leaves are dark green and glabrous, turning pale yellow and white in autumn, aromatic if crushed. The flowers are inconspicuous, fruits brown. The long shoots may hang to ground level and take root; this is how the bush gradually spreads.

**Pruning** If necessary the shoots can be pruned before they root.

## OSMANTHUS *(Oleaceae)* (E)

Elegant evergreen shrubs, some resembling hollies, from which they may be distinguished by their opposite leaves. They grow well in good ordinary soil and tolerate chalk.

*O. armatus* is a shrub reaching 3–4.6m (10–15ft) high. The dark green leaves are leathery and coarsely toothed, and the clusters of creamy autumn flowers are small but fragrant.

*O.* × *burkwoodii* (formerly *Osmarea)* is a shrub to 2.7m (9ft) high, rather dense with shining dark green leaves. The fragrant, white spring flowers are not abundant.

*O. delavayi* is altogether more elegant: a spreading shrub usually about 3m (10ft) high, with dark green leaves, spotted beneath. The flowers are fragrant, white, in terminal clusters which almost hide the foliage and appear without fail.

*O. heterophyllus* is an interesting shrub that grows well in shade, although the autumn flowers will be sparse. Glossy dark green leaves compensate for that. It is useful as a formal hedge plant.

**Pruning** These plants respond well to pruning after flowering, but the informal surface should be preserved by cutting over-long shoots back to laterals within the bush.

## OSMARONIA see OEMLERIA

## OSTEOMELES SUBROTUNDA *(Rosaceae)* (D)

A slow-growing shrub, 1.5–1.8m (5–6ft) tall in the open but not hardy and needs to be trained on a wall facing south, fan-wise and close to the surface. Grown thus the foliage is elegant and the white flowers, in branching corymbs appearing in early summer, stand out well.

**Pruning** Once the framework is established, pruning is directed to removing a few of the older branches after flowering.

## OSTRYA *(Carpinaceae)* (D)

With their attractive foliage, catkins and fruits, these make desirable trees.

*O. carpinifolia* (hop hornbeam) has the character of the hornbeam, with several botanical differences. The fruits, 5cm (2in) long, are attractive in autumn, as are the male catkins in spring. It readily forms a leader and makes a fine tree 15m (50ft) high.

*O. virginiana* (ironwood) is very like *O. carpinifolia*, but not as large or spreading.

**Pruning** No regular pruning required.

## OXYDENDRUM *(Ericaceae)* Sorrel tree (D)

This tree grows to 9m (30ft) in northern temperate zones and tends to be more shrub-like. The leaves are lanceolate, 15cm (6in) long, and the small white flowers, very like those of *Pieris*, are borne in late summer or autumn. This plant is definitely calcifuge and is not worth attempting except where the soil is acid, preferably pH less than 6.0. Under the right conditions the leaves turn scarlet after flowering is over.

**Pruning** No regular pruning required.

## OZOTHAMNUS see HELICHRYSUM

## PACHYSANDRA *(Buxaceae)* (D, E, S/E)

Useful ground cover in shade, but they fail in any alkaline soil and only survive narrowly in that which is neutral.

*P. procumbens* (Allegheny spurge) is a deciduous plant with leaves 5–7.5cm (2–3in) long and nearly as wide. They appear at the top of stems up to 30cm (12in) long, which come without branching from a rootstock. The flowers are borne in spikes at the base of the stems, a rather untidy arrangement.

*P. terminalis* is similar but the flowers arise at the end of the previous year's shoots (even more untidy).

**Pruning** No regular pruning required.

### PAEONIA *(Paeoniaceae)* Paeony (D)

Mainly herbaceous, but there are a few woody species of this lovely flowering genus.

*P. delavayi* reaches 1.8m (6ft) and has, in early summer, a fine blood-red flower with golden anthers in a cluster which enhances the effect. It likes a rich soil, tolerating chalk, and is hardy.

*P. lutea* var. *ludlowii* has larger flowers and is a larger shrub – up to 2.4m (8ft) – than the type. It flowers in late spring rather than early summer. The foliage is fine and densely deployed but the flowers are sometimes few.

*P. suffruticosa* reaches 2.1m (7ft) and bears large, pale pink, single or semi-double, cup-shaped flowers. There are many hybrids.

**Pruning** This is largely cosmetic. The flowered stalks die back to the terminal bud of the new growth and can be cut away just above it, but there is no urgency for this unless the appearance of these stalks is offensive. It is done in early spring, along with the removal of any dead wood. The paeony blight *Botrytis paeoniae* must be taken seriously and infected shoots should be removed at once. Fungicides are effective but run the risk of producing tolerant strains of the fungus.

### PARAHEBE *(Scrophulariaceae)*

A genus of shrubs or sub-shrubs forming spreading mounds, not particular as to soil but needing sun.

*P. catarractae* Makes shoots up to 30cm (12in) and has dark green leaves and white flowers with a central area of crimson in racemes, appearing from late summer to early autumn.

*P. lyallii* is very similar but smaller, up to 15cm (6in). Both are hardy.

**Pruning** No regular pruning required.

### PARROTIA PERSICA *(Hamamelidaceae)* (D)

A genus with one species which is usually seen as a wide, spreading shrub, even when reaching a height of 12m (40ft). The smooth grey bark flakes in an attractive way. The ovate leaves, up to 13cm (5in) long, turn to gold and crimson in autumn. The flowers appear in early spring in clusters, with numerous red stamens which make a fine picture on the leafless branches.

**Pruning** It is questionable whether one should attempt to train a leader with a clean stem of 3m (10ft). *Parrotia* rarely looks ugly as a shrub, the branches tending to grow strongly outwards without overcrowding. If grown as a single specimen in grass, which suits it well, a problem will arise in time as the lower branches may lie almost at ground level and mowing may easily damage them. Miss Jekyll thought this difficulty was easily solved by having two men stretch a rope to lift the branches while a third did the mowing. Not many of us have access to this method.

### PARTHENOCISSUS *(Vitaceae)* (CL, D)

A small genus of climbers that climb by leaf tendrils, which either twine or carry adhesive pads on their extremities.

*P. henryana*, up to 10m (30ft) or more, has digitate leaves variegated with silvery-white along the midrib and main veins. It is best on a low wall where the leaves can be admired.

*P. quinquefolia* (Virginia creeper), a fine plant up to 15m (50ft) or more, has wonderful autumn colours.

*P. tricuspidata* reaches 25m (70ft) and has crimson autumn leaves.

**Pruning** All may be grown on walls or pergolas, but in the latter case annual pruning to build up a spur system is best carried out in midwinter, as there is then no risk of bleeding. On walls, they should be pruned annually in autumn to keep growths out of the gutters.

### PASSIFLORA CAERULEA *(Passifloraceae)* Passion flower (S/E)

A vigorous climber to 10m (30ft), more or less evergreen in southern Britain if grown against a wall. The leaves are palmate and the flowers, 7.5–10cm (3–4in) across, are white, blue and purple, beginning in early summer and continuing until autumn. 'Constance Elliott' is a fine cultivar.

**Pruning** The plant attaches itself by twining tendrils to wires or wooden supports, the main stems trained to uprights, the laterals hanging down with the flowers on the current year's growth. The laterals are pruned to a single bud at the base in spring.

### PAULOWNIA TOMENTOSA *(Scrophulariaceae)* (D)

This fast-growing tree reaches 15m (50ft) and forms a rounded crown. The purple foxglove-like flowers are in erect panicles which are formed in autumn but do not open until the following spring, and are

vulnerable to the changeable British winter and spring weather.

*P. tomentosa* 'Lilacina' has unlobed leaves and flowers of pale lilac.

**Pruning** Paulownias are especially tender when young and need protection while a leader is being formed but subsequently require full sun. They can be grown as foliage plants by cutting back the young shoots hard in spring, then selecting the best two new growths to grow on. If well fed and watered the two stems will grow to 3.7m (12ft) and will produce handsome leaves up to 90cm (3ft) across.

## PENSTEMON *(Scrophulariaceae)* (E, S/E)

There are a few half-woody shrubs in this large genus, most needing the shelter of a sunny wall or a place in a rock garden in full sun.

*P. heterophyllus*, which is semi-evergreen, reaches 25cm (10in) and is tender, but the cultivar 'Blue Gem' justifies taking a risk and 'Hidcote Pink' is equally desirable.

*P. newberryi* is a hardy dwarf evergreen, reaching 15cm (6in). It is ideal for the rock garden and bears scarlet flowers abundantly.

*P. pinifolius* is another evergreen, reaching 30cm (12in) high and with a spreading habit. The flowers are scarlet in midsummer. Perfectly hardy in full sun.

**Pruning** No regular pruning required. Winter damage can be cut back in spring.

ABOVE *Paeonia suffruticosa* 'Rock's Variety' is famous for its beauty – but also because it has been difficult, and often impossible, to grow from seed and has to be propagated by grafting. It is not freely available from nurseries, but meristem culture may change that. Whether such plants will prove as healthy as those grown from seed is uncertain. The picture shows 'Rock's Variety' flowering in spring

TOP RIGHT *Perovskia atriplicifolia* 'Blue Spire' should be cut to one or two buds in early spring. It has grey leaves with complementary slate-blue flowers

RIGHT *Philadelphus coronarius* flowering from behind a 1.8m (6ft) high wall. This plant had not been pruned for at least 10 years. It calls into question the statement often made that mock orange flowers on wood of the previous year. It does – but also on wood of earlier years

PERNETTYA MUCRONATA (*Ericaceae*) (E)

A shrub usually 90cm (3ft) high, with a suckering habit and dark green leaves, densely displayed. Many small white flowers in early summer are followed by clusters of berries, each about 12mm (½in) across, coloured white, pink to purple. A lime-free soil is essential for good results and full sun is desirable. There are several good forms including 'Edward Balls' (erect) and 'Thymifolia' (dwarf) with white flowers.

**Pruning** Pruning is confined to removal of dying stems and of unwanted sucker extensions.

PEROVSKIA ATRIPLICIFOLIA (*Labiatae*) (D)

A semi-woody shrub to 0.9–1.2m (3–4ft), with stiff, erect stems and grey leaves. The panicles of lavender-blue flowers in late summer compliment the leaves admirably. The shoots die down in winter nearly to the base.

**Pruning** Pruning is best delayed until early spring, when shoots are cut back to one or two buds from the base.

PETTERIA RAMENTACEA (*Leguminosae*) (D)

A shrub to 1.2m (4ft) after 10 years in optimum conditions. It has trifoliate leaves and is said to bear fragrant yellow laburnum-like flowers in early summer. It seldom does so, though hardy and apparently healthy.

**Pruning** No regular pruning required. The natural habit of growth should be allowed to develop.

PHELLODENDRON AMURENSE (*Rutaceae*)
Amur Cork Tree (D)

This tree needs a rich soil and does not tolerate drought conditions well. It makes a tree about 9m (30ft) high with corky bark, wide-spreading branches and bright green pinnate leaves. The winter buds are silver-hairy, and small yellow flowers are borne in early summer.

**Pruning** It is not easy to maintain a leader after the tree is 3m (10ft) high. Young growths are often injured by spring frosts, although the tree is almost winter-hardy. Damaged shoots can be removed once all danger of frost has passed.

PHILADELPHUS (*Philadelphaceae*)
Mock orange (D)

A genus of deciduous shrubs with opposite leaves of no great character. The flowers are mostly white, and many are deliciously scented. The species hybridise freely in nurseries or collections so that many plants sold as species are in fact hybrids. If the species are a platoon, the cultivars are a battalion.

All plants of the genus and their hybrids like a rich soil and tolerate, even enjoy, chalk, but can perform remarkably well under poor conditions. They appreciate full sun and flower best on young wood. Of the plants in cultivation, this is a selection guided by affection and long experience.

*P. coronarius* is a shrub to 3.7m (12ft) with creamy white, heavily fragrant flowers in early summer.

*P. insignis* flowers until midsummer, reaches 3m (10ft) and is good all round.

*P. microphyllus* is a stylish, small-leaved species to 90cm (3ft) high with a fragrance of pineapple.

Among the excellent **cultivars** are: 'Belle Etoile', a dense shrub to 1.2m (4ft), bearing single white flowers with maroon spots, very fragrant; 'Erectus', up to 1.2m (4ft), with single flowers, well displayed and fragrant, with the bonus of being extremely tolerant of dry conditions; 'Innocence', which wins first prize with ease. It is a vigorous shrub to 3m (10ft) with discreet creamy variegation of leaves 5–7.5cm (2–3in) long. The fragrant single flowers are most abundant in midsummer.

**Pruning** This follows an annual routine which comprises cutting away shoots which have flowered to a point at which a new shoot is developing and removing some of them, the oldest, to ground level, hoping that enough new growths will have formed to retain a good flowering form in the shrub. It must be said that flowering is not confined to the growth of the previous year and many large bushes of *P. coronarius* flower abundantly for years with no pruning. One has to decide the policy from experience of the individual plant, but give it adequate feeding every spring. The photograph on p83 shows a specimen over 40 years old flowering very freely, apparently unpruned.

If the plant becomes ugly with lengths of bare wood, cut everything nearly to the ground after flowering. There will be no flowers the next year, but after that it may be possible to restore good behaviour.

PHILESIA MAGELLANICA (*Philesiaceae*) (E)

A suckering shrub making wide thickets of stems up to 1.2m (4ft) high, with narrow rigid leaves. The crimson flowers are tubular in summer and autumn. It needs a moist and acid soil in partial shade, with some shelter, but is hardy except in the coldest places. In moist, maritime areas it can climb trees or rocks for 6m (20ft).

**Pruning** No regular pruning required.

PHILLYREA LATIFOLIA (*Oleaceae*) (E)

A shrub to 4.6m (15ft), occasionally a tree twice as high, with glossy dark green leaves densely disposed. It makes an impressive shape and bears inconspicuous white flowers in spring. If this all sounds rather boring, be assured that this is a shrub with that elusive quality – charm.

**Pruning** Light pruning, carried out after the flowers have faded, can help to maintain a neat rounded outline.

## PHLOMIS (*Labiatae*) (E)

A genus of herbs, shrubs and sub-shrubs with pleasing hooded summer flowers in axillary whorls. They need full sun and good ordinary soil.

*P. chrysophylla* is a small sub-shrub with yellowish sage-like foliage reaching 90cm (3ft) in height and spread. The flowers, borne in early summer, are golden.

*P. fruticosa* (Jerusalem sage) has grey-green foliage, yellow flowers, and grows to 90cm (3ft) high and rather wider.

*P. italica* is an upright shrub reaching 90cm (3ft), with oblong, very woolly leaves and pink-lilac flowers.

**Pruning** All these soon become untidy if not pruned. This should be done in spring after an inspection for signs of winter damage. If the old wood is healthy new growth quickly breaks. Any weak stems, or those with long and ugly woody shoots, can be removed at this time. Half-ripe cuttings taken in early summer root easily. *Phlomis* is not a long-lived subject.

## PHOTINIA (*Rosaceae*) (D, E)

The evergreen majority in this genus of shrubs and trees like a light soil and do well with chalk, but the deciduous group needs an acid soil.

*P. serrulata* is an evergreen shrub to 9m (30ft), occasionally more, with leathery leaves which are often red when young, and dark green later. Panicles of small white flowers are produced in spring. While frost-hardy in all milder districts it does not flourish except in maritime areas.

Hybrids between *P. glabra* and *P. serrulata* have been raised and named by the Fraser Nurseries in Birmingham, Alabama, USA. The first was 'Birmingham' and 'Red Robin' came later. Both are evergreen plants with young growths that are fairly hardy; both reach some 6m (20ft) and are tolerant of chalk.

**Pruning** If frost-damaged branches are cut back regeneration soon occurs. *P. serrulata* is apt to produce shoots from the base, growing up the centre, and these should be removed. Any pruning to restrict projecting growths should be done in mid-spring.

## PHYGELIUS (*Scrophulariaceae*) (E)

Grown for their attractive tubular flowers, these plants are best against a sunny sheltered wall.

*P. capensis* (Cape figwort) is an evergreen shrub to 1.2m (4ft) with leaves 13cm (5in) long and 5cm (2in) wide. The flowers are scarlet with a yellow throat and well displayed on erect panicles.

*P. aequalis* is a sub-shrub to 90cm (3ft) with late summer pendulous flowers on panicles 15cm (6in) long or more, salmon-pink outside, orange-yellow at the mouth. The cultivar 'Yellow Trumpet' has soft yellow flowers and is relatively hardy.

**Pruning** *P. capensis* is often cut to the ground in winter but revives and, once growth commences in spring, the dead shoots can be removed.

## PHYLLODOCE (*Ericaceae*) (E)

These dwarf shrubs are difficult to grow in England for the surprising reason that the summers are too hot, but do well in Scotland. They must have acid soil and plenty of moisture.

*P. × intermedia* is the most satisfactory, growing up to 23cm (9in) with solitary flowers on slender stalks during mid-spring, bright purple.

*P. nipponica* is a neat shrub 10cm (4in) high with white or pinkish flowers in umbels in late spring.

**Pruning** These plants produce strong growths from the base every year. Any that die are cut out completely. No other pruning required.

## × PHYLLOTHAMNUS ERECTUS (*Ericaceae*) (E)

This dwarf shrub, under 30cm (12in) high, is one of a series of intergeneric hybrids between *Phyllodoce* and *Rhodothamnus*. Solitary flowers of delicate rose are produced in mid-spring. It needs a moist, lime-free soil and summer heat makes it flag.

**Pruning** No regular pruning required.

## PHYSOCARPUS OPULIFOLIUS (*Rosaceae*) (D)

A shrub to 3m (10ft) high, this rather undistinguished plant produces flowers in clusters, white tinged pink in early summer. The cultivar 'Luteus' has leaves of a good golden-yellow when they emerge but all too soon they become green, as the type.

**Pruning** This consists of removing some of the older wood after flowering, as young shoots are freely formed at ground level.

## PICEA (*Pinaceae*) (CO, E)

Conifers with attractive 'needles' arranged in spirals on the shoots.

*P. abies* (Norway spruce) is a fast-growing conifer to 20–30m (60–100ft).

*P. omorika* (Serbian spruce) is a tall graceful tree to

15m (50ft) with drooping branches which curve upwards at the tips. It does well in any decent soil and tolerates chalk. Why is it not used more often in developments and streets?

*P. smithiana* is another splendid tree to 30m (100ft) with drooping branches, long leaves and long cylindrical cones.

**Pruning** No regular pruning required.

### PIERIS *(Ericaceae)* (E)

A genus of shrubs which require a lime-free soil and ample moisture. They are of dense habit with flower panicles that form in autumn, some with reddish buds through the winter, eventually opening during mid-spring to reveal white pitcher-shaped flowers. Some plants have leaves which open red, passing through cream to plain green.

*P. formosa* is hardy and slow-growing with an eventual height and spread of 3.7m (12ft). The flowers are produced abundantly in late spring, and young growths are coppery. *P. f.* var. *forrestii* grows to 3m (10ft) high and has produced the excellent cultivar 'Wakehurst'. It has vivid red foliage at first in early spring, with white flowers opening two or three weeks later.

*P. taiwanensis* is hardier and is not often damaged by spring frost. The young growths are bronze-red and the white flowers in mid-spring are very fine on a bushy dense plant up to 3m (10ft).

**Pruning** No regular pruning required. The plants should be allowed their natural habit, although they will respond to hard pruning in spring if absolutely necessary, provided the plants are strong and healthy.

### PILEOSTEGIA VIBURNOIDES (CL, E)

A climber with very few problems, accepting any fertile soil, and climbing by aerial roots. It is hardy, reaching 6m (20ft), with leather leaves and creamy-white flowers crowded in terminal panicles in late summer and autumn.

**Pruning** In spring any protruding branches can be shortened. In summer any extension growths which go beyond the allotted space can be cut back.

### PINUS *(Pinaceae)* (CO, E)

A large genus of conifers with a wide range of sizes. Some tolerate very poor soils but those with fine needles dislike shallow chalk soil.

*P. armandii* is 10–15m (30–50ft) tall with leaves in fives, and cones in clusters of two or three, becoming pendulous. It does well where there is no chalk.

*P. jeffreyi* is 20m (60ft) or more in height and conical with leaves in threes, long and bluish-green, and

*Phygelius capensis* is a sub-shrub, here shown flowering well in an open situation in late summer. It will probably be cut to the ground by frost in winter but revives reliably in spring, even if the evergreen leaves have been ruined

cones 20cm (8in) long. It is very handsome, but short-lived.

*P. nigra* (Austrian pine) reaches 20m (60ft), with dark brown bark and a dense head of dark green leaves. It is good in chalky soil and in bleak exposure. On sandy soils, *C. n.* var. *maritima* (Corsican pine) is very common and reaches 25–30m (82–100ft). The bark of old trees is heavily ridged and dark grey.

*P. pinaster* (maritime pine) is a sparsely branched, less hardy tree to 18m (60ft). The cones are solitary or in clusters, often persisting intact on the branches for several years.

*P. pinea* (umbrella pine) is a tree to 10m (30ft) with a characteristic umbrella-shaped head of spreading branches. The leaves are in pairs, the cones up to 30cm (12in) long.

*P. sylvestris* is a common tree of great beauty at its best, when seen as a large tall-stemmed specimen, 15–25m (50–82ft) tall. The young bark is reddish. It does best in good average soil, neither damp nor dry, nor more than a little chalky.

*P. wallichiana* (Himalayan pine) is a fast-growing tree to 18m (60ft), with cones 15–25cm (6–10in) long. An unusual-looking pine, it is said to be short-lived and declining at 100 years. Do not let that deter you, but note that it will not tolerate chalk.

**Pruning** It is very important to retain a single lead for as long as possible, with any rivals removed in spring. Any dying branches should be cut back right to the trunk. Species with attractive bark can be cleared of lower branches to show this to advantage.

### PIPTANTHUS NEPALENSIS *(Leguminosae)* (E)

A shrub to 2.4m (8ft) often grown against a wall, where it should be hardy in most years. The foliage is very like that of laburnum, as are the bright yellow flowers, yet somehow it lacks character.

**Pruning** This is confined to the removal of dead or damaged shoots in spring once growth has started.

### PITTOSPORUM *(Pittosporaceae)* (E)

A genus of shrubs and trees which are undemanding as to soil but not hardy enough for most temperate areas.

*P. dallii* is one of the hardiest species and makes a handsome foliage shrub 4.6m (15ft) high with

coarsely toothed, dark green leaves; the flowers are never produced in Britain. Nonetheless, it is worth growing in a sheltered position.

*P. eugenioides* makes an evergreen tree to 10m (30ft) in mild areas, with narrow leaves 12cm (5in) long and fragrant small flowers in mid-spring.

*P. tenuifolium* is most often seen as a hedge in sea-side towns. It responds to hard pruning in spring.

*P. tobira* is a good wall shrub to 6m (20ft) with bright, glossy leaves and creamy scented flowers. It is much used for hedging in southern Europe but is not hardy enough for that purpose in cooler areas. Nevertheless, its foliage merits a sheltered place.

**Pruning** These plants all grow freely from old wood, so hard pruning in spring is quite feasible.

PLAGIANTHUS LYALLI see HOHERIA

### PLATANUS *(Platanaceae)* (D)

A genus of a few species, in the main noble trees that have survived attempts to show that they cause allergic irritation of the bronchii, eyes, and even ears, as first hinted at by Dioscorides in around 50AD. Recently these trees were attacked in print by nature-lovers on the ground that they do not give a house to birds and other fauna, and should therefore not be planted any more in London, one of their favourite haunts.

*P. × acerifolia* (London plane) is a magnificent tree up to 21m (70ft) with mottled, flaking bark, a very big crown of curved branches and large, palmate leaves, variable in shape and size. The fruit clusters are at first bristly, later becoming smoother.

*P. orientalis* produces laterals very readily and large branches form at a low level, which has to be accepted and is attractive. The leaves are palmate with five large lobes and little variation in shape. Otherwise it is like *P. × acerifolia*.

**Pruning** In the nursery a leader can be established for *P. × acerifolia* without much difficulty and a clean stem of 2.4m (8ft) attained. Later this may be increased to 4.6m (15ft), as the character of the bark is a feature. *P. orientalis* tends to develop cavities in the older branches which should be shortened to avoid them breaking off. All *Platanus* regenerate with exceptional vigour after any lopping, as shown by the regular pollarding of some street trees, but this is not advisable as a long-term practice as it weakens the tree overall.

### PODOCARPUS NIVALIS *(Podocarpaceae)*
Alpine totara (CO, E)

A low shrub, rarely upright to 3m (10ft), of dense habit with dull green foliage. It makes good ground cover, particularly for a shady area.

**Pruning** No regular pruning required.

### POLIOTHYRSIS SINENSIS *(Flacourtiaceae)* (D)

A tree to 9m (30ft) or more, with fragrant flowers in late summer. The leaves are slender and pointed.

**Pruning** No regular pruning required. An attempt should be made to establish a leader, but it is not easy as branching is strong.

### POLYGALA CHAMAEBUXUS *(Polygalaceae)*
Milkwort (E)

A dwarf creeper 15–30cm (6–12in) high with flowers pea-like, creamy-tipped yellow through spring. It likes cool, moist, lime-free soil.

**Pruning** No regular pruning required.

### PONCIRUS TRIFOLIATA *(Rutaceae)* (D)

A bushy shrub to 4.6m (15ft), notable for the fierce spines, 2.5–5cm (1–2in) long, which arm the stems. The leaves have three or five leaflets; the flowers are fragrant (do not get too close) and pure white in late spring. The fruits are seen in mild gardens and look like small oranges. It is sometimes advocated as a protective hedge. It is a slow-growing plant and would need much patience to grow to an effective size, as well as being a peril to children and pets.

**Pruning** It can be trained and responds well to pruning, but grows slowly and should not need attention often. Dead wood should be cut out in spring and for hedging purposes it is clipped in early summer.

### POPULUS *(Salicaceae)* Poplar (D)

There are so many species that they are here classified into four groups, with one or two examples in each. All are deciduous.

1. Leuce Aspens, white and grey poplars. Includes *P. alba*, *P. canescens* and *P. tremula*.

*P. alba* is a tree seldom more than 9m (30ft) high, and is short-lived. The young shoots and lower surfaces of the leaves are covered with white wool.

*P. canescens* is a superb hybrid to 21m (70ft), and suckers all too readily.

*P. tremula* (aspen) is noted for quivering leaves, even on some still days. It makes a large crown with a fine display of yellow autumn leaves on a tree to 15m (50ft).

2. Leucoides

*P. lasiocarpa* grows to 12m (40ft), rarely more, with a rough trunk and very large leaves up to 25cm (10in) long and half as wide on a red petiole. Rarely recognized as a poplar, it is the best choice for gardens as it forms a very shapely tree.

*P. wilsonii* is similar.

3. **Tacamahaca** Balsam poplars. Includes *P. balsamifera*, *P. candicans* and *P. trichocarpa*. Most trees supposed to be *P. balsamifera* are *P. candicans*.

*P. trichocarpa* (black cottonwood) grows very rapidly to 30m (100ft) or more. The leaves give off the balsam scent and colour well (yellow) in autumn. A tendency to canker has been almost overcome in recent clones. Suckering may cause trouble.

4. **Aegiros** Black poplars.

*P. × canadensis* forms an important group of hybrids. Among the best are *P. × eugenii* and *P. × robusta*, both handsome in leaf and shape.

*P. nigra* (black poplar) is fast-growing to 25m (82ft) with diamond-shaped leaves, bronze when young, green in summer and yellow in autumn.

*P. n.* var. *italica* (Lombardy poplar) is usually planted in rows, though a single specimen has a better landscape effect. It is easily propagated from hardwood cuttings and is very fast-growing to 30m (100ft).

**Pruning** Straightforward, and poplars readily form a leader. If a clean trunk is made by pruning lateral shoots it should not exceed 4.6–6m (15–20ft), so that ladder work is sufficiently safe. Such pruning is often followed by the formation of epicormic growth which will need to be cut away every winter. Mistletoe often colonizes the tree but does no harm. *P. lasiocarpa* does not need pruning at all.

## POTENTILLA *(Rosaceae)* Cinquefoil (D)

The shrubby potentillas do well in any average garden soil and flower for several weeks from late spring to midsummer. 'Beesii' is a dwarf shrub to 75cm (2½ft) with golden flowers on silvery foliage. 'Elizabeth', bushy and about 90cm (3ft) high, has flowers of soft yellow. One of the best and most desirable is 'Katherine Dykes', up to 1.2m (4ft) high with profuse yellow flowers. 'Longacre' is a mat-forming shrub with large sulphur-yellow flowers. 'Tilford Cream' grows to 90cm (3ft) high and the flowers are cream. 'William Purdom' is a large shrub to 1.2m (4ft) high, with canary-yellow flowers in dense cymes.

**Pruning** Prune, not severely, in spring, reducing strong shoots by one-third. Weak growths can be removed to the base or cut back to strong growths.

## PRUNUS *(Rosaceae)* (D, E)

A genus of mostly deciduous shrubs and trees which includes plums, apricots, cherries, bird cherries and the evergreen cherry laurels. The leaves are alternate, the flowers white, pink or occasionally yellowish-white. There are five subgenera with botanical features which distinguish them. Generally speaking, they all enjoy a loamy soil and tolerate lime completely. They are hardy, with a few exceptions, and those that are deciduous need a southerly exposure with some shelter from north and east. Examples from the subgenera are given below.

1. *Prunus* Plums and apricots.

*P. cerasifera* (cherry plum) A round-headed tree to 10m (30ft) with white flowers in early spring. Good for hedging.

*P. serrulata*, a flat-topped tree to (12m) 40ft. The white double flowers appear in mid- to late spring.

2. *Armeniaea* Apricots.

*P. mume* (Japanese apricot) reaches 6m (20ft) and has single, pink, almond-scented flowers in early spring. The double form has pink flowers in late winter.

3. **Dwarf shrubs** Axillary buds in threes.

*P. incana* (willow cherry) is a shrub to 1.8m (6ft) with red flowers in spring.

4. **Trees or shrubs** Buds solitary in leaf axil.

*P. avium* (gean, mazzard) reaches 20m (60ft) and has white flowers in spring. It is used as a stock for orchard cherries. The leaves are conduplicate (folded together) in bud.

*P. padus* (bird cherry) has fragrant white flowers in terminal racemes 15cm (6in) long on a spreading tree 15m (50ft) high.

5. *Laurocerasus* Cherry laurels.

*P. lusitanica* (Portugal laurel) is a wide evergreen shrub 3m (10ft) or more high. The glossy dark green leaves have red petioles. The flowers are small, white and scented in early summer. It is hardier than *P. laurocerasus*, which is a similar shape and size.

**Pruning** Most *Prunus* only need regular pruning during the nursery stage but before that comes the choice of a site and of the appropriate sort of tree. This is such a large genus that it should be possible to find one even for a really small garden. *Prunus × cistena*, for example, grows to 1.8m (6ft) with pointed leaves, crimson at first, later bronze, and white flowers in mid-spring. Assuming that a need to prune has arisen, for example due to damage to a branch or unwanted spread, there are some indications of the best time of year for the task. The winter is the time for the fungus *Chondrostereum purpureum* (silverleaf) to attack pruning or other wounds, especially on plums, though all species of *Prunus* are susceptible. Any major pruning should, if possible, be planned for midsummer. A further advantage of this choice is that bleeding will not occur, as the rise of sap has ceased by then.

## PSEUDOLARIX AMABILIS *(Pinaceae)* (CO, E)

This fast-growing coniferous tree dislikes lime but is perfectly hardy, reaching 10m (30ft). At first sight it looks just like a larch, but it has clustered male catkins and large woody scales on the cone. After transplanting to its final position the tree must be fed and watered regularly.

**Pruning** Good training is essential, with care to establish a leader. The horizontal branches should not be shortened as they weep nearly to ground level, often laden with cones.

### PSEUDOTSUGA MENZIESII *(Pinaceae)*
Oregon Douglas fir (CO, E)

A magnificent tree to 25m (82ft), but is useless on poor, dry soils and hates chalk. Few gardens are large enough to accommodate it.

**Pruning** No regular pruning required. The tree grows to a good upright habit unaided, and should be allowed to form its natural irregular outline. Any damaged or diseased branches should be removed to the main stem.

### PSEUDO-WINTERA COLORATA
*(Winteraceae)* (E)

Related to *Drimys* and a shrub to 90cm (3ft) high. Bark almost black. Aromatic oval leathery leaves, pale yellowish-green above, flushed pink, edged and blotched with purple, glaucous beneath. It is for the milder areas only and best in woodland conditions.

**Pruning** No regular pruning required. Winter-damaged growths should be cut back to healthy growths in spring.

### PTELEA TRIFOLIATA *(Rutaceae)* Hop tree (D)

A shrub or tree with a height and spread of 7m (23ft). The leaves are trifoliate; the yellowish flowers are borne in corymbs in early summer and are very fragrant, as are the clustered fruits, which are winged and persistent. Once fallen they often lie on the ground through the winter. A background of deciduous shrubs or trees will enhance the autumn display. The cultivar 'Aurea' has leaves of soft yellow which later become lime-green.

**Pruning** No regular pruning required once established. A clear trunk of 90cm (3ft) with staking suits the poorly developed root system, as the plant may lean over if unsupported.

### PTEROCARYA *(Juglandaceae)* Wing nut (D)

Three species and one hybrid of this tree are available in Britain; all are very desirable and adapt well to local conditions. The emerging foliage is liable to be ruined by spring frost but is soon replaced.

*P. fraxinifolia* (Caucasian wing nut) has been known to reach 30m (100ft) high. It has a trunk with furrowed bark, leaves around 45cm (18in) long, with up to 13 pairs of leaflets, and greenish pendulous catkins, the females reaching 38cm (15in) long.

*P. × rehderiana* is a wide tree, up to 15m (50ft) tall, often surrounded by a grove of suckers. It seems to be more vigorous than either of its parents, and hardier. Very fine.

*P. rhoifolia* is very similar to *P. fraxinifolia*.

*P. stenoptera* is a fine tree to 23m (80ft), very similar to *P. × rehderiana,* of which it is a parent.

**Pruning** No regular pruning required, but large pruning cuts, if necessary, should be made in late summer to avoid bleeding.

### PTEROSTYRAX HISPIDA *(Styracaceae)* (D)

A shrub to 6m (20ft) high, occasionally a tree, with fresh green oval or obovate leaves and small white flowers on pendulous panicles in early summer.

**Pruning** It seems preferable to allow this plant to make a shrub rather than to train it as a tree. No regular pruning needed.

### PUNICA GRANATUM *(Punicaceae)*
Pomegranate (D)

Even in milder regions this summer-flowering shrub needs a sunny, sheltered wall where it will reach 1.8–6m (6–20ft), with scarlet funnel-shaped flowers – but not always fruit, and never any that can be eaten with enjoyment. The dwarf variety 'Nana' is hardier than the type and suitable for a rock garden. It forms a rounded shrub of 30–90cm (1–3ft) and flowers well but only sets fruit occasionally. If the climate continues to warm up, it will succeed in the twenty-first century.

**Pruning** Some of the older shoots may be cut back in summer; not in winter, as living wood cannot easily be distinguished from dead at that time.

### PYRACANTHA *(Rosaceae)* (E)

Shrubs with alternate leaves and white flowers. The fruits are yellow, orange or scarlet. The shrubs do well in any average soil and are nearly all hardy. Good species include:

*P. atalantioides*, up to 4.6m (15ft) with scarlet fruits but prone to fireblight.

*P. coccinea* 'Lalandei', up to 3.7m (12ft) with large orange-red fruits.

*P. crenato-serrata*, up to 4.6m (15ft) with red fruits.

*P. rogersiana* 'Flava', up to 3m (10ft) with yellow fruits.

**Pruning** Grown in the open they are usually left alone without pruning, and, if any is needed to restrict the size of the shrub, it is best to remove entire shoots as the cut ends are unsightly. The flowering performance is better with wall-training, for which pyracanthas would be ideal if the colour of the berries were less blatant. Fan-training with plenty of room between the shoots allows the formation of spurs which will fill the space completely. After flowering a light pruning removes wood which is protruding forward, but take care not to damage faded flowers or berries already forming. In autumn another pruning removes part of any shoots concealing berries and allows maximum colour display.

## PYRUS *(Rosaceae)* Pear (D)

The true pears include some of the largest trees in this family. The flowers are mostly beautiful, if rather fleeting, but the fruits – if one excludes those which are grown in the kitchen garden – are of little merit (however, see Fruit Trees & Bushes).

**P. communis** (common pear) is a tree up to 18m (60ft) high, with splendid tessellated bark and branches with short spurs which bear white flowers in mid-spring, abundantly enough to make a picture rivalling that of the apple. The fruit is often brownish and small but until recently was good enough to make perry in Worcestershire, where in Elizabeth I's reign nearly every lane was lined by these very long-lived trees.

**P. nivalis** (snow pear) is a tree up to 10m (30ft) with ascending branches. The white woolly leaves appear in mid-spring along with the pure white flowers. The fruits are small, round and yellowish.

**P. salicifolia** (willow-leaved pear) is a small tree to 7.6m (25ft) high, the younger branches pendulous, resembling *Elaeagnus*. The leaves are narrow and lanceolate, covered with a silvery-grey down when young, and the flowers are pure white in mid-spring, in corymbs. This pear is mostly grown as the cultivar 'Pendula', with branches more drooping than on the type.

**Pruning** No regular pruning required. If any, it should be in midsummer when the risk of fireblight is slight and there is time for small wounds to heal before winter. Removal of dead or diseased limbs of *P. communis* is arduous, the timber being very hard.

## QUERCUS *(Fagaceae)* Oak (D, E)

There are almost 450 species, trees and shrubs, but only about 70 are in cultivation. Two of these are British natives – *Q. petraea* and *Q. robur*, the latter the best-known and best-loved of large British trees. Oaks in general must have a deep rich soil to thrive and do best of all in one which is rather acid; at least we assume so, when considering the wonderful oaks of the eastern USA in their native areas, and compare them with their failure in many areas of Britain, some on alkaline soils.

**Q. acutissima** is a deciduous tree to 15m (50ft) with bright green leaves, slender and pointed. It grows well from seed.

**Q. canariensis** is a splendid deciduous tree to 21m (70ft), notable for its dark green, lobed, obovate leaves which do not fall until Christmas. It is perfectly hardy and easily cultivated but when grown from seed it is very likely to produce the hybrid *P. canariensis × robur*.

**Q. castaneifolia** forms a very vigorous and erect deciduous tree reaching 30m (100ft). It has oval, shining, dark green leaves.

**Q. cerris** (Turkey oak) is a very hardy deciduous tree that grows rapidly when young, eventually reaching 30m (100ft). The foliage is dark and rather rough to the touch but the appearance of the tree is handsome.

**Q. coccinea** (scarlet oak) is a deciduous tree to 21m (70ft) and probably requires acid soil to flourish. It is noted for brilliant red autumnal leaves, but this colouring is very variable among trees raised from seed.

**Q. frainetto** (Hungarian oak) is a fast-growing deciduous tree to 22m (70ft), more tolerant of sandy, neutral soils than most oaks and one of the best-looking of the genus, with large leaves up to 20cm (8in) long and deeply lobed.

**Q. × lucombeana** is a group of semi-evergreen hybrids, formerly classified as *Q. hispanica*. The cultivar 'William Lucombe' makes a noble spreading tree up to 25m (80ft), with dark green leaves.

**Q. ilex** (holm oak) is a superb round-headed evergreen tree up to 25m (82ft) that thrives in rather light soil and makes a very dense mass of foliage. It is hardy in milder regions and tolerates the seafront. It has only two faults: leaves are shed every day during early summer, and often later, and it is quite difficult to raise the tree from acorns, which need to be grown in pots for two or three years before planting out.

**Q. palustris** (pin oak) is a deciduous tree to 18m (60ft) with a dense but graceful crown. Leaves are glossy dark green, with good red autumn colour in acid or neutral soil but it does not thrive on chalk.

**Q. petraea** (durmast oak) is a deciduous tree to 30m (100ft) very similar to *Q. robur*, but distinguished by its long-stalked leaves and sessile fruits.

**Q. robur** (English or common oak) is a large fast-growing deciduous tree with a broad crown, and a height and spread of 25m (80ft).

**Q. rubra** (red oak) quickly makes a sturdy deciduous tree to 25m (80ft) with a broad crown. Autumn colour is variable, often a striking red lasting two or three weeks.

*Q. variabilis* is deciduous and capable of 24m (80ft) in height, but is usually less. The bark becomes corky after about 10 years. The leaves are oblong, up to 17cm (7in) in length, with bristly teeth, the upper surface dark green, glabrous, the lower felted grey. The tree is slender with an elegant habit.

**Pruning** Beyond developing a single leader, there is little to be done to these reliable trees. *Q. acutissima* makes a leader readily, needing little attention. Pruning of *Q. ilex* becomes necessary when lower branches spread too widely. It is straightforward, though often requires professional help. *Q. palustris* is best with a trunk clear to 3m (10ft) at least, as long branches droop gracefully. The early training of *Q. robur* is usually easy and very little pruning is called for until maturity, when die-back is apt to occur at the top of the tree, causing a 'stag-headed' appearance. The greater part of the tree is often unaffected and the cause is not obvious, though a fall in the water table is suspected. Removal of the 'stag heads' is eminently worthwhile and may retain the tree in fair health for many years. It is a job for professionals. Early training of *Q. rubra* aims at a clear trunk to 2.4m (8ft) or a little more. *Q. variabilis* needs little pruning. To display the corky bark one should remove low branches to give a clean trunk to 1.8m (6ft).

RHAMNUS *(Rhamnaceae)* Buckthorn (D, E)
This genus contains about 160 species of trees and shrubs grown mainly for their foliage. They grow in any average soil, tolerate drought quite well, and are mostly hardy.

*R. alaternus* forms a bushy evergreen shrub 2.4–3.7m (8–12ft) high with small, dark green leaves. It is not fully hardy. Most attractive is the cultivar 'Argenteo-variegata', with its green leaves, marbled grey with a creamy white margin. It is vigorous and hardy except in unusually severe winters, and even then it recovers in spring. One of the best variegated shrubs.

*R. cathartica* (common buckthorn) is a deciduous large shrub or small tree to 4.6m (15ft), exceptionally common on chalky soils, with shiny black berries in autumn.

*R. imeretina* is a deciduous shrub to 3m (10ft) high, spreading to 4.6m (15ft) with big oblong leaves up to 35cm (14in) long, dark green above, turning bronzy-purple in autumn.

**Pruning** No regular pruning required. Generally the buckthorns can be allowed to develop without interference and *R. alaternus* in particular makes a shrub with a very neat, informal surface, with branches to ground level.

RHAPHIOLEPSIS *(Rosaceae)* (E)
These spring- to early summer-flowering trees all require some shelter, full sun and well-drained but fertile soil.

*R. indica* is tender but given shelter in mild, maritime zones it may grow to 1.5m (5ft) high and rather wider, freely producing clusters of pink, starry flowers.

*R. umbellata* is a good deal hardier, a rounded shrub to 1.5m (5ft), and carries pure white scented flowers.

*R. × delacourii* is rounded, 1.8m (6ft) high, and has leathery leaves and charming rose-pink flowers in spring, continuing into summer. It is hardy in milder areas and very desirable.

**Pruning** No regular pruning required. Best left to their natural habit, branches of these slow-growing shrubs may sometimes die back and should be cut out. If unbalanced growth is produced, it can be cut back to within the bush in spring.

RHODODENDRON including AZALEA *(Ericaceae)* (D, E, S/E)
This huge genus of shrubs, mainly grown for their beautiful flowers, presents a formidable assignment for any writer, let alone one who has not lived in a garden which included rhododendrons as a feature since he was 10 years old. With over 500 species in cultivation in Britain, and new cultivars being developed all the time, the choice is enormous and is best guided by a specialized listing. Rhododendrons like best a soil with pH5, and will not tolerate any amount of lime in the soil. It is not worth attempting their culture in a garden with limy soil when there are many calcicole lime-lovers ready to give no such trouble. Those that have smooth peeling bark, such as *R. thomsonii*, seem to peel off their dormant growth buds or at any rate lose them for no obvious reason. The hardy hybrids such as 'Pink Pearl' like to grow in full sun and have no need of the pruner.

*R. luteum (Azalea pontica)* is deciduous, reaches some 1.8m (6ft) and will perform admirably in neutral sites, provided the soil is rich. It has exquisitely fragrant, yellow, funnel-shaped flowers in spring.

*R. yakushimanum* If you have room for only one rhododendron, choose this dome-shaped evergreen or one of its hybrids. It grows to 90cm (3ft), with abundant pink, funnel-shaped flowers, speckled green within. Christopher Lloyd suggests planting three for foliage and flowers.

**Pruning** Fortunately it is agreed among experts in this field that regular pruning is not needed, except to correct a miscalculation in the choice of site and the distance from neighbouring shrubs and trees.

Plants that are deprived of adequate light may suffer from die-back, and dead wood should be cut away. Any plants that have become drawn up by the lack of light may be cut back hard and will soon produce new shoots. Dead-heading is advised after flowering, a period as busy as any in the gardening calendar, using finger and thumb, and taking care not to damage the young growth or any buds which are about to open, but there is no hard evidence that it makes the plant flower more abundantly than if it is left alone.

## RHODOTYPOS SCANDENS *(Rosaceae)* (D)

A shrub to about 1.8m (6ft), bearing ovate leaves with long points and deeply toothed margins. Flowers appear in late spring until midsummer and are pure white, resembling roses, followed by black fruits. It flowers on shoots thrown up from the base in the previous year.

**Pruning** Prune after flowering, cutting the oldest shoots to their point of origin, the others by half their length.

## RHUS *(Anacardiaceae)* Sumach (D)

A large genus with few species worthy of the garden, and some of these are disappointing as the autumn colour of the foliage is apt to be spoiled by the untidy appearance of the leaves. The toxic properties of the sap are known, especially in *R. vernix* (poison sumach) which should not be grown, but it is wise to assume that the sap of any sumach is poisonous and to wear rubber gloves for any pruning.

*R. typhina* reaches 4.6m (15ft) and, as it withstands pollution, is frequently planted in cities. The flower panicles are not to everyone's taste.

*R. verniciflua* (varnish tree) is a very handsome specimen to 15m (50ft), with smooth pale brown bark when young, pinnate leaves to 60cm (2ft) long and large leaflets. The flowers and fruit are negligible. It becomes more beautiful with age.

*R. potaninii* is a very vigorous tree to 12m (40ft) with large leaves turning red in autumn. Flowers and fruit are seldom seen.

**Pruning** No regular pruning required. *R. typhina* will form a small tree if trained with a 1.2m (4ft) clear stem. The cultivar 'Dissecta' can be cut back in spring to the ground, and will produce handsome leaves 90cm (3ft) long on stems 1.8m (6ft) high. *R. potaninii* can only be trained with a little difficulty because it is very vigorous, but can be made to form a clear stem to 1.5m (5ft) and then a good crown. It is remorseless in producing suckers but these can be used to make new plants.

## RIBES *(Grossulariaceae)* (D, E)

The numerous species are mostly deciduous, a few evergreen and can be divided into two groups, distinguished by differences of botanical characteristics – currants and gooseberries. The latter have spines at the joints, of some interest when starting to prune. Here some of the better garden plants are listed alphabetically.

*R. alpinum* (mountain currant) is a deciduous shrub of dense habit, 1.8–2.7m (6–9ft) high and thornless, dioecious in flowering, with red fruits, not recommended for eating. It is hardy, tolerates shade well and maintains its good outline in poor soils. It could be a useful hedge plant.

*R. × gordonianum* is a vigorous and hardy deciduous shrub, growing only to 90cm (3ft) high. The flowers are bronze red on the outside, yellow within; an acquired taste perhaps.

*R. laurifolium* is a thornless and dioecious spreading evergreen, reaching 90cm (3ft) high. The flowers in late winter are greenish-yellow, the males more ornamental than the females.

*R. odoratum* (buffalo currant) is a medium-sized evergreen shrub of loose growth. The leaves are shining green.

*R. sanguineum* is an unarmed deciduous shrub to 2.4m (8ft) high. The leaves are unremarkable, the flowers red in mid-spring. The cultivar 'King Edward VII' remains as good as any, with flowers of splendid crimson two weeks later than 'Pulborough Scarlet', which is described as having flowers of Bengal rose. One could grow both.

*R. speciosum* is a deciduous shrub up to 1.8m (6ft), the most beautiful of the gooseberries. It is very early into leaf, in late winter. The flowers are rich red in pendulous clusters.

**Pruning** For *R. alpinum* pruning is hardly needed except for a hedge, when overlong shoots should be reduced. *R. laurifolium* requires no pruning. *R. sanguineum* and its cultivars are best pruned immediately after flowering. Cut the older shoots, perhaps one quarter of the whole plant, to 2.5–5cm (1–2in) from the ground with secateurs. After that a good mulch, including manure, is indicated. Neglected shrubs may be hard pruned, removing all top growth in the dormant season and foregoing a year of flowering. Better still, take 30cm (12in) cuttings of the current year's growth in late autumn and insert in the open ground; or, an even better option, persuade the owner of a healthy plant a few years old to let you have a cutting. *R. speciosum* is worth growing against a south-facing wall, though fully hardy, as it is possible to train young shoots from the base to replace the oldest ones, which should be cut out. Tie

LEFT *Quercus ilex* (holm oak), a noble tree that has
been trained into cylinders at Arley Hall, Cheshire, a
surprising feat
ABOVE This picture shows it growing freely to
maturity at Fonmon Castle, Glamorgan, Wales

them in to produce a fan form. Flowers are borne on
one-year-old wood so this training can be carried
out after flowering. Feeding in spring is necessary.

## ROBINIA *(Leguminosae)* (D)

Deciduous trees and shrubs with pinnate leaves,
pea-type flowers and often spiny stems. All do well
in ordinary, not too rich soil; too much feeding
makes them grow coarse and unshapely, with brittle
branches. They are hardy and, if on their own roots,
can be propagated from suckers which are readily
produced. If grafted, as they usually are, on roots or
stems of *R. pseudoacacia*, any suckers will be of
the latter.

*R. hispida* (rose acacia) is a tree reaching 2.4m
(8ft) which in the wild suckers freely, but for some
reason in nurseries is grafted as a standard on
*R. pseudoacacia* to form a small, thornless tree
which is very liable to storm damage. The flowers
are held on short racemes in late spring and are deep
rose in colour.

*R. kelseyi* is a thornless shrub or small tree to 2.4m
(8ft) with rose-coloured flowers in early summer
and red pods. A handsome shrub but too brittle for
culture as a tree.

*R. pseudoacacia* (false acacia) is a tree to 24m (80ft)
with deeply furrowed bark, and spines 2.5cm (1in)
long. The white flowers appear in long racemes in
early summer. It thrives in any soil that is not too
moist and makes very hard trunks. When young it
grows rapidly and may lose branches in a storm.
Cultivars in some instances avoid the brittleness
which prevents *R. pseudoacacia* from living to old
age. 'Bessoniana' is about 15m (50ft) high with a
rounded crown, and considered the best street tree,
but is shy flowering. 'Frisia' is about the same
height, has no obvious faults and carries golden
leaves which do not fade in summer. 'Umbra-
culifera' (mop-headed acacia) reaches 6m (20ft) and
is not suitable for exposed sites but is often used in
borders, associated with herbaceous plants. It is
grafted to make a small standard and rarely flowers,
but has a good rounded crown.

**Pruning** No regular pruning required. *R. pseudoacacia* should have a leader so that a more or less
straight trunk is formed, and no laterals should be
allowed to make rival growth. All this involves regular inspection and prompt action if necessary,
preferably in winter.

ROMNEYA *(Papaveraceae)* (D)

This would be thought of by most non-botanical gardeners as a herbaceous plant but one should not miss a chance to refer to this wonderful plant.

*R. coulteri* (California tree poppy) is a semi-shrubby plant with succulent herbaceous stems 1.2–2.4m (4–8ft) high. It spreads by suckers in a mild setting. The leaves are glaucous and lobed, the flowers fragrant, solitary or in pairs 10–13cm (4–5in) across, the petals like 'crumpled silk', according to Arnold Forster, with a mass of golden-yellow stamens. The soil should be deep, rich and well-drained. Chalk is acceptable.

*R. trichocalyx* is altogether daintier and has more finely divided leaves. Other botanical differences entitle it to rank as a species. An earlier edition of Bean (1938) described it as 'a better plant for colder situated gardens, being of hardier constitution, not too gross in habit and cultivated with less trouble.'

**Pruning** Though *Romneya* is hardy, at least in milder areas, it is best to grow it against or near to a south- or south-west-facing wall. The stems are cut back in a hard winter but the rootstock survives and will usually produce new shoots and flowers in the next summer. Leave the old growth until spring when it can be removed with a little of the live shoot. This can safely be done every year.

ROSA see Roses.

ROSMARINUS OFFICINALIS *(Labiatae)*
Rosemary (D)

A shrub of dense habit, at times 1.8m (6ft) high or even more. The only species, but there are forms and cultivars. The leaves are glossy green above, white below, fragrant when crushed. The flowers are blue in late spring. The following cultivars are of note: 'Benenden Blue' and 'Miss Jessopp's Upright', hardier than most with broad leaves; 'Prostratus', tender and trailing; and 'Severn Sea' with arching branches and a good blue flower, but rather tender. It is strange that no standard text refers to the gilded rosemary, *R. o.* 'Aureus' which was in Britain in the reign of Elizabeth I. It has splashes of gold on the leaves, and is just as hardy as the type. Some do not like it.

**Pruning** Rosemaries may be pruned immediately after flowering, the shoots being reduced by up to one half, that which remains becoming more compact. If there is winter damage or shoots have become leggy, a quite drastic pruning into living wood will produce regeneration. Propagation from cuttings is easy and, if in doubt, it is better to be able to introduce a new plant.

RUBUS (CL, E) (D, E, S/E)

There are numerous species of these shrubs and woody climbers, but few qualify for admission to the garden. Those few do so by virtue of their attractive habit of growth, their foliage, or the covering of white or purple bloom on the stems and, in the case of the climbers, for their handsome foliage and some for an elegant form. Those with edible fruits, and grown specifically for them, are considered in Fruit Trees & Bushes. That group includes blackberries, dew berries, loganberries and raspberries. All *Rubus* prefer a rich soil and none objects to lime.

*R.* 'Benenden' is a vigorous, thornless, deciduous shrub producing annual stems 2.4m (8ft) or more high, which in late spring or early summer bear pure white flowers 5–7.5cm (2–3in) wide. It seems to do best in full sun and is a faultless plant.

*R. cockburnianus* is a vigorous deciduous shrub to 3m (10ft) high with purple, arching stems covered by a white bloom. The fern-like leaves are attractive but the flowers are not. The fruits are black. It is perhaps not as good as *R. thibetanus* (see below).

*R. flagelliflorus* is an evergreen climber with long scandent stems to 1.8m (6ft) in a season, white-felted when young. The ovate leaves are shallowly lobed and finely toothed, the lower surface covered by a yellow-white felt. The black fruits in autumn are edible. An elegant plant when trained up a post or tripod.

*R. henryi* is similar and needs the same management.

*R. lineatus* is a deciduous to semi-evergreen lax shrub, about 1.2m (4ft) high and valued for its fine foliolate leaves, dark green above and covered with a silvery down below. It is not entirely hardy and merits a sheltered position.

*R. thibetanus* is an erect, deciduous shrub to 2.4m (8ft) with purplish stems covered with blue-white bloom. The pinnate leaves are up to 23cm (9in) long with seven to thirteen leaflets, making quite a dense head to the stems; the flowers are of little account. It is hardy and undemanding.

*R. tricolor* is a semi-evergreen ground-covering shrub reaching 60cm (2ft) with pleasant, shining, dark green leaves. The flowers are white, 2.5cm (1in) across, but are seldom seen in the shady sites for which the plant is used. Given a good soil and enough moisture the shoots, which are covered in brown bristles, extend rapidly and root on contact with the soil. Altogether a desirable ground cover.

**Pruning** This should be guided by the knowledge that they flower on growth of the previous year, though some retain their canes for several years, flowering less well. New shoots appear each year and stems which have flowered are cut to the ground if these replacements are adequate. In large clumps the young shoots may be thinned out. Shoots of the climbers *R. flagelliflorus* and *R. henryi* should be cut to the ground after the fruits are gathered.

## RUSCUS (*Liliaceae*) (E)

These are not, strictly speaking, shrubs or even sub-shrubs, as they have no woody base or stems. However, they are welcome here as they survive in any soil but certainly benefit from feeding with manure or compost. They are usually doomed to live in very shady places but whether they would perform to better effect if afforded the lifestyle of a sunny border does not seem to have been recorded.

*R. aculeatus* (butcher's broom) forms an erect shrub to 90cm (3ft) high, with cladodes which are not leaves but flattened stems, spine-tipped, borne on the upper branches of the ascending stems. The flowers are very small, dull white. It bears round red berries, not often seen in cooler climes, partly because female plants are rare and this is a dioecious plant.

*R. hypoglossum* is not very different, although rather smaller, but perhaps even more tolerant of shade and dry conditions from the competition of tree roots.

**Pruning** Pruning of both species is confined to the cutting down of dead or unhealthy stems in early spring. There is no need to thin out the stems.

## RUTA GRAVEOLENS (*Rutaceae*) Rue (E)

This is a sub-shrub with a little wood at the base and in the branches. It grows to 90cm (3ft). The leaves are glaucous, the flowers in terminal corymbs, dull yellow (but go well with the leaves). The cultivar 'Jackman's Blue' is often supplied and is smaller than the type, with blue-grey foliage.

**Pruning** When well grown in good soil with lime, and cut back throughout to the last season's origin in spring, it is a very handsome plant. It has very irritant effects on the skin of some people, who should wear gloves to handle it or – better – keep away if a less sensitive helper is at hand.

## SALIX (*Salicaceae*) Willow (D)

A large genus varying in size from tiny shrubs hugging the ground to very large forest trees. Many like a damp site and all need a good loam, but few flourish on chalk.

*S. aegyptiaca* is a vigorous large bush or small tree to 3.7m (12ft) with a dense head and grey felted shoots. In late winter it bears bright yellow catkins.

*S. alba vitellina* 'Britzensis' (scarlet willow) is narrowly upright to 25m (82ft) with pale leaves.

RUBI

The result: vigorous new stems, for flowers or winter impact, depending on variety

In early spring, cut old growth almost to ground level. Mulch well

The young shoots in winter are bright orange-scarlet.
*S. caprea* (goat willow) is a large shrub or small tree, to 3m (10ft), notable in early spring (but not at other times) for the large yellow male catkins. The female's silver catkins are pussy willow.

*S. daphnoides* (violet willow) forms an erect tree to 12m (40ft). Very rapid-growing at first, with purple-violet shoots overlaid with a plum-coloured bloom. Catkins appear in early spring.

*S. elaeagnos* forms a dense shrub with linear leaves, the catkins appearing with them in mid-spring. It has no special attraction of colour but its form is very charming. Its only drawback is its size – 3.7m (12ft) high and across, which makes it difficult to place in a smallish garden.

*S. exigua* (coyote willow) is a shrub or small tree to 3.7m (12ft) with slender leaves, silvery silky.

*S. helvetica* is a small shrub with orange buds and grey-green pubescent stems and leaves, usually grafted on a 1.5m (5ft) standard and producing a rounded head. Very effective in formal designs.

*S. hookeriana* develops into a shrub or small tree with stout, red-brown branches, leaves glossy green above, white felted beneath.

*S. lanata* (woolly willow) is a bush to 1.2m (4ft) high with ovate, silver-downy leaves and stout yellow-grey catkins in spring. A good combination.

*S. magnifica* is a small tree with large oval leaves, which suggested magnolia to E.H. Wilson. A very handsome plant, but not fully hardy.

*S. purpurea* (purple osier) has a cultivar 'Gracilis' with silver-grey leaves on a dense bushy shrub with a height and spread of 1.5m (5ft), very good as a hedge.

*S. repens* **var. argentea** forms a shrub to 1.8m (6ft) in cultivation, spreading by underground stems. The leaves are silvery-silky.

*S. sachalinensis* 'Sekka' is noted for the fasciated growths in some of the stems, which are brownish-red on plants grown in sunlight. It is very vigorous, reaching 4.6m (15ft) high and 10m (30ft) across, and needs plenty of space.

*S. viminalis* (common osier) should not be ignored, though cultivated mainly for basketwork. It makes a vigorous large shrub or small tree up to 10m (30ft) with long straight shoots. The tapering leaves, dark green and glabrous above and covered with a silvery grey down beneath, are agreeable, especially when the catkins appear in spring.

**Pruning** The coloured young shoots of *S. alba vitellina* 'Britzensis' are more striking if hard pruning is carried out in early spring every year or other year. *S. caprea* regenerates freely if pruned but becomes untidy in response. *S. daphnoides* can be pruned in

*Salix alba* 'Chermesina' has bright red-orange stems in the first year of growth, less so in the second year. For the best winter effect it should be cut to the ground each year in late winter and well manured after that and at every annual pruning

the first few years to produce a framework of branches and, when this is achieved, pruned hard in early spring, but every other year, to gain the best effect from the shoots. *S. exigua*, *S. helvetica* and *S. lanata* are best without pruning, and *S. hookeriana* need only be pruned to make space.

SALVIA *(Labiatae)* Sage (E, S/E)
Most are herbaceous or so little woody that they are not included. Those listed here are sub-shrubs that form a permanent woody framework. All the sages like full sun and a light soil.

*S. guaranitica* is a shrub with erect stems to 1.2m (4ft). Leaves ovate and long racemes of deep blue flowers from late summer into autumn. An excellent hardy plant.

*S. fulgens* (cardinal sage) has heart-shaped leaves and long racemes to 90cm (3ft) of brilliant, almost strident, scarlet flowers in late summer.

*S. involucrata* 'Bethellii' reaches 60–75cm (2ft–2½ft) and has bright crimson flowers borne on racemes from midsummer into autumn.

*S. microphylla* is probably identical with *S. grahami* and forms a shrub to 1.2m (4ft) high with ovate, dull green leaves. The flowers, borne on terminal racemes, are bright red at first, later magenta. Not entirely hardy in most temperate regions unless in a sheltered spot.

*S. officinalis* is an almost evergreen shrub 30–60cm (1–2ft) high. It is covered in a down which gives it a grey appearance, and has aromatic, wrinkled leaves, with flowers in whorls on terminal racemes, purple from early summer. Good cultivars are 'Icterina', leaves variegated yellow and pale green; and 'Purpurascens', with leaves purple when young.

**Pruning** Pruning is cosmetic only, but *S. officinalis* benefits from being cut well back in early spring and will break readily from old wood. None of the others is repeat-flowering but they are worth dead-heading for tidiness' sake.

SAMBUCUS *(Caprifoliaceae)* Elder (D)
These large shrubs or small trees, mainly grown for their leaves, like good soil, not dry, and not too much shade.

*S. nigra* (common elder) is too often dismissed as a weed since the seeds are distributed by birds and

germinate profusely. That is certainly a nuisance but is forgiven as one drives on a summer day down a quiet country road and sees on each side the marvellous spectacle of numerous large bushes in full creamy flower arising from the hedges. This shrub grows to 6m (20ft), with pinnate leaves and flowers which have an odour not too agreeable. The berries are round and black. The form 'Laciniata' (parsley-leaved elder) is a good cut-leaved variety. The excellent *S. n.* 'Guincho Purple' has leaves coloured bronze-purple.

*S. racemosa* (red-berried elder) is not as vigorous as *S. nigra*, reaching 3m (10ft). It bears yellowish-white flowers in mid-spring but seldom the red berries, which are abundant in France and Switzerland. The cultivar 'Plumosa Aurea' has deeply cut golden leaves, bronze when young, and is very handsome.

**Pruning** All the desirable elders require feeding in early spring after pruning, which is usually needed. The older growths are cut to near ground level while one-year shoots are cut by about one-third of their length. If the shrub longs to be a tree it is quite manageable, but growths from low down, up to 1.2m (4ft) from the ground, have to be removed and some above that cut back moderately.

SANTOLINA *(Compositae)*
Lavender cotton (E)

These are low-growing evergreen sub-shrubs with dense foliage and button-like flower heads (often removed) on long stalks in midsummer. They need a sunny position.

*S. chamaecyparissus* is a dwarf species under 60cm (2ft) high with leaves crowded on the shoots, the whole covered by a white felt. The flowers are bright yellow. *S. neapolitana* and *S. pinnata* are probably varieties of *S. chamaecyparissus*.

*S. rosmarinifolia* (formerly *S. virens*) forms an evergreen bush to 60cm (2ft) high with bright green leaves and bright yellow flowers in midsummer. The plants, if grown in an enclosed area, have a very agreeable scent.

**Pruning** Pruning is carried out in the autumn, cutting off old flowerheads and stalks. If this is neglected dead stems and leaves collect and may kill the plant. If deterioration continues, hard pruning may restore the vitality of this shrub. If that fails, a new plant is the solution.

SARCOCOCCA *(Buxaceae)* Sweet box (E)

All are worthwhile but the following are the most highly regarded. They are all hardy plants.

*S. confusa* is a densely branched shrub to 1.8m (6ft)

high, much less in shaded conditions, though it will still remain healthy with shining foliage. The modest white flowers in midwinter are very fragrant if the weather is mild and are followed by black berries.

*S. hookeriana* var. *digyna* is a suckering shrub to 90cm (3ft) and has smaller flowers in early spring; the berries are black.

*S. humilis* is similar, but with shorter and broader leaves. The berries are blue-black.

*S. ruscifolia* reaches 1.2m (4ft) high, has very dark shining leaves, milk-white flowers in midwinter and round crimson berries.

**Pruning** No regular pruning required. Dead shoots should be removed at the base, preferably in spring, but thinning is not required.

SASSAFRAS ALBIDUM *(Lauraceae)* (D)

In northern temperate gardens this forms an aromatic suckering tree 10m (30ft) high or more, reported to be perfectly hardy though the unfolding leaves may be ruined by frost. It requires lime-free soil and some shelter, best provided in woodland. It has a tidy conical habit and dark green leaves which colour well (yellow) in autumn.

**Pruning** During the early stages the trunk is gradually cleared of branches up to 2.4m (8ft) to display the furrowed bark. Suckers may appear at some distance and can be potted up.

SATUREIA MONTANA *(Labiatae)* (E)

A bush about 30cm (12in) high, aromatic with narrow leaves, greyish-green, flowers in midsummer, white to purplish.

**Pruning** No regular pruning required.

SCHIMA WALLICHII *(Theaceae)* (E)

This is an evergreen tree, 18m (60ft) high in its native China but in cultivation only 1.8m (6ft). It is a handsome plant with ivory-white flowers in late summer, like those of a camellia, but only fit for a mild and wet climate, with no lime in the soil.

**Pruning** No regular pruning required, although it is tolerated. It should be trained fanwise on a south-facing wall.

SCHISANDRA RUBRIFLORA (CL, D)

This woody-stemmed climber twines to 3–6m (10–20ft) and produces deep crimson flowers on pendulous stalks in spring to early summer, borne in the leaf axils of new shoots. Drooping scarlet berries follow in late summer. It is hardy and may be trained fanwise on a wall to 1.5–1.8m (5–6ft) and then allowed to hang down.

**Pruning** It is reduced by cutting out the weakest

and oldest shoots in winter, before new growth commences.

## SCHIZOPHRAGMA (*Hydrangeaceae*) (CL, D)

Two climbers closely allied to *Hydrangea*, needing a good loamy soil which does not dry out, and a wall or tree trunk to which they can fasten themselves by their aerial roots.

*S. hydrangeoides* climbs to 12m (40ft) and has broadly ovate leaves 10–15cm (4–6in) long which are coarsely toothed. The flowers are small, yellowish-white in a broad cymose inflorescence with pale yellow bracts in midsummer.

*S. integrifolia* climbs to about the same height but has larger flowerheads up to 30cm (12in) across, freely borne in midsummer.

**Pruning** These climbers may be grown against a wall, not necessarily a sunny, sheltered one, and may need the help of a wire system as the main growths enlarge. From the framework produced by early pruning, long and self-clinging extension growths are formed and may reach up to 90cm (3ft) in a season, with short laterals at their base. In addition, branched laterals grow from the main framework and are the flowering growths on which the buds can be seen in winter at the end of the spurs. During the dormant season many extension growths may be removed, only those useful for filling space being retained.

## SCIADOPITYS VERTICILLATA (*Taxodiaceae*)
Umbrella pine (CO, E)

A slow-growing tree up to 12m (40ft) with reddish-brown inner bark revealed as the surface comes away. Horizontal branches bear clusters of rich, glossy green foliage, with fused pairs of leaves arranged in whorls like the spokes of an umbrella. If your appetite is whetted and you garden on chalky soil, be warned that this is a plant you cannot raise.

**Pruning** The best form has a single leader and makes a very shapely small conical tree, but some plants produced rival leads and these are best dealt with early, preferably before the plant reaches 3m (10ft).

## SENECIO (*Compositae*) (CL, E, S/E)

A genus of over 1000 species, although some have been transferred to the genus *Brachyglottis*. They have been retained here for convenience and familiarity. Most of these shrubs do well in a light sandy soil, tolerating chalk, but only a few are really hardy and are sun-lovers.

*S.* **Dunedin hybrids** (now *Brachyglottis* Dunedin Hybrid Group) is particularly outstanding in the cultivar 'Sunshine', which reaches 75cm (2½ft) with non-wavy leaves, white-felted flower stalks and involucral scales. The flowers are bright yellow and profuse. It is almost hardy and very reliable.

*S. monroi* (now *Brachyglottis monroi*) is slightly larger, to 90cm (3ft), a much-branched shrub with wrinkled leaves and yellow flowers.

*S. scandens* is a semi-evergreen, semi-woody climber, the only climbing senecio grown in Britain. It makes scandent stems up to 1.8m (6ft) long and bears small, bright yellow groundsel-like flowers in panicles during autumn. It is best planted to scramble over something which is not precious, as it is not a first-class plant though it is pretty in the same way as is groundsel.

**Pruning** No regular pruning required for the shrubby types, but most plants benefit from hard pruning every four years or so in spring. Winter-damaged wood should be cut out at the same time. *S. scandens* benefits from fairly hard pruning in spring to get rid of dead stems, but an eye should be kept on the soft new growths which may need some tying to enable them to climb.

## SHEPHERDIA ARGENTEA (*Eleagnaceae*)
Buffalo berry (D)

A shrub to 3.7m (12ft) high with branchlets often spine-tipped. The leaves are oblong, silvery, scaly and opposite, the flowers insignificant in early spring, followed by scarlet, allegedly edible berries.

**Pruning** It is slow-growing and should be trained to a single stem, which will make it look tree-like. It is often compared unfavourably with *Elaeagnus* but it is not without charm and has no bad habits. It grows slowly and rarely needs pruning.

## SKIMMIA (*Rutaceae*) (E)

A small genus of evergreen shrubs or small trees all of which like a rich, moist soil and moderate shade. As they are dioecious, it is necessary to plant one male to every three or four females to achieve a good crop of fruits, but there is an exception to this in *S. j. reevesiana* (see below).

*S. japonica* is a small, dense shrub up to 1.5m (5ft) with obovate leaves and small flowers. It is dioecious, so female plants need a male to achieve fertilization. The fruits are bright red. 'Nymans' is a very free-fruiting cultivar. These shrubs are well suited to forming a clump and a mixture of forms and cultivars would work well as all are similar.

*S. j. reevesiana* is no more than 60cm (2ft) high and unusual in the genus in being monoecious, producing good, abundant crimson fruits without a male plant being needed.

**Pruning** No regular pruning required, and plants

should be allowed to grow to their natural habit, but any cosmetic pruning is for the spring.

### SOLANUM *(Solanaceae)* (CL, E) (D, E, S/E)

The plants of this large genus are grown for their small attractive flowers and fruits. Two climbers are good garden plants.

NOTE It is wise to assume that the fruits of all shrubby and climbing solanums are poisonous to humans and animals. Fatal cases of children eating the fruit of *S. laciniatum* are documented.

*S. crispum* is a vigorous climbing shrub with scrambling stems to 1.8m (6ft) long. The flowers are 2.5–4cm (1–1½) inches across, rich purple-blue borne in loose clusters through midsummer, sometimes into autumn. It likes chalk and should be grown against a sunny, sheltered wall. 'Glasnevin' is an improved cultivar.

*S. jasminoides* is a less hardy but faster-growing climber and must have protection of a sunny wall. It can reach 6m (20ft) and produces pale slate-blue flowers in clusters.

*S. laciniatum* (kangaroo apple) is a sub-shrub reaching 1.5m (5ft) high with lanceolate, deeply cut leaves and violet-purple flowers in mid- to late summer. The fruits are egg-shaped, green at first, later yellow. A tender plant, best grown as an annual from seed. It will not survive the winter in most areas.

**Pruning** No regular pruning required for shrubby species, but frost-damaged growths can be cut out in spring. Climbers should have any weak wood cut out in spring (not after flowering) to allow plenty of time for new growth to ripen before winter.

### SOPHORA *(Leguminosae)* (D)

These trees and shrubs have attractive foliage and flowers but may require some shelter, particularly when young.

*S. davidii* is a rounded shrub to 3m (10ft) high, with pinnate leaves and terminal racemes of blue and white, pea-like flowers in early summer. In cultivation it seems to like sun and a rich soil. Once through the first three or four years it is perfectly hardy.

*S. japonica* grows to 24m (80ft), and can be trained as a tree but will not flower for 30–40 years. When it does it is outstandingly beautiful, its regular rounded crown carrying a dense mass of creamy-white bloom on panicles which stand out from the foliage.

**Pruning** No regular pruning required but, if absolutely necessary, it should be in late summer as spring cuts will bleed.

### SORBARIA *(Rosaceae)* (D)

A genus of hardy flowering shrubs, all of which need a rich soil with moisture.

*S. aitchisonii* has established itself as the best species. A shrub to 3m (10ft), it has pinnate leaves with 11–23 leaflets and white flowers in mid-summer on panicles.

*S. arborea* is similar, but is considered the best of the genus by some.

**Pruning** is carried out in winter, removing some stems which have flowered, reducing the number which grow from the base and ultimately improving the display of flowers. *S. arborea* suckers freely and these growths have to be removed unless the plant grows in a wild area.

### SORBUS *(Rosaceae)* (D)

A genus with about 120 species of shrubs and trees, with attractive foliage, flowers and berries. They require only ordinary soil, preferring chalk and an open position; the rowan group is intolerant of drought and prolonged heat.

*S. aria* (Section Aria) (whitebeam) is a tree to 12m (40ft), occasionally more, with a dense head of oval, greyish-white leaves, later bright green above with a white felt below, turning to gold in autumn. The dull white flowers are borne in corymbs, followed by beautiful scarlet fruits that are soon taken by birds. The branches have an erect habit, making a well-shaped crown. The cultivar 'Lutescens' develops leaves covered by a creamy-white down which becomes green by late summer.

*S. aucuparia* (Section Sorbus [Aucuparia]) (rowan, mountain ash) forms a tree to 15m (50ft), but more commonly a neat grower to 9m (30ft) with pinnate leaves and white flowers, followed by bright red fruits, soon taken by birds. The cultivar 'Beissneri' has coppery-brown bark of trunk and branches and leaves that colour yellow in autumn.

*S. cashmiriana* (Section Sorbus [Aucuparia]) is a small, slow-growing tree, rather open in branching, with soft pink flowers in late spring, larger than most others. The fruits are like white gleaming marbles, and persist until they decay, as they seem not to be attractive to birds.

*S. domestica* (service tree) is a tree to 15m (50ft) with a broad crown, pinnate leaves and insignificant flowers. The fruits are shaped either like a pear *(pyriformis)* or an apple *(maliformis)*.

*S. hupehensis* (Section Aucuparia) is a tree that can reach 15m (50ft), though it usually makes less. The large leaves have a blue tinge but the flowers are inconspicuous, followed by round fruits, 5mm (¼in) across, usually white, sometimes faintly pink. It is easily propagated from seed and its early growth is rapid.

*S.* 'Joseph Rock' is a tree of uncertain origin, certainly in Section Aucuparia, reaching 10m (30ft) high and fine in its structure. The leaves turn red-copper or orange in autumn, and the globular fruits change from green to yellow by mid-autumn. An excellent tree deserving good soil and adequate moisture.

*S. reducta* (Section Aucuparia) is a dwarf shrub up to 60cm (2ft), spreading by underground runners from which rise erect stems, bearing leaves with red petioles and shining dark green leaflets, which turn reddish in autumn. Though said to be easily grown in any good moist soil, it has proved a failure on two occasions with us, in spite of every care. Perhaps it is calcifuge.

*S. torminalis* (Section Aria) grows quite quickly in the first few years and should be allowed ample space. The leaves are like those of a maple, sharply lobed, strikingly dark green, turning bronze-yellow in autumn. This tree self-sows in woodland but the seedlings do not develop well unless transplanted to open ground.

**Pruning** No regular pruning required, except in the course of training. *S. aria* should be trained early on to establish a leader with a clear trunk to 1.8m (6ft). *S. domestica* is best grown as a standard with a clear stem to 1.8–2.4m (6–8ft) and a central lead. *S. hupehensis* produces a leader without training. *S. torminalis* forms a leader with little training but opens out at 1.8m (6ft) if not stem-trained.

## SPARTIUM JUNCEUM (*Leguminosae*)
### Spanish broom (D)

This shrub thrives in a sunny position with rather dry soil. It has a loose habit with rush-like stems to 3m (10ft) bearing inconspicuous leaves and fragrant, bright yellow, pea-like flowers 1cm (¹⁄₂in) long, in terminal racemes 30cm (12in) throughout summer.

**Pruning** It needs to be pruned in spring just before new growth appears. After the first year of planting out the growth is cut back by half. This is continued each year, taking great care not to cut into the old wood. If the plant becomes old and straggly it may be cut back nearly to the ground and will regenerate moderately, but it is time to think of a replacement. It is a good seaside shrub.

## SPIRAEA (*Rosaceae*) (D)

A large genus from which many well-known species have been stripped, but it still contains many good shrubs, graceful in habit and in foliage, less exciting

in flower. All do well in good soil, tolerating chalk and a sunny position, though some perform adequately in partial shade, eg *S. bumalda*. The pruning regime can be separated into two distinct categories according to the flowering season of the shrub, and they are so listed here. Those which flower on wood of the previous year include:

*S.* × *arguta*, a plant of rounded habit reaching 2.4m (8ft). The flowers are pure white in small clusters in late spring.

*S.* × *cinerea* 'Grefsheim' is smaller than *S. arguta* but resembles it, flowering earlier.

*S. nipponica* is very vigorous and reaches 1.5m (5ft) or more with cluster of pure white flowers in early summer. Very fine.

*S.* × *vanhouttei* is liable to frost damage in low-lying places, but is otherwise very hardy, with arching stems reaching 1.8m (6ft) and abundant white flowers in early summer.

**Pruning** These are pruned back to two or three buds immediately after flowering. The flowered stems of *S. nipponica* can be cut right back as the shrub is very vigorous and will produce plenty of new shoots. It should be well manured. Only the older stems of *S.* × vanhouttei should be cut back.

Those which flower on the current year's shoots include:

*S. japonica*, mainly known by its numerous cultivars, the best-known being 'Anthony Waterer'. This is one of the best plants, with flowers of carmine-pink covering the surface. Though often described as a dwarf shrub reaching 1.2m (4ft) it can be pruned in spring to 30–60cm (1–2ft) with a good result.

*S. douglasii* reaches 1.8m (6ft) with dark rose flowers in summer.

**Pruning** These are pruned to two or three buds in early spring, at which time any weak or unhealthy shoots are cut away entirely. In the case of *S. douglasii* it may be advisable to cut the whole plant right down every few years and start again, manuring well.

## STACHYURUS (*Stachyuraceae*) (D)

These flowering shrubs do best in a neutral to acid soil and benefit from some shelter. The flowers are borne before the leaves appear.

*S. chinensis* is very similar to *S. praecox*, which is better-known and is considered by some to be a better plant. It is certainly more widely available. It flowers about two weeks after *S. praecox* so you should have both.

*S. praecox* grows to around 1.2m (4ft) high and produces drooping racemes of between 12 and 20 pale yellow flowers in late winter.

**Pruning** These plants are hardy, but will flower even better if trained to the surface of a wall, though that might be thought wasteful. Older branches can be removed after flowering, but not every year.

### STAPHYLEA (*Staphyleaceae*) (D)

These spring-flowering shrubs produce attractive bladder-like fruits and require moist, fertile soil.

*S. colchica* is a shrub to 3m (10ft) high with erect branches. The white flowers are borne in erect panicles, followed by the fruit, an inflated capsule 10cm (4in) long.

*S. pinnata* is similar to *S. colchica* but has smaller capsules containing larger seeds. In a hot summer the leaves may turn an attractive foxy brown, persisting for several weeks.

**Pruning** These shrubs do not require regular pruning but young growth from the base may be thinned and the best shoots allowed to develop, while older growths are removed to make way. This is usually done in winter.

### STAUNTONIA HEXAPHYLLA (*Lardizabalaceae*) (CL, E)

A strong-growing climber, capable of reaching 10m (30ft) by twining. It is best grown against a sunny, sheltered wall with a wire system, so that the stems may hang down from the top strand and display the fragrant violet-tinged white flowers, male and female on separate racemes. It is related to and very like *Holboellia*, which has rather better leaves but less good flowers.

**Pruning** Fruits are occasionally seen. Weak growths are removed completely in winter.

### STEPHANANDRA (*Rosaceae*) (D)

These summer-flowering shrubs are fully hardy and attractive all year round.

*S. incisa* is a shrub to 1.2m (4ft), notable for its triangular leaves with margins cut into deep lobes, dense panicles of tiny green-white flowers in early summer and also for the pleasant brown stems in winter.

*S. tanakae* is a perfectly hardy shrub to 3m (10ft) and has slender arching stems with leaves less often lobed, and small but plentiful white flowers in early summer. The leaves turn light brown in autumn. A pleasant plant in a quiet way.

**Pruning** After flowering old growths are cut back almost to ground level and good mulching ensures that young stems will be produced.

### STUARTIA (*Theaceae*) (D)

A genus of very beautiful trees and shrubs but not easy to grow well, for reasons not always apparent. Certainly it would be rash to attempt them in chalky soil, but even in the best peaty loam they are often not robust. They need sun, and a clearing in woodland may be the most suitable site.

*S. malacodendron* is among the best species and is a shrub or small tree to 4.6m (15ft) with leaves 5–10cm (2–4in) long and solitary flowers with white petals, purple stamens and blue anthers in midsummer.

*S. pseudo-camellia* is a tree to 10m (30ft), with thick leaves turning red and yellow in autumn, flowers white, solitary, stamens white, orange anthers. These flowers are short-lived but are soon replaced through summer. Shelter from wind is necessary, as is sun but combined with shade, plus moist soil.

*S. sinensis* forms a large shrub or small tree to 12m (40ft) with very attractive flaking bark, and fragrant, white, rose-like flowers in summer.

**Pruning** No regular pruning required. The trunk of *S. pseudo-camellia* may be cleared of any branches below 1.8m (6ft).

### STYRAX (*Styracaceae*) (D)

A genus of deciduous flowering trees and shrubs. All need a lime-free soil with humus added, and a sheltered site. Not all are hardy.

*S. hemsleyana* is a small tree to 12m (40ft) with open branching, and broad leaves with deep veins. The flowers are white with yellow anthers, borne in long racemes in early summer.

*S. japonica* forms a shrub or small tree to 12m (40ft) with wide-spreading branches and bell-shaped flowers, pure white, hanging from the underside of the branches. It readily makes a tree and when in flower is spectacular seen from below. This tree needs shelter and some temporary cover if spring frosts threaten.

*S. obassia* is similar to *S. hemsleyana*, but slower-growing to 12m (40ft) and slower to flower.

**Pruning** No regular pruning required. A leader should be trained for *S. hemsleyana* from the start since branches develop at a low level.

### SYCOPSIS SINENSIS (E)

A bushy shrub reaching 2.4–3m (8–10ft) with leathery leaves. The flowers are small and monoecious, and petal-less, but with showy yellow stamens and red anthers in late winter.

**Pruning** No regular pruning required. This shrub branches freely from the base, and should be encouraged so that the flowers can be seen at close quarters. If pruning is needed because of damage, regeneration is adequate.

## SYMPHORICARPOS (*Caprifoliaceae*) (D)

A genus of rather commonplace species, but with some worthy hybrids and cultivars.

*S. albus* is usually grown as *S. a.* var. *laevigatus*, a coarse shrub to 1.2m (4ft) high with pure white globose fruit, which ripens in autumn and is unattractive to birds. It is much used for dark corners and unattractive areas, where it makes a dense thicket.

*S. × chenaultii* is best seen as the cultivar 'Hancock', which is procumbent and layers freely. It is an excellent ground cover to 90cm (3ft), as seen in London under plane trees.

*S. Doorenbos hybrids*, all 0.9–1.5m (3–5ft), are a series of seedlings from various species and *S. × chenaultii*, the most successful being *S. × doorenbosii* 'Mother of Pearl' and 'White Hedge'.

**Pruning** No regular pruning required; it is not easy, in any case, because of the suckering habit. Occasional digging out may be helpful, but why not accept defeat – and a thicket?

## SYRINGA (*Oleaceae*) Lilac (D)

A genus of hardy deciduous shrubs and small trees, flowering in late spring and early summer. They appreciate good soil, especially chalky earth, and full sun. The majority are vigorous and grow rapidly.

*S. × josiflexa* is a race of hybrids, the best of which is perhaps 'Bellicent', reaching 3.7m (12ft) with very large panicles of rose-pink fragrant flowers.

*S. meyeri* 'Palibin' is a dwarf, slow-growing shrub with a height and spread of 1.5m (5ft) and violet-purple flowers in early summer in panicles up to 10cm (4in) long.

*S. × persica* forms a shrub 1.8m (8ft) or more high, bushy and rounded, with lanceolate leaves and lilac flowers which are moderately fragrant and produced in late spring. A splendid sight in the spring after a hot summer in the previous year. 'Alba' has white flowers.

*S. vulgaris* (common lilac) is a shrub or small tree to 6m (20ft) high, with erect branches, ovate leaves and richly scented lilac flowers. It is so common and easy to grow (without pruning) that it is often, even usually, taken for granted, but it has more charm and character than many of the bloated garden lilacs.

**Garden Lilacs** (Vulgaris group) are a group of cultivars to about 4m (13ft), raised in the last 100 years, a large number by the company of Lemoine in Nancy, and some of the earliest remain in every list – 'Souvenir de Louis Spaeth', with single, deep wine-red flowers; 'Charles Joly', with double, dark reddish-purple flowers; 'Michel Buchner', with double, pale rosy-lilac flowers; and 'Madame Lemoine', with double white flowers.

**Pruning** The *vulgaris* lilacs flower from buds formed in the previous season. As they open the growth buds immediately below them begin to grow quickly and may be quite long as the flowers fade. It helps to remove the faded blooms, but taking care not to damage the developing growths which will produce the next season's flowers. If much damage occurs there will not be sufficient time in the ensuing season for flowers to develop. Overgrown or misshapen branches may call for drastic pruning to 60–90cm (2–3ft) above ground level. There should be rapid regeneration if the soil is in good condition, but no flowers can be expected for two years.

## TAMARIX (*Tamaricaceae*) (D)

A genus of shrubs and small trees, easy to grow in any good loam in inland areas, though they are natives of hot, maritime regions. Two species represent the different flowering habits of the genus.

*T. parviflora* is a shrub to 4.6m (15ft) high with arching branches, sessile leaves, and flowers in racemes up to 5cm (2in) long, with rosy-pink petals borne on the old wood in late spring. It is absolutely hardy and flowers freely every year.

*T. ramosissima*, also known as *T. pentandra*, has the same general character as *T. parviflora*, growing to 4.6m (15ft) with rosy pink flowers but on wood of the current year. It is hardy and reliable.

**Pruning** *T. parviflora* is pruned after the flowers fade and any tidying up may be done at the same time. *T. ramosissima* is pruned in spring before new growth starts. Damaged branches may be cut away at the same time and regeneration should follow.

## TAXODIUM DISTICHUM (*Taxodiaceae*)
### Swamp or bald cypress (CO, D)

A large tree to 25m (80ft) with reddish-brown bark, and the trunk buttressed at the base. The leaves are flattened, arranged in two opposite ranks, spirally on the persistent branchlets. Though it grows quite well in average soils, it belongs in bogs and marshes and tolerates damp conditions.

**Pruning** No regular pruning required.

## TAXUS BACCATA (*Taxaceae*)
### Common yew (CO, E)

This evergreen species grows well on chalk soil, but equally well on acid soils given good drainage. It is equally obliging in shade and forms a very long-lived tree seldom over 15m (50ft) high. The bark is brown-red and a rounded or spreading head of branches bears glossy, dark green leaves. The fruits have a bright red aril and are poisonous. There are many cultivars.

*T. b.* 'Adpressa' is a fine shrub of spreading habit with small, dark green leaves 1cm ($^1/_2$ in) long. It will reach 1.5m (5ft) in 10 years.

**Aurea group** describes all the golden-leaved and gold-variegated forms. *T. b.* 'Aurea' itself can be grown as a dwarf and makes a neat conical shape.

*T. b.* 'Fastigiata' (Irish yew) is a columnar tree of great merit reaching 10–15m (30–50ft). The leaves start out all round the branchlets and are dark, dull green. The cultivar 'Fastigiata Aureo-marginata' is even more popular but lacks the gravitas of the plain tree.

**Pruning** No regular pruning required for specimen plants. Fastigiate types can be tied in to emphasize their narrow form, preferably using plastic bands. To maintain a neat outline they can be pruned in late summer with secateurs. (See also Hedges & Topiary.)

TELOPEA TRUNCATA *(Proteaceae)*
Tasmanian waratah (E)

A shrub or tree to 6m (20ft) with leathery leaves and rich crimson flowers in terminal heads in early summer. 'It thrives where the rainfall is above average and the soil acid' (Bean, 1980), and needs the same conditions as rhododendrons: sun above and shade at the root.

**Pruning** No regular pruning required.

TETRACENTRON SINENSE *(Tetracentraceae)* (D)

A tree to 12m (40ft) of spreading habit with ovate or heart-shaped, pointed dark green leaves. The flowers are tiny but numerous, forming a yellow, catkin-like, pendulous spike. It is moderately hardy and tolerates lime but grows better without it, in average loam. It should be sited in the open on a lawn or in a woodland clearing, the lower branches being encouraged so that the catkin-like spikes may be displayed in summer.

**Pruning** No regular pruning required.

TEUCRIUM *(Labiatae)* (E)

These shrubby flowering plants need full sun and well-drained soil to give them the best chance of coming through winter unscathed.

*T. chamaedrys* (wall germander) is a semi-shrubby plant to 20cm (8in), woody at the base with a creeping rootstock and erect stems, bearing bright green hairy leaves and small rosy flowers from midsummer to mid-autumn.

*T. fruticans* (shrubby germander) is less hardy and usually grown against a wall in a light soil. It has a spreading habit, reaching 1.8m (6ft) high and twice as much across.

Pruning *T. chamaedrys* is useful for ground cover and is best cut back in spring, using shears for a large mass but secateurs if avoiding an edge to a lawn or path, with the object of presenting an informal outline. *T. fruticans* should be lightly pruned after flowering and any shoots killed in winter cut away in spring.

THUJA PLICATA *(Cupressaceae)*
Western red cedar (CO, E)

This fast-growing conifer reaches 20–30m (60–100ft) and has a naturally conical shape. The cultivar 'Hillieri' is a slow-growing dense bush with leaves in irregular whorls, certainly interesting, reaching no more than 90cm (3ft) in height and spread.

**Pruning** No regular pruning required. *T. plicata* makes a natural central lead and is well clothed with spreading branches to the base, so there is nothing for the keen pruner to do, unless it is grown as a hedge (see p122).

THUJOPSIS DOLOBRATA *(Cupressaceae)* (CO, E)

A small evergreen tree or shrub of dense conical habit reaching 10–20m (30–60ft). With large sprays of silver-backed leaves and rounded blue-grey cones, it is an attractive plant.

**Pruning** Some specimens form a central leader better than others. Try to remove rivals as soon as they are spotted.

THYMUS *(Labiatae)* Thyme (E)

These evergreen prostrate and mound-forming shrubs have aromatic leaves. They thrive in sunny, fairly well-drained conditions.

*T. serpyllum* (more properly known as *T. praecox arcticus*) is a sub-shrub only 2.5–5cm (1–2in) high, woody at the base with trailing stems and rosy-purple flowers on upright stems from summer to autumn.

*T. vulgaris* (garden thyme) is 15–30cm (6–12in) high with a woody base, and greyish down on shoots and leaves. Lilac or pale purple flowers are borne in whorls on a terminal spike in summer.

*T.* × *citriodorus* (lemon thyme) is an old garden plant making a bush to 30cm (12in). The lemon scent remains as strong as ever.

**Pruning** None of these plants requires any regular pruning beyond some gentle tidying up when the shrub has finished flowering.

TILIA *(Tiliaceae)* Lime, linden (D)

Noble trees which grow well in any fertile soil, are hardy and tolerate hard pruning and pleaching.

*T. cordata* is a tree to 18m (60ft) high, usually

smaller, but occasionally reaching 30m (100ft). The leaves are rounded, finely toothed, dark green, and the flowers yellowish-white in midsummer. A splendid tree, not planted often enough.

*T. × euchlora* reaches 21m (70ft) and forms a large crown, with the outer branches pendulous, often sweeping the ground. The leaves are large, dark green and shiny, while the flowers, borne in midsummer, are yellow and attractive to bees. It is strikingly free from aphid attack but has come under a cloud in recent years, through a damaging disease of uncertain origin.

*T. × europea* (common lime) is a vigorous tree to 35m (115ft) and was once popular for avenues and parks. It is now out of favour as it is liable to aphid attack, their excrement turning black on the leaves, making these unsightly and early to fall.

*T. japonica* has a dense leafy crown to 15m (50ft) and flowers profusely in midsummer.

*T. olivera* forms a spreading tree, perhaps not more than 15m (50ft) high in cultivation.

*T. petiolaris* is a very vigorous tree up to 30m (100ft), sometimes more. The branches are pendulous and produce a very graceful outline. The leaves are dark green above, white beneath, and the flowers in late summer are very fragrant.

*T. platyphyllos* reaches 30m (100ft) and has bigger leaves than most others and an impressive outline. The cultivar 'Rubra', with red twigs in winter, is even better.

*T. tomentosa* (European white lime) is notable for the silvery white felt on the underside of the leaves. It grows quickly to 25m (80ft) and in time becomes handsome.

**Pruning** The pruning of limes is straightforward. Initially the object is to establish a single leader and shorten, if necessary, any laterals, removing any that are becoming upright. If damaged or badly placed limbs on mature trees need cutting back, the work should be done in midsummer to allow time for the wound to heal before winter. *T. × europea* produces suckers at the base, often arising from large burrs. These suckers can be removed, a tedious task, but the burrs cannot.

**TORREYA CALIFORNICA** *(Taxaceae)*
Californian nutmeg (CO, E)

A small evergreen tree, its conical form well furnished to ground level with shining dark green leaves rather similar to those of yew.

**Pruning** A lead should be trained in the nursery stage, when the tree should have protection from frost. If this leader is killed numerous laterals take over and the shape is lost.

**TRACHELOSPERMUM** *(Apocynaceae)* (CL, E)

Two species of these flowering woody-stemmed, twining climbers are in gardens in Britain. They need wall protection and a good soil. The leaves are oval and a dark, glossy green.

*T. asiaticum* climbs by twining, to 6m (20ft) if allowed. The fragrant tubular flowers are 2.5cm (1in) across, creamy white in summer.

*T. jasminoides* is less hardy, but will reach 9m (30ft) in the right position. It has pure white, very fragrant flowers produced on small laterals from the old wood in summer.

**Pruning** Pruning for both these plants consists of removing some weak growths and cutting back extension growths above the wall or coming forward from it, to a point just above a flowering stem.

**TRACHYCARPUS FORTUNEI** Chusan Palm (E)

This striking, long-lived palm can reach 3.7–5m (12–15ft) in mild areas. It is woody and hardy, its stem clothed by the disintegrated bases of the leaves, which can persist for many years.

**Pruning** No regular pruning required.

**TROCHODENDRON ARALIOIDES** *(Trochodendraceae)* (E)

A large shrub or tree, branching freely from the base. The foliage is described as 'recalling that of a tree ivy' (Bean, 1980, p621), and the flowers, in an erect terminal inflorescence, are vivid green. It needs lime-free soil and shelter from wind. It has done well in Suffolk, Hampshire, Gloucestershire and Cornwall.

**Pruning** No regular pruning required and the leading growths should never be cut back.

**TSUGA CANADENSIS** *(Pinaceae)*
Eastern or Canada hemlock (CO, E)

This tree reaches 4.6m (15ft) and tends to branch low down, forming a rounded head. It is lime-tolerant but grows best in areas of high rainfall. Cultivars are legion, including 'Jeddeloh' with light green foliage and a semi-prostrate habit, spreading 75cm (2½ft).

**Pruning** No regular pruning required. This tree looks best if clothed in foliage to the base, so the stem should not be cleared.

**ULEX** *(Leguminosae)* (D)

A genus of spring-flowering shrubs allied to the brooms. They appear evergreen because their almost leafless shoots remain green all year.

*U. europaeus* is a bushy shrub that is naturalized on huge areas of moorland, doing best on the poorest soils and growing to 1.2m (4ft) or so. The side branches end in a strong sharp spine. The leaves are insignificant but the flowers, calyx and petals are bright yellow in late spring, when they are at their height, though they show a little in late winter on wood of the previous year. 'Flore Pleno' (double-flowered gorse) needs the same conditions and is more compact. It bears semi-double flowers which last a long time in mid-spring, and produces no seed, which makes it suitable for gardens with thin soil. Propagation has to be by cuttings.

*U. gallii* is a dwarf shrub under 60cm (2ft). It flowers from late summer to autumn.

*U. minor* is a dwarf or even prostrate form, rarely over 30cm (12in), which flowers in early autumn. It must be grown on very thin soil.

**Pruning** Pruning of gorse depends on the season of flowering. If it is spring (*U. europaeus* and *U. e.* 'Flore Pleno'), prune immediately the flowers are over, giving time for ripening new wood. If flowering is in autumn (*U. gallii* and *U. minor*) prune, not too hard, in early spring.

ULMUS *(Ulmaceae)* (D)

At one time large, stately specimens of elm were a characteristic part of the British landscape, but not any longer; the arrival in the late 1960s of the aggressive strain of Dutch elm disease has altered the appearance of a large part of the country. It seems likely that no species escaped entirely and exact information is hard to gather. Some of the species previously grown are simply not obtainable any more.

Dutch elm disease is now known to be due to the fungus *Ceratycystus ulti*, transmitted from infected trees by the elm bark beetles *Scolytus scolytus* and *Scolytus multistriatus*. It is considered possible that the disease has been present in a relatively mild form for several centuries, but was definitely identified in 1927 in Hertfordshire. In the mid-1930s there was increased severity of the disease in many areas. Certainly in Worcestershire many trees were killed, and others disfigured but left alive as the attack receded. By the late 1940s the disease was quite mild and the onset of the aggressive form began acutely just before 1970, later traced to elms imported from Canada with the bark still intact. By 1979 about half the total elm population of 23 million reckoned to exist at the onset of this outbreak had died. Around 1980 there was evidence that regenerated elms were growing to 3m (10ft) or more, and by 1990 specimens 9m (30ft) tall and in good health were recorded in Hertfordshire. The author grew *V. americana* and *U. procera* from cuttings of dying trees in 1972 and these plants

are healthy, but as yet only 6m (20ft) high.

*U. glabra* (wych elm) makes a large tree to 30m (100m) with arching branches, very handsome and good for exposed coastal situations. It self-seeds.

*U. procera* (English elm) was a sad loss to the countryside. To watch its disappearance was an extremely painful experience and nothing can replace this superb tree to 35m (115ft), stout yet graceful, densely leafy, the leaves turning a fine yellow in autumn. The leafless tree is impressive and beautiful in a modest way when the first flowers appear in late winter.

*U. pumila* makes a small tree to 7.6m (25ft). It is probably immune to elm disease.

**Pruning** No regular pruning required, mainly because there are no trees large enough to merit it.

UMBELLULARIÀ CALIFORNICA *(Lauraceae)*
California laurel (E)

This is a tree to 30m (100ft) in California, though it makes less than 18m (60ft) in more northerly and temperate climates. It makes a dense head of branches bearing leathery leaves, pungent when crushed, and said to cause headache if inhaled for more than a few minutes. This tree needs a warm position in good soil, or otherwise it may suffer spring frost-damage.

**Pruning** In early life it should be trained to a single stem with a stake. The laterals are usually well-formed and need no pruning.

VACCINIUM *(Ericaceae)* (D, E)

A genus of shrubs requiring an acid soil, not rich, and tolerating some shade. Their flowers are pleasant but not remarkable. All are hardy in the west of Britain. All those mentioned here are evergreen, although there are deciduous members of the genus too.

*V. floribundum* is a shrub reaching 1.2m (4ft) in height, with dark green leaves and rosy-pink flowers in early summer on the lower sides of shoots, followed by tiny red berries. The young growths are red-tinted.

*V. ovatum* (box blueberry) is a shrub of 3.7m (12ft) in temperate regions. The white flowers grow in short racemes in early summer, followed by round black berries. The leaves emerge coppery-red and later become shining green.

*V. vitis-idaea* (cowberry) is a dwarf, creeping shrub with small leaves similar to those of box, dark green above, pale beneath. The flowers are white, tinged pink in short racemes, borne all through summer, followed by red berries, edible but bitter. A good ground cover in shade.

**Pruning** The smaller plants of this genus, including those above, need no pruning, except for the removal of poor growths in spring, but some larger deciduous shrubs tend to retain weak elderly shoots which should be cut away in winter.

## VIBURNUM (*Caprifoliaceae*) (D, E, S/E)

A large genus with many species worthy of culture. Most are grown for their flowers, but the fruits are fine in a few, limited by self-incompatibility which requires pollination from a plant of a different clone and the presence of an active insect to carry it out. Corrugated foliage is a feature of *V. rhytidophyllum* and some hybrids of it, notably *V.* 'Pragense', where the leaves are dark green and shining. Some give a good display of autumn colour, especially *V. opulus*, sadly often thought too coarse for the garden. If so it is the garden which needs modifying. Here is a selection of worthy, reliable plants; a few have been omitted because they favour an acid soil or are doubtfully hardy.

*V. betulifolium* is a tall, erect deciduous plant to 3m (10ft) with corymbs of white flowers, not impressive, in early summer. In autumn the long branches are weighed down by bunches of red fruits, making them arch over. The fruits last until winter, but the self-incompatibility must be allowed for.

*V. × bodnantense* is a rather gaunt, upright deciduous shrub to 3m (10ft) producing, from late autumn, clusters of aromatic rose-tinted white flowers, which may be damaged by severe frost.

*V. × burkwoodii* is a vigorous, easily grown semi-evergreen shrub to 2.4m (8ft) in height and spread, with fragrant white flowers from late winter to late spring.

*V. × carlcephalum* is a good rounded shrub to 3.7m (12ft) with leaves that often colour well in autumn and very fragrant large pink flowerheads in late spring (though beginning in early spring in mild regions).

*V. cinnamomifolium* has the most handsome leaves of the evergreens and a height and spread of 4.6m (15ft). The flowers are small and white in early summer but are uninteresting.

*V. odoratissimum* is very similar in size and appearance but rather tender. Fragrant white flowers on large panicles arrive in late summer and the older leaves colour in winter.

*V. opulus* (guelder rose) is a deciduous bushy shrub with a height and spread of 3.7m (12ft). The maple-like leaves colour splendidly in autumn. The flowers, produced in early summer, are white and in flattened heads, followed by red translucent fruits, lasting into the winter. It chooses boggy sites.

*V. plicatum* 'Mariesii' has strikingly tabular branches on which the white flowers are crowded on the upperside. A splendid plant with a height and spread of some 3.7m (12ft).

*V.* 'Pragense' is an elegant evergreen with shining dark green corrugated leaves, with a height and spread of 3m (10ft). The flowers are creamy-white in spring and early summer, not bad.

*V. rhytidophyllum* is an evergreen shrub to 3.7m (12ft) high with corrugated leaves, dark green above, grey hairy beneath. Creamy flowers in cymes appear in late spring. Single specimens do not fruit readily. It should be in rich soil (chalk is tolerated) and given shelter from storms.

*V. sargentii* 'Onondaga' reaches 1.8m (6ft) and has young leaves coloured deep bronze and red flower buds. Stylish is the word.

*V. tinus* is a bushy evergreen now represented by several cultivars of great merit including 'Eve Price', with a height and spread of 3m (10ft), smaller leaves than the type and bright pink flower buds; and 'Lucidum', a vigorous shrub with large leaves. Unfortunately it is only really successful in the milder regions.

**Pruning** If shrubs are healthy there is no need for regular pruning in most cases. *V. betulifolium* has negligible flowers but the flowerheads will not be cut back as you will be hoping for a crop of fruits. *V. × bodnantense* produces stems from the base freely, which permits removal of old and unproductive wood. This is best carried out in early spring, at the end of flowering, and that applies to the other winter and spring-flowering shrubs, including *V. × burkwoodii*, *V. × carlcephalum* and *V. juddii*. *V. cinnamomifolium* and *V. adoratissimum* will need only a mild tidying in early spring. Any pruning of *V. opulus*, rarely needed, is done in early spring. *V. plicatum* should be approached with great care as nothing must be done which will disturb the tabular structure of the stems. Only dead or diseased wood should be cut away. *V. rhytidophyllum* produces shoots from the base and these have to be removed unless some of the older growth needs to be cut off. In general it is grown from a central main stem and laterals may be shortened if they seem to be failing. *V. sargentii* 'Onondaga' needs no pruning. It develops slowly in an elegant way. *V. tinus* only needs pruning if it is outgrowing the space allotted to it. As it ages or is damaged by frost, some hard pruning in spring is indicated and it will regenerate vigorously.

## VINCA (*Aponyanaceae*) (E)

A genus of sub-shrubs and herbaceous perennials. Those described here are flowering evergreen sub-shrubs with slender trailing stems and glossy, oval leaves, used for trailing and ground cover in often quite unpromising sites, such as the dry shade of hedge bases.

*V. difformis*, although evergreen, may die back in winter, but in our Somerset garden in the shade of *Quercus ilex* it persists, with rather scanty pale violet-blue flowers from autumn to spring, spreading widely but reaching only 30cm (12in) high.

*V. major* (greater periwinkle) is a shrub with flowering stems erect up to 60cm (2ft) high. The bright blue flowers appear in late spring and continue until autumn.

*V. minor* is, unsurprisingly, smaller with a height of 15cm (6in). The long trailing stems root readily, allowing it to spread over an indefinite area, and the flowers are bright blue, from late spring to summer and intermittently until autumn. The cultivar 'Azurea Flore Pleno' has flowers of a lovely sky-blue, and double. Like all the vincas it flowers much more freely in full sun but will still perform in shade.

**Pruning** The slender stems mat together after a time so the only possible method of pruning is to shear over the whole plant, cutting back quite hard. This can be undertaken every two years, in spring, and the plant will benefit greatly.

VITEX *(Verbenaceae)* Agnus castus (D)

A shrub of spreading habit with dark green, narrow leaves and fragrant, tubular, violet-blue flowers produced in late summer and early autumn in large panicles. It is only hardy in the open in mild areas but does fairly well in maritime places. No doubt it needs more sun than Britain offers.

**Pruning** Flowers are produced on wood of the current season: annual pruning in spring is indicated, cutting back all growth to 2.5–5cm (1–2in) from the framework of branches.

VITIS *(Vitaceae)* (CL, D)

A large genus of climbers, most of them vigorous, that climb by twining tendrils and will cover walls, pergolas, fences and hedges. They need well-drained reasonably rich soil, preferably chalky, and will tolerate some shade.

*V. coignetiae* is a very vigorous plant climbing to 15m (50ft) by twining tendrils. The ovate leaves can be 30cm (12in) long and 50cm (20in) across, dark green above, covered by rust-coloured tomentum below. The flowers are insignificant but, in a good season, will be followed by bunches of small black grapes with a purple bloom, although they are not dessert fruit. In autumn the leaves turn brilliant crimson and scarlet. It is without rival among vines.

**Pruning** Depends on the way in which the plant is trained. If over a stump or a disused rock garden, it may be left to cover the whole area before it needs any cutting back. On a pergola some shortening of the long shoots is necessary, as they are too untidy and liable to get in the way. The cut is made to leave five or six leaves. These shortened stems are hard pruned in the dormant season before midwinter, after which bleeding can occur.

WEIGELA *(Caprifoliaceae)* (D)

A popular genus of hardy, flowering shrubs related to honeysuckle.

*W. florida* is a shrub to 2.7m (9ft) high with arching branches. The leaves are oval to 10cm (4in) long, and the flowers are borne in clusters, reddish on the outside, paler within, from late spring to early summer. It has produced many successful hybrids and cultivars, including 'Foliis Purpureis' with purple-flushed leaves and 'Variegata', with leaves edged creamy white and pink flowers. Both are more compact than the type.

*W. middendorffiana* is a fine shrub to about 1.5m (5ft) with sulphur-yellow flowers spotted orange within, in cymose clusters during late spring. It may be damaged by spring frost. Among the hybrids, all about 1.5m (5ft high), are some of the oldest: the still-popular 'Abel Carrière', with deep carmine flowers; 'Eva Rathke', with crimson-red flowers; and 'Looymansii Aurea', rather weak in growth with golden leaves and pink flowers.

**Pruning** As a rule it pays to prune these plants immediately after flowering to allow time for new growths to ripen before autumn. If the stool from which new shoots develop becomes weak it may be cut right back and will respond by producing new growth, which may be so abundant that the weakest members can be removed. This is then left until midsummer, otherwise a fresh crop of weak stems may appear. Be on the lookout for reversion of growth on variegated forms and cut it out at once. Good feeding is essential in spring for all weigelas, whether or not this system of pruning is adopted.

WISTERIA *(Leguminosae)* (CL, D)

A small genus of woody-stemmed, twining climbers with large, showy, unequally pinnate leaves and masses of pea-like scented flowers in elegant axillary or terminal racemes. They are hardy in the southern half of Britain and are not particular about soil, but must have a sunny position. They can live to a great age.

*W. floribunda* climbs by twining clockwise to 9m (30ft). The leaves are up to 38cm (15in) long, and the fragrant, violet-blue, early summer flowers are

*Vitis* arch in the lower garden at Powys Castle. Each pillar supports a different vine, notably *V. coignetiae* with leaves that turn crimson in autumn

in slender racemes 13–25cm (5–10in) long. The cultivar 'Alba' has white flowers, tinged lilac on the keel. 'Multijuga' has pale violet flowers with a yellow mark at the base, in racemes about 60cm (2ft) long.

*W. sinensis* has pinnate leaves, 25–30cm (10–12in) long with usually 11 leaflets. The flowers appear in late spring, mauve or lilac in racemes 20–30cm (8–12in) long. The cultivar 'Alba' has white flowers.
**Pruning** All the wisterias have the same pruning system, whatever the type of training adopted – wall, pillar, pergola, as a tree or as a bush. For the first three of these the main growths are tied to supports, keeping them 30cm (12in) apart and making sure that they do not twine together or, if they do, cutting one away. In midsummer the laterals, which by then are long trailing growths, are reduced to three buds, except for any that may be required to fill the allotted space. In the following winter cut back the leader to 90cm (3ft) from the highest laterals, which are cut back at this time to two buds. The shortening of laterals, and of the leader if it is necessary because of space, takes place each year in

midsummer, later rather than earlier. It can be spread over several weeks and the winter pruning follows as before. Wall training makes it possible to train the main laterals horizontally, and this ensures maximum flowering. Feeding is desirable in spring, though mature plants manage without it in good soil. (See illustrations on pp112–13.)

**XANTHOCERAS SORBIFOLIUM (*Sapindaceae*) (D)**
A large erect shrub or small tree to 6m (20ft) high, with white flowers in late spring in erect panicles, reminiscent of horse chestnut. It grows well in any good soil, tolerating chalk. In the open it needs summer heat to perform really well.
**Pruning** No regular pruning required. It is subject to coral spot disease and affected branches should be cut back immediately.

**XANTHORHIZA SIMPLICISSIMA**
**(*Ranunculaceae*) (D)**
A hardy shrub with creeping roots and erect stems to 60cm (2ft) high. The bright green pinnate leaves with three or five leaflets are handsome and the tiny purple flowers, in panicles, appear in early spring. It does well in semi-shade but dense shade is too much for it. It needs adequate moisture and can be used as ground cover.
**Pruning** No regular pruning required.

WISTERIA

1 At planting in winter.
Cut back the most
promising shoot to 1m
(3ft) from the ground

2 In summer train that shoot to be the
vertical leader. Train four laterals to 45°
and tie them in. Cut away any shoots
from the base

3 The following winter cut back the
leader to 45cm (18in) from the highest lateral. Bring down the laterals
to the horizontal

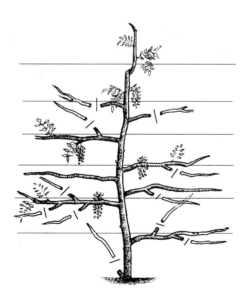

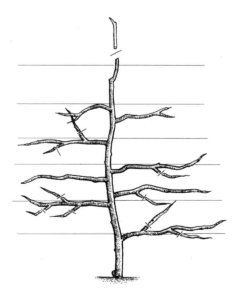

4 In summer tie in any new laterals horizontally.
In late summer cut back sub-laterals to about
15cm (6in)

5 In winter cut back the leader to 1m (3ft) from the
highest lateral. Cut back sub-laterals to 2–3 buds

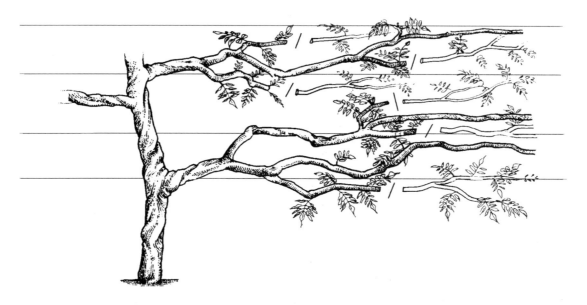

6  In midsummer cut back all extension growths to 15cm (6in)

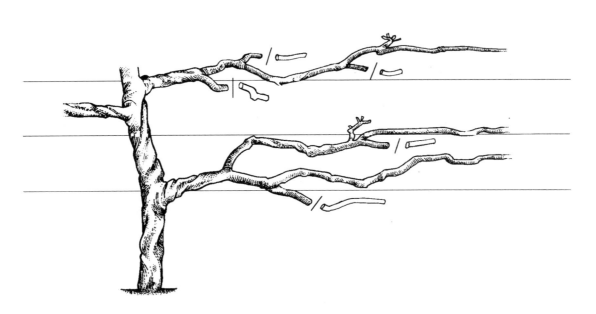

7  In winter prune these same growths again to 10cm (4in). Repeat
steps 6 and 7 each year

YUCCA *(Liliaceae)* (E)

It is difficult to think of this genus as shrubby and Graham Stuart Thomas reasonably excuses his inclusion of it in his *Perennial Garden Plants* by saying that it 'resembles a shrub so little and so little has been written about it'. As pruning is the excuse for this book and plays virtually no part in the culture of *Yucca*, little will be written about it here either.

ZANTHOXYLUM *(Rutaceae)* (D)

A genus of trees and shrubs, little known though not without merit, characterized by the strong, usually disagreeable odour of the crushed leaves and the spines on young branches and leaf-stalks. The leaves are pinnate and the most handsome feature.

**Z. americanum** (toothache tree) gained its popular name because the bark and seed capsules were chewed to ease toothache. It is a shrub to 3m (10ft) with pinnate leaves up to 15cm (6in) long, and leaflets in 5–11 pairs. The yellow-green flowers are inconspicuous, followed by black fruits. This plant needs rich soil to flourish. It has an upright habit and a single leader should be established without difficulty.

**Z. piperitum** (Japan pepper) has a tidy bushy habit, and the 11–23 leaflets are conspicuous. It reaches some 1.8m (6ft).

**Z. planispinum** has leaves with a winged petiole and three or five leaflets, and the spines are broad and flattened. After a hot summer there are small red fruits. It reaches 3m (10ft) or more in height and spread.

**Pruning** No regular pruning required and the plants should be allowed plenty of space to achieve their natural habit. Dead wood builds up as the plant matures and this should be removed, particularly as it is prone to coral spot disease.

ZELKOVA *(Ulmaceae)* (D)

The species in cultivation all have smooth trunks and coarsely toothed leaves, rough to the touch. They should have a deep rich soil and some shelter.

**Z. carpinifolia** is a large tree to 30m (100ft) that divides not more than 30cm (12in) above ground into many erect branches, which seem to suffer no ill-effect from this crowding and present a remarkable picture. The trees are exceptionally healthy, which is just as well because the removal of single limbs would be extremely difficult.

**Z. serrata** is relatively common. It can be trained to have a clean stem of 1.8–2.4m (6–8ft), the branches being almost erect, but the outer ones are spreading and pendulous at their extremities. A slow-growing tree to 20m (60ft), it is alleged to develop elm disease but is still much the most easily obtainable.

**Z. sinica** grows to 10m (30ft) or more and has grey bark that flakes with age, with small leaves pink in spring.

ZENOBIA PULVERULENTA *(Ericaceae)* (D)

A rather untidy shrub to 1.2–1.8m (4–6ft) with young shoots and leaves covered by glaucous bloom. The white, bell-shaped flowers are produced in clusters in early summer. It is perfectly hardy, but must have a lime-free soil with a little shade. It does not tolerate drought.

**Pruning** This consists of removing the dead flowers and a little of the stem on which they form. If the plant is elderly and failing, it may respond to hard pruning, followed by a rich lime-free mulch.

# Hedges & Topiary

The original function of the hedge was to keep out intruders, men or animals, as expressed in Hamlet's 'there's such divinity doth hedge a king that treason can but peep to what it would'. In Britain hedges were familiar in Anglo-Saxon times and increased through the Middle Ages. It has been shown that the count of species of shrub in a 27m (30yd) length of hedge gives the approximate age of that hedge to the nearest century – for every species counted, add 100 years. The shape of the enclosure, too, can help to date a hedge. Curved shapes are usually older than those defined by straight lines. Many are at least 1,000 years old and comparatively few date from the parliamentary enclosures of the eighteenth century.

## FARM HEDGES

The practical value of hedges was modified by the invention of barbed wire in the nineteenth century, and further reduced by the emphasis on arable farming during and after the Second World War. Thousands of kilometres of hedge were grubbed up to create large and easily managed fields, and consequently the laborious practice of 'laying' hedges to keep them stockproof almost disappeared.

Fortunately, however, it is still practised with, apparently, regional differences in style and pattern and is most frequently applied to *Crataegus monogyna* or thorn hedges which otherwise become bare and gappy at the base. Stakes made of *Salix viminalis*, the common osier, are driven in at intervals of 1.8–2.4m (6–8ft), having first been debarked because willow will root at any time of year and soon outgrows the hedge. Selected long growths of hawthorn are then partly split with a billhook low down on the trunk and trained horizontally by weaving them in and out of the stakes. This is repeated every four years and in other years the hedge is 'brushed' (lightly clipped) each autumn. Strong seedlings are not discouraged in a hedge of this type, except for those of elder *(Sambucus nigra)*, which is apt to kill plants close to it.

## GARDEN HEDGES

Other uses for the hedge ensure that it survives and is an almost essential element in all but the smallest gardens. It may define the boundary of the property and keep out stock, cats, dogs, foxes, raccoons in the USA and, of course, man, who often wants to know what goes on within.

The Anglo-Saxon desire for privacy calls for a hedge 1.8m (6ft) high, but in a tiny garden this is overwhelming and quite impractical. A wall may seem a less troublesome if more expensive alternative to a hedge and offers opportunities for growing climbers, but has at least one drawback: in windy conditions air is forced upwards and, as it drops on the other side of the wall, may form a damaging vortex, a violent eddy round an axis, which is bad for any plant in its path. A hedge, on the other hand, filters and slows down the airstream. However, in order to achieve worthwhile noise abatement, a hedge must be too thick to be practical for most gardens. Unfortunately, concealing the source of the noise does not reduce the noise itself or its impact.

One other point arises. It was discovered, or at least became well known 50 years ago, that cold air moving down a slope would be held to some extent by an obstruction, even a hedge. Making sizeable gaps in the hedge could allow the air to pass through, so reducing the danger of frost on the slope above the barrier, and thus was of great value to the cherry and other fruit orchards in valleys. Sadly, the cherry orchards have mostly disappeared.

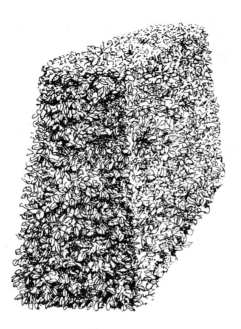

A formal hedge, showing the 'A' shape, known as a batter, that allows maximum light to reach the base of the hedge

## PLANNING A HEDGE

Our first consideration is to decide whether it is appropriate to the site in question: whether it should be formal or informal, tall or short, and whether or not it should divide the garden into 'rooms', each with its own character and acting as extensions of the house. Whatever the decision, most garden hedges will need regular and reasonably skilled pruning, with very few exceptions. Many shrubs and some trees can be used for hedging but the list that follows contains some which are of proven merit as far as growth and response to pruning are concerned.

## ACER CAMPESTRE Field maple (D)

An excellent plant for an informal hedge if cattle are kept away. Rabbits chew the bark and can kill a large stem close to the ground. Maple is much used on the continent of Europe. Why not more in Britain?
**Pruning** Prune with secateurs and a double-action lopper, reducing strong shoots by one-third and removing any that are weak. Once a year is enough, in the dormant season, not before leaf fall as the yellow autumn colour is good.

## AUCUBA JAPONICA (E)

The green-leaved form is much preferred by right-minded people to the variegated form. It makes a good evergreen hedge even in poor soil and shade. If you can put a male near females you should have a fair crop of egg-shaped fruits.
**Pruning** If fruits are produced, pruning should be delayed until early winter and then comprises removal, with secateurs, of shoots arising from ground level or slightly higher. Clipping results in some leaves being partly cut and the result is unsightly, so use of *A. japonica* for formal hedging is not advised.

## BERBERIS DARWINII (E)

If well treated and fed, this is a splendid, if spiny, shrub for hedging. It has pleasant dark glossy green leaves and golden or orange flowers leading to worthwhile blue fruits, taken by birds only in dry spells.
**Pruning** If there is a good crop delay pruning until late summer, cutting back the shoots which have flowered and bringing them in line with the new shoots which are developing.

## BERBERIS × STENOPHYLLA (*B. darwinii* × *B. empetrifolia*) (E)

This forms a dense mass of spiny stems producing arching shoots to 3m (10ft) when mature. The flowers are yellow-orange – not the best of colours – and the fruits are remarkable. However, the habit and healthy nature of this plant recommend it. It has been suggested that berberis hedges could act as a disincentive to burglars and other intruders. This may well be so, but they are not to be recommended for gardens where children play.
**Pruning** This is undertaken as the flowers fade.

## BUXUS SEMPERVIRENS Common box (E)

This dense bushy plant will, in time (although not less than 200 years) make a tree 9m (30ft) high. For a hedge it is among the best choices. The cultivar 'Suffruticosa', with a dwarf habit and small leaves, is traditionally used for edging flower beds and was often planted to form the pattern in knot gardens created in the sixteenth and seventeenth centuries, and occasionally today.
**Pruning** *B. sempervirens* normally needs clipping only once a year. High summer is usually recommended for this but experience following the advice of James Hancock, head gardener at Powys Castle, Wales, has confirmed that early summer is better, and the fragrance of the new growth which results is pleasant. Ted Bullock at Felbrigg Hall (both of these are National Trust gardens) finds that it is easier to cut box when it is wet. He has managed to renovate old box hedges by cutting back to 10cm (4in) in early spring and feeding with fertilizer when there are signs of renewed growth. 'Suffruticosa' needs frequent clipping to maintain the dwarf state. If it is left unpruned

it will grow into a handsome light green bush of 1.2–1.5m (4–5ft).

### CARPINUS BETULUS Hornbeam (D)

The best deciduous, formal hedge plant in temperate climates, it is tolerant of most soils, including heavy clay, and is planted at intervals of 45cm (18in). The leaves, which turn yellow in autumn, are retained through the winter.

**Pruning** It makes good growth almost from ground level so that early training is easy, with clipping back in late summer after the first two years.

### CHAMAECYPARIS LAWSONIANA (E)

A popular hedging plant which blotted its copy book by showing a tendency to eventually become bald in the lower part. There are many cultivars, such as 'Green Hedger', an easily managed plant, though the bright green colour will not appeal to everyone.

**Pruning** This is best cut with secateurs during mid- to late summer.

### CRATAEGUS (D)

*C. monogyna* (common hawthorn) and *C. oxyacantha* may, perhaps both forms of one species, make the traditional English hedge. They are easy to grow from seed and plant out, and arm themselves with repellent thorns.

**Pruning** They accept much pruning and can be cut back as severely as is necessary when dormant. The slasher mounted on a tractor has become a sad necessity, but hedges recover fairly well in the next spring. The old practice of laying such a hedge is described at the beginning of this chapter.

### × CUPRESSOCYPARIS LEYLANDII
### (*Cupressus macrocarpa × Chamaecyparis nootkatensis*) (E)

This hybrid took many people by surprise when its vigour exceeded all expectations, and continues to do so: it grows to 18m (60ft) in 25 years. In fact, it makes an excellent specimen or screen when given plenty of space but has gained a reputation as a garden thug through being planted in plots that are simply too small for it. The Leyland cypress and its clones are very hardy and tolerant of sea winds.

**Pruning** As a formal hedge it behaves well, but should be transferred from open ground – not a container – and then attached to a bamboo pole tied to a wire stretched along the hedge site. Once the central leaders reach 30cm (12in) beyond the height required for the hedge they are cut back to 15cm (6in) below that height in early summer, with the laterals cut back moderately at this time and for each subsequent pruning.

### ELAEAGNUS PUNGENS (E)

The cultivar 'Maculata' is a popular shrub the green leaves of which have a patch of rich yellow in the centre. Admirably hardy and not unduly vigorous – but would you get tired of it shouting at you every time you opened the garden door?

**Pruning** If you do choose to plant it, you should look out for reversion of the foliage to plain green, which is all too common and needs urgent action, cutting off all stems which show this change immediately. Trim with secateurs during summer.

### ESCALLONIA VIRGATA (D)

This attractive early summer-flowering shrub has arching branches and white flowers. It is very hardy and should make an elegant informal hedge, but dislikes chalky soil.

**Pruning** Prune lightly after flowering.

### EUONYMUS JAPONICUS
### Japanese spindle tree (E)

This is most often seen as cultivar 'Ovatus Aureus', a gold-variegated form, only fully hardy in the mildest temperate climates and flourishing by the seaside. Grown as a formal hedge it is unattractive, but if allowed some freedom to spread it is better. Predictably the type with dark, polished leaves makes a good formal hedge.

**Pruning** Both are trimmed in mid-spring.

### FAGUS SYLVATICA Common beech (D)

The most popular deciduous formal hedge, it is a little behind the hornbeam in vigour, not as healthy or prolific in lateral growth but splendid when the leaves open, their colour an unmatched fresh green. It needs well-drained but fertile soil.

**Pruning** It should not be pruned in the first three years after planting. Once established, pruning takes place in late summer. Mixed hedges of the type with its form 'Purpurea' or 'Riversii', the leaves of which open pale red in spring, becoming purple before long, have charm but seem to be difficult to manage. Perhaps this is because of slightly different growth rates in the various forms.

### FORSYTHIA × INTERMEDIA (D)

The cultivar 'Spectabilis' can reach 3m (10ft) high and across and needs plenty of space, but the upright growth predominates and plants can be put in 1.8–2.4m (6–8ft) apart.

**Pruning** Prune immediately after flowering, taking away all flowered stems except those which are two to three years old, and feeding to encourage the young shoots from the base.

### FUCHSIA MAGELLANICA (D)

'Riccartonii' is a plant of uncertain origin but over the last 150 years has established itself as fully hardy in the mild areas of Britain and Ireland, particularly the south-west where the flowers with scarlet sepals and violet corolla, on semi-wild hedges, make an unforgettable impression. In many inland districts it is cut to the ground by frost each winter but by the end of spring is growing strongly. It needs plenty of moisture, not unknown in south-west Ireland.

**Pruning** Prune back hard to a formal outline just as growth commences in spring. The rapid growth will soon produce a softer outline with plenty of flowers.

### GRISELINIA LITTORALIS (E)

This shrub is from New Zealand and is only hardy in maritime areas in Britain, where it makes a dense growth of stems. This characteristic, along with its tolerance of salt winds, makes it a good choice for a windbreak near the sea.

**Pruning** Removal of some stems from the outside in early summer encourages growth near the centre.

### HIPPOPHAE RHAMNOIDES Sea buckthorn (D)

A native of the British coast, tolerant of salt-laden winds but able to flourish in average conditions inland. Grey scaly twigs and orange-coloured fruits (ignored by birds) are attractive in winter and the grey-green leaves in summer are equally so.

**Pruning** As a hedge it may be cut to size in spring.

### ILEX AQUIFOLIUM Common holly (E)

This makes an excellent hedge, formal or informal, and is tolerant of pollution and of any type of soil. 'J. C. van Thol' is an excellent cultivar with dark green, hardly toothed leaves and is just as satisfactory as common holly as a hedge. Some berries will form on the surface of the hedge but may have to be sacrificed if needs be in order to keep a formal outline.

**Pruning** Unless the hedge is very long, use secateurs to avoid damaging leaves, cutting back longer shoots individually in spring. This is time-consuming but not boring.

### LAURUS NOBILIS Bay laurel (E)

Noble it is, but only fully hardy in the fortunate areas. However, neither is it wholly tender in many places, where it is cut to the ground in a severe winter but revives in the next spring. This would ruin a few years' topiary work. In the mild areas so often mentioned here it tolerates wind.

**Pruning** This is best done in midsummer to maintain shape.

**BELOW** *Fagus sylvatica* and *F. sylvatica* 'Riversii' together make a wonderful tapestry hedge of green and purple. A problem may arise because the rate of growth of *F. sylvatica* is considerably more rapid than that of 'Riversii', but there are examples with a good regular outline. Prune in late summer to shape
**RIGHT** *Fagus sylvatica* makes a good opening for a path. Beech grows fairly fast, but annual clipping should suffice once the spheres have been formed. On each side of the opening one upright stem is allowed to grow above the line of the hedge, and is cleared of branches for about 30cm (1ft) of its length once it has reached the required height. The branches above this are then cut back in late summer to produce the spheres

### LAVANDULA ANGUSTIFOLIA
### Common lavender (E)

This plant is often recommended for hedging but in most of Britain the uncertain climate makes it difficult to keep tidy.

**Pruning** It should not be pruned after flowering but in spring, when new growth has appeared.

### LIGUSTRUM OVALIFOLIUM (E)

Tolerates dim light, poor soil and neglect. This and its price explain its popularity as a hedge in town gardens. The flowers have an unpleasant odour. The

gold-variegated form has a bright yellow margin reviled by good-taste gardeners.

**Pruning** Hedges of either form need pruning two or three times a year, once in early spring and perhaps twice in summer.

### OLEARIA TRAVERSII (E)

Performs very well in maritime areas, even on poor soil in exposed positions, and can reach 5.5m (18ft). The shoots and undersurface of the leaves are covered in a dense white felt. The leaves are oval, leathery and dark green.

**Pruning** It needs cutting back by a half after two years in spring, after that as necessary at that time. Not worth trying inland.

### POTENTILLA (D)

There are good hybrids and garden varieties, mostly related to *P. fruticosa*. The majority reach a height of 0.9–1.2m (3–4ft) but there are considerable variations in size and vigour. A hedge is, therefore, best when composed of one subject only and the following are well established in the trade:

**'Abbotswood'**, white flowers. A dwarf cultivar of *P. davurica*, 30cm (12in) high.

**'Elizabeth'**, soft yellow flowers. A large hybrid to 1.2m (4ft).

**'Jackman's Variety'**, reaching 1.2m (4ft) with bright yellow flowers.

**'Katherine Dykes'**, up to 1.2m (4ft) with canary-yellow flowers. A *P. fruticosa* cultivar.

**'Primrose Beauty'**, 90cm (3ft) with pale primrose flowers. A *P. fruticosa* cultivar.

**'Tilford Cream'**, 1.2m (4ft) with cream flowers.

**Pruning** This is certainly valuable: in spring weak shoots are removed and strong healthy stems shortened by half.

### PRUNUS (D, E)

*P. laurocerasus* (cherry laurel) is best grown as a specimen 'unmolested by the pruner' (Bean, 1976, p378). However, the cultivar 'Otto Luyken' grows only to 1.2m (4ft) and makes a compact hedge when planted at 90cm (3ft) intervals.

*P. lusitanica* (Portugal laurel) is very hardy. The dark oval leaves are handsome, the racemes of flower in summer not so. It makes a good hedge but is subject to silverleaf disease.

**Pruning** Trim with secateurs during midsummer.

### QUERCUS ILEX (E)

Makes an excellent hedge in the milder areas in any soil which is not heavy. It should be grown from acorns, which are abundant after a hot summer. They are planted in open ground and on germinating are put singly in pots and grown on for a season or two (not more). Then they are planted out where they are to grow. *Q. ilex* resents transplanting and at more than 15cm (6in) is unlikely to survive.

**Pruning** No pruning is needed for two to three years and then only light trimming in spring.

### RIBES SANGUINEUM (D)

This can make an informal hedge, if one of the lower-growing cultivars (1.2m/4ft) is used, such as 'King Edward VII', which bears scarlet flowers in mid-spring.

**Pruning** Prune immediately after flowering, using secateurs. The weak shoots are cut away and the stronger ones retained as far as possible, only the flowered portion being removed. The outline of the shrub should be fairly symmetrical but not formal.

### ROSMARINUS OFFICINALIS (E)

At first it seems a good idea to grow rosemary as a hedge but it does not readily lend itself to the discipline, however slight, of hedge life. A visit to Provence shows that it needs prolonged heat and sun to give its best. In cooler and wetter climates it cannot be relied on to produce a hedge of uniform quality.

**Pruning** Necessary in spring, cutting well back into the healthy but not old wood. A light trimming after the flowering helps to keep the plants in shape.

### SANTOLINA CHAMAECYPARISSUS
Lavender cotton (E)

Grows 30–60cm (1–2ft) high, with dense leafy stems, both stems and foliage covered in a thick white felt. The flowers are bright yellow, in a head on a stalk up to 15cm (6in) long. A row of the shrubs hardly qualifies as a hedge but makes an attractive strip of planting 60cm (2ft) wide.

**Pruning** The flowers may have to be sacrificed in favour of pruning in spring, preserving a rounded shape. In a few years the plant becomes untidy and cuttings should be kept in readiness for replacement.

### TAXUS BACCATA Common or English yew (E)

Yew makes the great formal hedges of Britain and has no rival among the evergreens. In the USA it is not considered reliable in regions more rugged than Long. Island and the cultivar 'Repandens' is often used as well as the species *T. cuspidata*. The virtues of *T. baccata* are that it is hardy; it regenerates even from the oldest wood and survives annual pruning for many years (the hedges at Levens Hall in Cumbria with their topiary have been pruned every year since 1692); it is unrivalled in producing a regular formal outline of great beauty, austere but not gloomy.

## PLANTS FOR HEDGES

| | | DISTANCE APART AT PLANTING | | APPROXIMATE PRUNING TIME |
|---|---|---|---|---|
| | | CM | IN | |
| I D | *Acer campestre* (field maple) | 45 | 18 | Dormant |
| I E | *Aucuba japonica* | 75 | 30 | None. Shape in spring |
| I E | *Berberis darwinii* | 60 | 24 | After flowering (berries) |
| I E | *Berberis × stenophylla* | 60 | 24 | After flowering |
| F E | *Buxus sempervirens* (box) | 30 | 12 | Early summer |
| F E | *Buxus sempervirens* 'Suffruticosa' (for edging) | 15 | 6 | Summer |
| F D | *Carpinus betulus* (hornbeam) | 60 | 24 | Dormant |
| I D | *Chaenomeles speciosa* and cultivars | 80 | 30 | Spur in spring, long shoots in summer |
| I/F D | *Crataegus monogyna* (hawthorn) | 60 | 24 | Summer |
| F E | × *Cupressocyparis leylandii* (Leyland cypress) | 60 (75) | 24 (30) | Summer |
| F E | *Cupressus macrocarpa* (Monterey cypress) | 60 | 24 | Summer |
| F/I E | *Elaeagnus pungens* 'Maculata' | 60 | 24 | Mid-spring |
| I D | *Escallonia virgata* | 75 | 30 | After flowering |
| I E | *Euonymus japonicus* (Japanese spindle bush) | 45 | 18 | Mid-spring |
| F D | *Fagus sylvatica* (common beech) | 45 | 18 | Late summer |
| I D | *Forsythia × intermedia* 'Spectabilis' | 90 | 36 | After flowering |
| I D | *Fuchsia magellanica* 'Riccartonii' | 60 (75) | 24 (30) | Mid-spring |
| I/F E | *Griselinia littoralis* | 60 | 24 | Early summer |
| I D | *Hippophae rhamnoides* (sea buckthorn) | 75 | 30 | Spring |
| F E | *Ilex aquifolium* (common holly) | 45 | 18 | Spring |
| F E | *Ilex aquifolium* 'J. C. van Thol' | 45 | 18 | Spring |
| F E | *Juniperus communis* (common juniper) | 45 | 18 | Spring |
| I E | *Juniperus virginiana* (red cedar) | 150 | 60 | (Screen) Spring |
| F E | *Laurus nobilis* (bay laurel) | 60 (75) | 24 (30) | Midsummer |
| I E | *Lavandula angustifolia* (common lavender) | 45 | 18 | Spring |
| I E | *Lavandula stoechas* (French lavender) | 30 | 12 | None |
| F E | *Ligustrum ovalifolium* (oval-leaf privet) | 45 | 18 | Spring and summer |
| F E | *Lonicera nitida* | 37 | 15 | Several times, spring to late summer |
| I/F E | *Olearia* | 45 | 18 | Late spring |
| I D | *Philladelphus coronarius* | 75 | 30 | After flowering |
| I D | *Potentilla* cultivars | 60 | 24 | Mid-spring |
| F E | *Prunus lusitanica* (Portugal laurel) | 60 | 24 | Spring |
| F E | *Quercus ilex* (holm oak) | 45 (60) | 18 (24) | Summer |
| I D | *Ribes sanguineum* (flowering currant) | 75 | 30 | After flowering |
| I E | *Rosmarinus officinalis* (rosemary) | 45 (60) | 18 (24) | Spring and summer |
| F E | *Taxus baccata* (common yew et al) | 45 (60) | 18 (24) | Autumn |
| I E | *Teucrium chamaedrys* (wall germander) | 15 | 6 | Spring |
| F E | *Thuja plicata* (Western red cedar) | 60 | 24 | Late summer |
| F/I E | *Viburnum tinus* 'Eve Price' | 60 | 24 | Spring |

I = Informal  F = Formal  E = Evergreen  D = Deciduous

The only serious problems arise from:

1. Waterlogged ground, which can be fatal.

2. Infestation by the yew scale insect, which can damage sizeable areas but will respond to spraying with malathion.

3. Honey fungus infection, which is not common but threatening if it does occur.

4. Gnawing by rodents, which can cause the death of moderate-sized stems and is thought to explain the wavy outlines of some ancient yew hedges.

5. It is widely but not universally known that yew, when eaten, can be fatal to cattle (and probably man) but it is also clear that cattle can eat the shoots without coming to any harm. Semi-dried twigs and foliage are more dangerous than green ones. It appears that the poison – probably the alkaloid 'Taxine' – is virulent when the stomach is empty, and perhaps only then. The lesson is clear.

**Pruning** In spite of these problems a yew hedge is very little trouble apart from the rather tedious labour of pruning, but that occurs only in autumn. Nowadays the task is made shorter, if no less laborious, if petrol-driven cutters are used. They are, however, very heavy to manipulate on the upper part of the hedge. The renovation of aged yew hedges is now established as a successful enterprise, though the method was advocated as long ago as 1879 in *The Garden* (p432). There is an outstanding example at Powys Castle undertaken by James Hancock, the head gardener. The most important yew hedges were planted just before the outbreak of war in 1914. They suffered neglect in the two World Wars and, when the castle came into the care of the National Trust in 1952, many of the formal hedges had grown to a width of 2.4m (8ft). The process of repair began with cutting back (stem pruning) one side of the hedge to the main trunk, removing all branches and reducing the tops to the required height. In the following spring the yew started to sprout and after three years there was healthy and quite dense growth. Then the other side of the hedge was treated in the same way. The final, excellent result, after just 12 years, was hard to believe. The hedge was, of course, well fed during the pruning operation.

### TEUCRIUM CHAMAEDRYS Wall germander (E)

Herbaceous at the top and woody at the base, the plant is useful as an edging 30cm (12in) high to a bed or border, seen at its best in midsummer. The leaves are bright green and the flowers, on a terminal raceme, have a rose-coloured corolla with the lower lip of a darker shade.

**Pruning** Cut it back in spring, preferably using secateurs to avoid destroying the natural outline, which is irregular.

*Parterre in Tuscany, Italy. Here, box encloses blue gravel – effective and labour-saving*

### THUJA PLICATA Western red cedar (E)

Makes a good hedge planted at 90cm (3ft) intervals.

**Pruning** In midsummer of the second season after planting light pruning of the whole plant is carried out, in time for the new wood to ripen before winter. After that the leader is only beheaded when the required height is reached, at which stage the sides of the hedge are trimmed.

### VIBURNUM TINUS (E)

Since *V. tinus* is such a variable shrub, it is preferable to use one of the cultivars 'Eva Price' or 'Gwenllian', preferably propagated from a single plant by cuttings. The leaves are dark green, and the carmine buds open to pink flowers at any time from midwinter to mid-spring.

**Pruning** Pruning is not often needed but the plant responds readily even from old wood, and such a measure is undertaken in late spring.

## TOPIARY

The history of topiary is quite fascinating. Its popularity has waxed and waned literally over centuries and has marked significant changes in society and societal attitudes to gardening and leisure.

The word 'topiary' came originally from the Greek *topos*, meaning a place, which the Romans adapted to 'topiarius', referring to the man who looked after the place, hence the gardener. The practice of topiary dates back at least to Roman times, and must have appealed to the Roman liking for order. In the garden of the Pliny the Younger (AD61–113), for example, box hedges were clipped into shapes, some of them spelling the name of the gardener or his master, and trees were planted in patterns, most notably the arrangement known as the *quincunx*, with one tree at each corner of a square and one in the middle, thus:

Topiary came to Britain with the Romans, but with the collapse of the Roman empire this kind of gardening ceased until the Normans brought it back after 1066. It had never died out in France (Gaul) and soon became fashionable again in England. By 1592 the word topiary was used to mean the training of trees

or shrubs into ornamental or fantastic shapes, a trend that coincided with the new commercial wealth and its display in Elizabeth I's reign. In the next century, French and Dutch influence was absorbed, producing designs of increasing sophistication culminating in the style seen at the garden of Levens Hall in Cumbria. This garden was laid out by Guillaume Beaumont, a pupil of Le Nôtre, and has been maintained without a break until this day.

The short reigns of William of Orange and Mary Stuart (1689–1702) saw the high point of British topiary. Beaumont had already designed the semi-circular garden at Hampton Court, the royal residence. Soon the landscape movement of Lancelot 'Capability' Brown and later Humphry Repton, with its emphasis on the 'natural', led to much topiary being grubbed out, and there was little interest in it until mid-Victorian times. Again, new wealth with cheap labour encouraged ostentation, which found its expression in topiary and massive bedding schemes. Towards 1900, again, there was a strong surge of interest, recorded in the *Book of Topiary* by Curtis and Gibson (1904), the latter being the gardener in charge of Levens Hall. After the First World War, however, increasing wages, cost of materials and taxation led to the disappearance of many topiary gardens, a loss much aggravated by the Second World War.

Soon after, however, interest in gardening increased and continues to do so. It had always been a British 'thing' and the working class (no longer a term to be bandied about readily), with more money to spend, developed a taste for topiary along with their traditional bedding-out. This is well recorded in the book *Brilliant Gardens* by Candida Lycett-Green and Andrew Lawson (1987), which contains many examples of topiary in gardens all of modest size, but developed with great skill and feeling.

### Requirements for Topiary

A hedge or shrub is often the starting point. Perhaps some wayward growth from a hedge suggests the beginning of a cone or ball, and one ball leads to another. We are not concerned here with the initial training and development of hedges, but must consider those plants which are suitable for the training which leads to an ornamental feature.

First, the site should be level, with shelter from strong winds. This is best provided by a hedge which filters the air and reduces its speed for a distance about twice the height of the hedge. The undesirable effect of walls in this respect is discussed on p115.

Second, exposure to sunlight for several hours a day is necessary for, if part of a plant is always in shade, its growth will be relatively retarded. When choosing a site, remember that a view from above is always effective, either from the house as at Chastleton, Oxfordshire, and Lytes Cary, Somerset, or from a raised terrace as at Blickling, Norfolk, or Athelhampton, Dorset.

Third, plants should be hardy, comparatively slow-growing, and dense in form and habit. When propagating, cuttings should be taken from a single plant to ensure uniformity of vigour and appearance; seedlings may vary in colour and form.

### PLANTS FOR TOPIARY

Most deciduous plants may be dismissed as unsuitable, though they can be and sometimes are used for topiary, especially in the USA – but they are losing ground there. *Crataegus monogyna* (hawthorn) and other species such as *C. phaenopyrum* (Washington thorn) are the most frequently used deciduous plants. They are reasonably dense but not when leafless and their growth is not easy to control. They tend to produce long straggling shoots needing frequent attention, though this may be a specifically British problem. Deciduous plants come into their own, however, for training as large architectural features, such as archways, tunnels and pleached stilt hedges.

That leaves evergreen but, obviously, not all are suitable. In addition to the requirements mentioned above, of hardy, slow, dense growth, plants for topiary must respond well to pruning, sometimes hard pruning, have reasonably pliable young growth, and reasonably small neat leaves that clothe the shoots well. It is, perhaps, stating the obvious to point out that the smaller and more detailed the final shape, the smaller the leaves should be. So although holly is fine for large spheres and other simple shapes, small spirals and cones are best tackled in yew or box.

### Recommended Plants

#### BUXUS SEMPERVIRENS BOX (E)

This needs a well-drained soil and some protection from northerly winds. It stands clipping well as long as no frost is threatened and can be used to produce sophisticated shapes. It is slow in growth and may take 10 years to reach 1.2m (4ft). This may discourage many, but it is a choice plant for topiary.

#### × CUPRESSOCYPARIS LEYLANDII
#### Leyland cypress (E)

An extremely vigorous plant which needs no encouragement and stands up to wind and coastal weather. Rather surprisingly, it responds to clipping (not too vigorous) and can be restricted to a formal outline by trimming three times during each growing season. All the same, it is best confined to large and simple designs.

CUPRESSUS MACROCARPA Monterey cypress (E)
This is somewhat tender and performs best in maritime areas. It stands clipping well enough but is apt to be untidy.

FAGUS Beech (D)
*F. sylvatica* in Britain and *F. grandifolia* in the USA are only suitable for architectural subjects such as arches or pillars. Beech grows quite rapidly, can easily become too tall and needs a skilled topiarist to handle it. Hornbeam *(Carpinus betulus)* is similar to beech but the dead leaves, retained in winter if the plant is pruned as a hedge, are less attractive.

ILEX AQUIFOLIUM Holly (E)
This species is very hardy, tolerates poor soil and atmospheric pollution, and grows quite rapidly. It can be clipped either in spring or in late summer and responds well with new growth. The use of secateurs is recommended, removing whole leaves rather than cutting through them with shears, as the cut leaves die back unattractively. In the USA, at Disneyland and elsewhere in the south, *I. opaca* and *I. vomitoria* are much used, but neither of these plants succeeds in Britain.

JUNIPERUS COMMUNIS Common juniper (E)
This has upright growth to 3m (10ft) and will keep a regular outline without much clipping. It tolerates chalk and rather poor soil.

LAURUS NOBILIS Bay (E)
This fine plant is not fully hardy in Britain, except in coastal areas. Elsewhere it may be cut to the ground in a severe winter, but almost invariably shoots in spring and can reach 1.2–1.5m (4–5ft) in two years. For topiary it needs clipping with secateurs to produce a good outline and is seldom seen in this role, except as 'lollipop trees' formed of a sphere on top of a bare stem.

LIGUSTRUM OVALIFOLIUM Privet (E)
Although it is often despised by elite gardeners for its suburban image, it is a satisfactory foliage plant, with dark glaucous leaves. The cultivar 'Aureum' is the plant which gardeners really love to hate, but it is the most popular of all shrubs for brightening dark corners. Slower in growth than the type and easier to shape, it produces a colourful picture, if not exactly golden. It will need more frequent clipping than yew or box if a neat shape is to be maintained, but since it is faster growing, satisfactory shapes can be formed more quickly. There are fine examples of ambitious privet topiary, even in Britain, but the best

are found where the summers are really hot – Italy and the USA.

LONICERA NITIDA Chinese honeysuckle (E)
This dense evergreen shrub seldom grows beyond 1.2–1.5m (4–5ft). It is tolerant of most soils and weather and can be used for simple architectural shapes, but it responds to clipping with rather too much enthusiasm for it to be usable for detailed shapes, and it will require clipping several times during the season.

Until 20 or 30 years ago, it was offered by nurserymen as cultivar 'Ernest Wilson', though named simply as *L. nitida*. Since then, however, the cultivar 'Baggesen's Gold' has been much more popular, though the colour is not of the best, reverting to green in shade, and the plant is low-growing which limits its use for topiary. The best choice for topiary may be the cultivar 'Elegant', which is not easy to find but grows to 90cm (3ft) with horizontal branches and leaves of matt green.

TAXUS BACCATA Yew (E)
Although botanically a conifer, yew bears no cones. This great plant, already described on pp120–2, forms a dense outline and bears repeated clipping even if this continues for centuries, as at Levens Hall. Although reputed to be slow-growing, growth is rapid enough to produce a respectable 1.8m (6ft) tree in 10 years from a 30cm (12in) pot-grown plant, yet clipping is only needed once a year. Feeding with manure is essential in the early stages.

The special virtue of yew for topiary is shown in the well-defined lines, edges and curves of the best geometric examples. The golden forms are especially useful for the geometric designs. A plain *T. baccata* with *T. b.* 'Aurea' either grown through it, or grafted at 90cm (3ft), became popular as the trademark of the garden designer Thomas Mawson (1861–1933). Healthy examples still survive at Duffryn Garden in Cardiff, South Wales.

THUJA PLICATA Western red cedar (E)
A hardy and fast-growing tree, it makes a dense head of medium green colour. It is used for topiary in the USA.

FIRST STEPS
The most important rule of topiary for the amateur is to keep everything simple – cylinders, pyramids, cubes, cones and spheres are straightforward. Do not distort the natural shape of the tree or shrub more than is necessary.

After planting, deciduous specimens such as

A handsome yew hedge with 'roofing'. Beautifully maintained, it is trimmed every autumn and in summer is decorated in front with tobacco plants

hawthorn, beech and hornbeam should be cut back in early spring if their growth is upright. Hawthorn (and privet, although evergreen) are cut to 15cm (6in) from the ground in spring of the first and second years, then in each subsequent spring about 10–15cm (4–6in) is cut away each year. Beech and hornbeam need less severe pruning, to 30cm (12in) perhaps in the first year, leaving 45cm (18in) of stem in the second year. When the desired height is reached, prune each year to keep that height, and also cut back laterals to produce the required shape (see the table on p121 for timing).

Evergreen plants are not pruned in the first year, but straggly branches are clipped as necessary.

Feed and water all specimens every month. Subsequently, during the first three to four years, do not allow too much increase in height – probably 15–20cm (6–8in) a year is enough. Clip three to four times each year. Box, holly and yew are first cut in early summer then every six weeks. Beech and hornbeam are clipped in midsummer but, as they mature, defer this until late summer or early autumn. Use secateurs for bay, holly and laurel, and prune in late winter to early spring if strong growth is needed.

## Free shaping of young trees

This technique is best for simple designs that are broader at the base than the top, such as cones or pyramids. Only use bamboo or wire if it cannot be avoided; such aids are mainly needed in complex designs. Clear out dead wood and leaves from the inside of the plant to promote air circulation and penetration of light. A good shape for beginners is a cone or pyramid. The outline follows that of many trees, and allows further development from the main leader. Use string as a guide for cutting a straight line.

Spheres and cubes are not very difficult and look effective on a bare stem. A circle or crown can be created as follows. First, produce a life-size or scaled drawing, from which a metal frame can be made, ideally using a local blacksmith. When the frame is complete, get him to insert a strong metal rod to fix the completed design to the ground and to position the shape at the desired height. As the plant grows, tie it to the frame, spacing the branches evenly. As the shoots expand through the frame, start clipping, once more remembering to clear leaves from the inside.

## Container-grown topiary plants

The best containers are wooden tubs of oak, cedar or cypress, measuring say 53 × 53 × 53cm (21 × 21 × 21in). There should be 10 drain holes, each about 15mm ($\frac{3}{4}$in) in diameter, and the tub should be raised

on blocks 5cm (2in) high. Put a layer of broken crocks and gravel at the bottom, and top this with a layer about 10cm (4in) deep of light-textured soil. The plant, if not container-grown already, should have a wrapping of sacking round the root ball. If so, do not remove or loosen the wrapping. Place the plant on top of the soil, making sure it is in the middle of the container. Fill the space round the root ball with a light soil enriched with compost and a little general fertilizer. Firm it down by treading, so that the soil level is about 5cm (2in) below the rim of the tub. Water well and add a layer of mulch to protect the roots from heat and cold and to stifle weeds. Water daily for a week, then once a week. Keep the plant and its container in partial shade for one year, and do not apply any more fertilizer.

Yew topiary at Hidcote, Gloucestershire. Lawrence Johnston never discussed the ideas behind his twenty-one 'gardens within a garden'. However, this kind of topiary was already common in both Europe and the USA by the time he began to create his famous garden, so the concept was not original

Mature subjects are best pruned when the effect on the plants of removing leaves will be diminishing; that is, late summer. Some plants will need clipping more than once, for the sake of tidiness, but this does place an extra strain on the victim. Spring pruning is indicated for plants that have been damaged, perhaps by frost, which is a serious threat to all topiary. Manuring, followed by a long-acting fertilizer, should follow the pruning in this unhappy situation.

# Roses

## PRUNING PHILOSOPHIES

It is easy to make rose pruning sound difficult. The subject *is* difficult because it requires a knowledge of the various kinds of rose and their habits and it takes time to achieve that. The act of pruning, however, is not difficult given the right tools, well maintained (see pp9–12): secateurs, long-handled for some climbers, loppers for any stems over 1cm (¹/₂in) in diameter, and a pocket saw for any over 3.5cm (1¹/₂in). A very sharp pruning knife helps in neatening any untidy cuts, especially as these cuts should be close, but not too close, to a bud.

## WHEN TO PRUNE

Roses that are never pruned may perform quite well for five years, but the stems will become long and spindly, the flowers smaller. All carefully recorded experience would support the assertion that pruning once a year makes most roses perform well and enables them to live a long and useful life. But the questioning of accepted practices is always useful. When do we have to do it? In 1933 William Robinson, a most influential gardening author, set down the following rather controversial and combative view in the preface to *The English Flower Garden*, his last major work (1933):

> A delusion is that the plants must be pruned late in the spring . . . they are left all the winter to be knocked about [by the weather] . . . it is a much better practice to prune all our Roses before Christmas, if possible, and set them to work to make roots.

This is all very well, but there arises the matter of climate differences, especially noticeable in Britain with its wide ranges of temperature and rainfall, and of microclimates, often related to hills, plantations or lakes. Robinson's garden at Gravetye in Sussex had, and still must have, a benign micro-climate related to southerly slopes and woodland, with relatively mild winters. Under these conditions pruning at any time in the dormant period (mid-autumn to late winter in Britain) would be safe. In less favoured conditions, however, pruning before late winter would run the risk of damage to the exposed shoots caused by frost, while leaving the pruning until mid-spring would involve a risk from late frosts to young immature shoots: hence the now accepted routine pruning for the majority of roses just before spring. If the

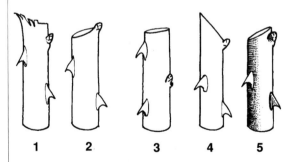

1  This ragged cut made too far from the bud, may lead to die-back

2  A cut too close to the bud may allow infection to enter and could damage the bud

3  A cut too far from the bud may lead to die-back

4  A cut sloping the wrong way directs rainwater on to the bud, which becomes moist and may rot

5  CORRECT: The cut ends not more than 0.5cm (¼in) above the bud

weather is unfavourable, pruning may be delayed for a couple of weeks. During this period new growth will develop slowly and is able to resist most late frosts.

CLASSIFICATION

Roses are classified below as suggested by the World Federation of Rose Societies. The listing consists of a selection of good examples with their date of introduction if this is known.

**Species** Wild roses, mostly once-flowering.

*R. foetida*, *R. glauca (rubrifolia)*, *R. hugonis*, *R. paulii*, *R. pomifera*, *R. primula*. *R. spinosissima (pimpinellifolia)* (Burnet or Scotch rose); naturalized on sand dunes in Britain. Small leaves and flowers, but they have charm. Varieties include 'Double Pink'; 'Double White'; 'William III', pink-purple. *R. s. altaica* reaches 1.8m (6ft) and has given rise to a number of hybrids, including 'Frühlingsgold' (1937). 'Stanwell Perpetual' (1838) a cross between a Burnet rose and probably a damask, is hardly that, but it does repeat over a long period. All the Scotch roses flourish without routine pruning, but occasional thinning of shoots when overcrowded is beneficial.

**Gallicas** (Old garden roses, Gallica). Summer-flowering only.

'Charles de Mills'; 'Gloire de France'; *Rosa mundi*, before sixteenth century; 'Tuscany'.

**Damasks** (Old garden roses, Damasks). Summer-flowering only.

'Ispahan', 'Mme Hardy' (1832); 'St Nicholas' (1950, found in Yorkshire).

**China roses** (Old garden roses, China roses). Perpetual flowering.

'Fellemberg' (1857); 'Mutabilis', an amazing rose, with single flowers changing colour from red to buff to pink to copper; 'Old Blush China' (c1789) another remarkable plant, flowering in every month, always on Christmas Day at Tintinhull, almost disease-free.

**Bourbon roses** (Old garden roses, Bourbons). Most, and all those listed here, have a second flowering in autumn.

'Boule de Neige' (1867); 'Mme Isaac Pereire' (1880); 'Zéphirine Drouhin' (1868), the thornless rose, will reach 3.7m (12ft) against a wall. Coppery young leaves, double cerise flowers, fragrant, repeat flowering.

**Portland roses** (Old garden roses, Portlands). Two flushes of bloom, often some at intervals as well.

'Portlandica' (c1790); 'Mme Knorr' ('Comte de Chambord') (1863), double pink with an edge of lilac.

**Hybrid Perpetuals** (Old garden roses, Hybrid Perpetuals). Not, in fact, perpetual, flowering twice.

'Reine des Violettes' (1860); 'Souvenir du Docteur Jamain' (1865); 'Mrs John Laing' (1887), double fragrant pink flowers.

**Tea Roses** (Old garden roses, Tea Roses). For greenhouse or conservatory, except in mild climates.

**Hybrid Tea Roses** Bush roses, large-flowered and recurrent.

'Shot Silk' (1924); 'The Doctor' (1936); 'Grace de Monaco' (1956); 'Wendy Cussons' (1963); 'Peace'

FIRST STEPS IN PRUNING ROSES

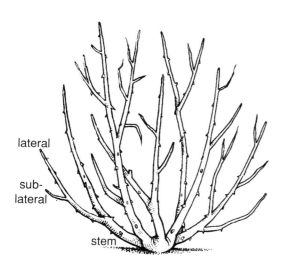

Look out for stems likely to rub against each other and remove the more expendable ones completely and promptly

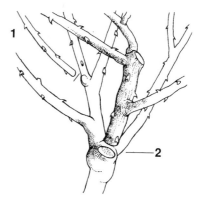

1 Cut out any wood which is dead or diseased. Prune into wood which looks healthy and examine the cut surface. If it is at all brown, cut further down into the stem
2 If you reach a point where there is no healthy bud above which you can cut, the whole stem must be sacrificed

(1939) very large pale yellow flowers edged pink, leaves dark and glossy – very prone to blackspot, needs light pruning.

**Albas** (Old garden roses, Albas). Summer-flowering only.

*Alba maxima*; 'Celeste', late eighteenth century, very fine shrubs with soft pink flowers; 'Königin von Danemark' (1826).

**Centifolias** (Old garden roses, Provence, Centifolias). Summer-flowering only. Lax flowers and leaves. These are cabbage roses, developed in Holland in the seventeenth century and featured in Dutch paintings of that period.

'Rose de Meaux' (before 1800), small leaves and pink flowers becoming darker on opening; 'Fantin Latour', pale pink double flowers, a splendid tall bush.

**Moss Roses** (Old garden roses, Moss Roses). Summer-flowering only.

'Common Moss' (1727); 'William Lobb' (1855), tall enough for a pillar, double purple-crimson flowers.

**Rugosas** Shrub roses, repeat-flowering, classed as modern garden roses.

*R. rugosa* (c1796); *R. r.* 'Alba'; 'Blanc Double de Coubert' (1892), white, no hips; 'Roseraie de l'Hay' (1901), wine-red, no hips; 'Frau Dagmar Hastrup' (1914), pale pink, good hips. All these are in the top class, very healthy, reliable and with excellent foliage.

**Polyanthas** Bush roses, polyanthas, recurrent. 'Little White Pet' (1829) (a sport of 'Felicité et Perpétué, but polyantha habit); 'Nathalie Nypels' (1917), semi-double pink flowers, low but spreading, good repetition; 'Yvonne Rabier' (1910), double white flowers, well scented, robust.

**Floribundas** Bush roses, cluster-growing, recurrent.

'Rosemary Rose' (1945); 'Frensham' (1946); 'Iceberg' (1958), the best white rose, prune lightly; 'Arthur Bell' (1965), bright red flowers, dark purple foliage, tolerates some shade; 'Margaret Merril' (1977), white fragrant flowers tinged pink in the bud, easy to grow.

**Grandifloras** Bush roses, cluster-flowering, recurrent. Average height 1m (3½ft). A dubious class.

'Queen Elizabeth' (1945); 'John S. Armstrong' (1961).

**Hybrid Musks** Shrub roses, recurrent. Two main flushes of bloom.

'Pax' (1918); 'Penelope' (1924); 'Buff Beauty' (1919).

**Modern shrub roses** Shrub roses, recurrent and non-recurrent.

'Nevada' (1927); 'Golden Wings' (1956); 'Cerise Bouquet' (1958); 'Constance Spry' (1961).

**Ramblers** Climbing roses, non-recurrent, summer-flowering only.

'François Juranville' (1906); 'Seagull' (1907); 'Albertine' (1921); *R. filipes* 'Kiftsgate'.

**Climbers** Climbing roses, recurrent and non-recurrent.

'Zephirine Drouhin', bred in France in 1868, is probably the best of the Bourbons and still widely available. This deliciously scented rose has no thorns and produces shoots 2.4m (8ft) or more long; it is best grown on a wall. The cerise-pink flowers are semi-double and produced continuously. It has a reputation for attracting mildew and blackspot, but that is probably exaggerated. It is nevertheless a lovable plant

1. Noisette climbers, all recurrent. 'Gloire de Dijon' (1853); 'Mme Alfred Carrière' (1879).

2. Large-flowered climbers, flower more than once but later blooming seldom equals the first. 'Lady Hillingdon' (1917); 'Mermaid' (1918); 'Mme Gregoire Staechelin' (1927); 'New Dawn' (1930); 'Guinée' (1938); 'Parkdirektor Riggers' (1957); 'Helen Knight' (1977).

**Miniature roses** Miniature roses, bush and climbing, all recurrent. Height of most 25–30cm (10–12in).

'Easter Morning' (1960); 'Nozomi' (1972); 'Swany' (1978); 'Snow Carpet' (1980).

### PRACTICAL PRUNING OF NEWLY PLANTED ROSES

It is worth visiting one or more rose collections during the flowering period before deciding which roses to grow. The plants will have been given the best cultivation and pruning, and it is possible to form an idea of the height and spread to be expected, as well as seeing the real colour rather than relying on a photograph.

If you are able to collect the plants from the nursery you have a better chance of planting in autumn, the best time. Delivery by a nursery is apt to be uncertain, but it must be between autumn and early spring. In advance of delivery you can prepare the ground, but delay planting until a still, dry, fairly warm day. These do not happen at weekends.

Equipped with secateurs, a knife, lopper and pocket saw, you are ready for action. If this is autumn or winter examine the root system, cut away any roots that are coarse (without rootlets) or damaged and then plant; that is all. Pruning of shoots follows in early spring and that applies also to any plants that arrive in late winter. For most, pruning is severe, cutting back main shoots to two to four eyes, about 15cm (6in) from the ground. At this stage it may be as well to name the exceptions to this cruel first-year routine.

1. Any growing in poor, thin soil. Prune very lightly.
2. True ramblers, such as 'Dorothy Perkins'. Prune all strong shoots to 23–38cm (9–15in).
3. Ramblers with growth high on the plant and very little at the base. Prune to 22–38cm (9–15in).

4. Climbers and ramblers which are sports of Hybrid Teas and Noisette roses, all recurrent, such as 'Gloire de Dijon', 'Mme Alfred Carrière'. *No* pruning, as they may revert permanently to the bush form.

5. Large-flowered climbers the late flowering of which is poor, such 'Lady Hillingdon', 'Mermaid' and 'Helen Knight'. 'New Dawn' does repeat well. *No* pruning. Remember that these five exceptions to the rule of severe pruning refer only to the first year.

### PRUNING OF ESTABLISHED ROSES

At any time of year keep a look out for dead wood and remove it completely (the pocket saw may be needed). Cut back diseased wood to healthy-looking wood. Examine the cut end and if it is brown cut further to another bud, and so on until the pith is white. Even then there must be a bud above which to make the cut – if not the whole stem must be cut away. Do not overlook shoots that cross others and rub against them or look like doing so. One of the two must be sacrificed. Look out for suckers. Most roses grown in nurseries are grafted onto a rootstock, *R. multiflora* or a wild species. Shoots may arise below the graft, forming suckers which may extend and may even take over from the grafted rose. The difference between sucker foliage and that of the grafted rose is usually easy to detect. The leaves of the sucker are normally lighter green with several leaflets and the thorns

may be of a different shape. Cutting a sucker at ground level simply encourages new and diffuse growth. None of these tasks has to wait for a pruning session but can be carried out as soon as the problem is noticed.

### PRUNING OF SUMMER ROSES

This is a subject of some importance and one of the commonest pruning operations. As with dead-heading of herbaceous subjects, it calls for some knowledge of the structure and habit of the plant, and unfortunately attracts the attention of eager volunteers who lack this qualification. The object is to remove all flowers as they fade – this also removes the seed or seeds. Once the seed-containing hips begin to form the energy of the plant is directed to their development, and the formation of new shoots and flowering stems is inhibited by growth-regulating hormones. There is also some danger of disease arising in the dead flowerhead if it is left to rot. As a rule, it is possible either to cut off individual roses at the origin of their stems or to remove a whole truss, for example of the floribunda rose 'Iceberg', carrying five or six blooms. In the latter case the stem should be traced down to a promising bud and cut off just above it. In all dead-heading, never leave an unsightly length of stem which may lead to dieback. In some instances, and a good example is the polyantha-type rambler 'Little White Pet', individual blooms open and die

SUCKERS

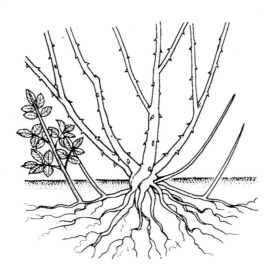

Suckers can emerge from the roots of a rose grafted at ground level. Remove at their origin

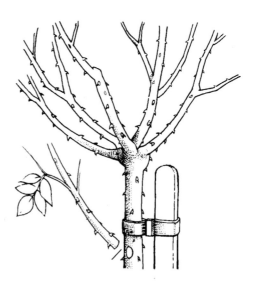

A sucker arising on the main stem of a standard rose. The foliage is that of the rootstock plant. Remove at its origin

after a very short life and dead-heading is indicated two or three times each day, unless brown is your favourite colour.

The contra-indication to dead-heading is the formation of attractive hips. *R. canina*, the dog rose, and *R. rubiginosa*, the eglantine, are the oldest to carry distinguished hips, but in modern gardens *R. glauca* is held in affection for its red young stems, grey-green leaves and red-brown hips. Rugosa roses vary. The following bear excellent hips: 'Alba', 'Frau Dagmar Hastrup', *R. rugosa* itself, and 'Scabrosa'. Hips are negligible (so dead-heading desirable) on 'Blanc Double de Coubert', 'Roseraie de l'Hay' and probably most others.

### ROUTINE PRUNING OF ROSES THAT FLOWER ON CURRENT SEASON'S WOOD

Roses that flower on the growth of the current season make up the majority of garden roses, but their pruning is subtly different in the different groups. They include: China, Bourbon, Portland, Hybrid Perpetual, Tea and Hybrid Tea, Rugosa, Polyantha, Floribunda, Grandiflora, Hybrid Musk and Miniature roses.

**China roses** are rather tender and are best grown against a wall, when they will reach 2.4m (8ft). Pruning is best done at the start of spring, cutting the main shoots to 20–25cm (8–10in) long and removing any thin stems (less than the diameter of a pencil).

**Bourbon roses** need to be pruned between late winter and early spring (mid-February to mid-March in Britain). The star of this group is 'Zéphirine Drouhin', which has no thorns, cerise-pink, quite fragrant flowers, and a long flowering season. It produces shoots 3.7m (12ft) long, and has coppery young leaves. Pruning involves cutting back the side shoots by two-thirds and main shoots by one-third. Dead-head all fading flowers.

**Portland roses** are not numerous. Perhaps 'Comte de Chambord' has undergone a sex change and emerged as 'Mme Knorr', none the worse. There are two flushes of bloom. Give routine early spring pruning and dead-head immediately after the first flowering.

**Hybrid Perpetuals** Famous as exhibition roses in Victorian days but are still going strong in borders today. Make a note of 'Mrs John Laing' (1897) with soft pink, fragrant double flowers. Prune those which are vigorous in early spring as you would Bourbons, others as you would Hybrid Teas but less severely.

**Tea Roses** are tender and dislike hard pruning but should have a mild dose in early spring. 'General Schablikine' (1878) sounds sinister and is only picked out because his performance in the south of France is marvellous (not helpful to readers who do not travel). Prune in early spring. 'Lady Hillingdon', with double apricot-yellow flowers and coppery new leaves, is now grown in her climbing form as a rule and is given a warm place against a wall. Prune in spring.

**Hybrid Teas** need the routine early spring pruning. There do not seem to be any exceptions but there surely must be as there are thousands of these roses, with very variable characters.

**Rugosas** are indispensable. Life would be diminished without them for there is no substitute. Happily it is agreed that they normally only need light pruning in spring to improve their shapes, but if they go into a decline they respond well to drastic pruning to 60cm (2ft). Then you must live without flower for a year. Dead-head 'Frau Dagmar Hastrup', which has pale pink flowers, with discretion as very good crimson hips follow. Leave at least half the hips to develop. Hips are negligible on 'Blanc Double de Coubert' and 'Roseraie de l'Hay'. Dead-head them as soon as the flowers fade – it can be a tedious job.

**Polyanthas** accept the early spring pruning and none is better than 'Nathalie Nypels' (she was Dutch), who manages to produce fragrant pink semi-double flowers continuously through summer. That judgement was almost overturned by the arrival of 'Margaret Merril' (English) with not-quite-double, splendidly scented flowers, white with a shade of pink. Prune as for Hybrid Teas.

**Floribundas** (cluster-flowered) have a very strong team including 'Frensham' (1946) with good, dark green leaves and clear red flowers in groups, hardly clusters.

It is not easy to calculate the extent of pruning but important to attempt it. Cutting off too much each year may weaken the plant, at first hardly perceptibly but within three or four years quite obviously. Being too gentle, on the other hand, leads to big bushes with thin, weak shoots. A compromise may produce a good collection of clusters, but not always. The advice of pruning some shoots lightly for early flowering and others severely to produce basal growths for flowering late in the season may solve the problem, but once more not always. This pruning must be done in late winter to early spring in the second year, and in the same period of each year thereafter. All the main one-year-old shoots are reduced by one-third and any older wood cut to 15–23cm (6–9in), while any laterals which remain are shortened by 10–15cm (4–6in). 'Iceberg', justly famous for its long and repeated flowering, dislikes hard pruning (as does the Tea Rose 'Peace'). This kind of pruning produces long shoots with few flowers. Given light pruning, taking off about 30cm (12in) from the main shoots each year, it makes a fine well-shaped bush to 1.5m (5ft) high, repeat-flowering but only slightly fragrant. 'Rosemary

## ROSA CHINENSIS AND SOME OLD HYBRID TEAS

Pruning is aimed at encouraging growth from the base

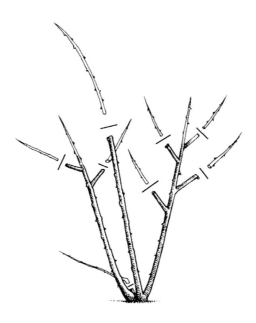

1 In early spring of the second year long growths are cut back by one-third of their length and laterals to 15cm (6in)

2 Flowering takes place on laterals of old wood. Summer prune

3 In the third and following years, long growths are cut back by one-third of their length and laterals to 15cm (6in) in early spring

4 Each autumn, cut back long growths by up to one-third of their length. Remove badly placed growths completely

## ALBAS, CENTIFOLIAS, DAMASK, MOSS ROSES AND SOME MODERN SHRUB ROSES

These flower mainly on lateral and sub-lateral shoots of second-year or older wood. Most do not repeat flower, but some will do so on laterals of the current year

1 In early spring of the second year cut back any weak or damaged shoots

2 In the following summer, flowering takes place on laterals of old wood. Summer prune to encourage the formation of new laterals which may flower later in the season

3 In late summer, flowering takes place on laterals produced this season

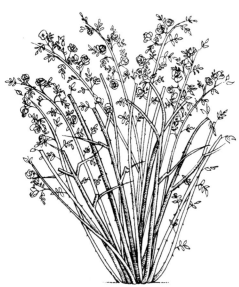

4 In subsequent years, summer prune as before. Spring prune as necessary (see step 1), and shorten any over-long shoots

SPECIES ROSES AND CLOSE HYBRIDS,
*R. SPINOSISSIMA*, *R. RUGOSA*, GALLICAS,
HYBRID MUSKS

**These flower on the current season's growth and
need quite severe pruning**

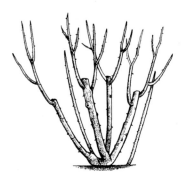

1 In early spring of the second year, lightly trim the
strongest shoots

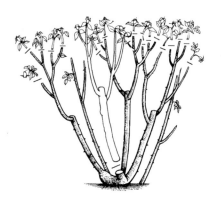

2 In autumn, cut out elderly shoots which flowered
poorly and shorten laterals to 10cm (4in)

3 In subsequent years, summer prune and cut out
weak growths, especially in the centre of the shrub

Rose', with very dark, almost purple, foliage, bears trusses of red flowers which recur reliably in partial shade, and that shade does not seem to have any bad effect. Instinct suggests that this rose should not be hard-pruned.

**Grandifloras** Mainly American, including 'Queen Elizabeth' (1945). Very tall with large china-pink flowers in clusters, which last well after picking. It is probably *the* favourite rose, in Britain at least. The pruning of Grandifloras is the same as for Floribundas, from which they differ mainly in height.

**Hybrid Musks** The pioneer was the Reverend Joseph Pemberton of Havering Atte Bower in Essex. Soon after 1900 he started breeding, using two German roses 'Aglaia' and 'Trier', both with *R. moschata* and *R. multiflora* in their family tree. Crossing them with a selection of Teas, Hybrid Teas and Hybrid Perpetuals, he produced an entirely new breed which at first was known as 'Pemberton Roses'. The best are not easy to pick out but 'Pax' (1918), 'Buff Beauty' (1919) and 'Penelope' (1924) are widely grown. The Hybrid Musks do benefit from pruning by living on into a floriferous old age. In the late winter remove any stems that are filling the centre of the plant; the rest can be cut back by one third. These roses are successful in borders of perennial herbaceous plants as single specimens, and will also do well as an informal hedge.

**Modern Shrub Roses** A group of mixed character with a suggestion of Centifolia in 'Constance Spry' (1961). 'Nevada' (1927) arches to 2.4m (8ft) with round dark leaves and very large, creamy white single flowers in abundance, only modestly repeating. 'Cerise Bouquet' (1958) has grey-green leaves and big clusters of semi-double, crimson, fragrant flowers. It blooms only in summer but for a long time and makes a beautiful arching shrub, 2.4m (8ft) high. These shrubs all benefit from pruning in early spring.

CLIMBERS AND RAMBLERS

**True Ramblers** These flower in early summer on the laterals of long shoots arising from the base. These roses include 'Dorothy Perkins' (1901), once the best-known rose of all, and 'American Pillar', both hybrids of *R. wichuraiana*. They are summer-flowering only, mainly on the wood of last year and slightly on older wood. The flowers are small.

At planting – if in late winter to early spring – prune all strong shoots to 25–38cm (10–15in) from the ground. If planting has been in autumn or early winter, delay pruning until the time just indicated. Strong shoots will develop by early summer and they should be tied to horizontal wires at intervals as they grow. There will be no flowers that year. In the

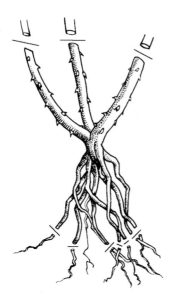

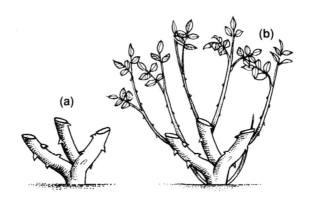

At planting, cut away any damaged roots and coarse roots with few rootlets. Cut main shoots back by 5–7.5cm (2–3in)

(a) In early spring, cut shoots back to around 15cm (6in) from ground level
(b) By early summer vigorous new shoots have been produced

In autumn, flowered stems are cut back by one-third of their length. Any weak shoots are removed entirely

In subsequent years, in early spring cut out dead or diseased wood, and any inward-pointing, crossing or weak shoots. Cut remaining shoots back to 15–23cm (6–9in)

SUMMER PRUNING OF HYBRID TEAS

INCORRECT: cut stems are too long

CORRECT: cut stems are correct length, and are cut to a
strong, outward-facing shoot or bud

SUMMER PRUNING OF FLORIBUNDAS

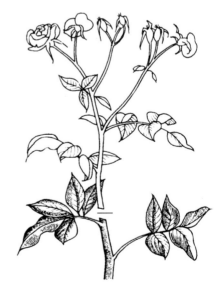

INCORRECT: individual flowers only have been
removed

CORRECT: whole flower truss is removed to a strong,
outward-facing shoot or bud

FLORIBUNDAS

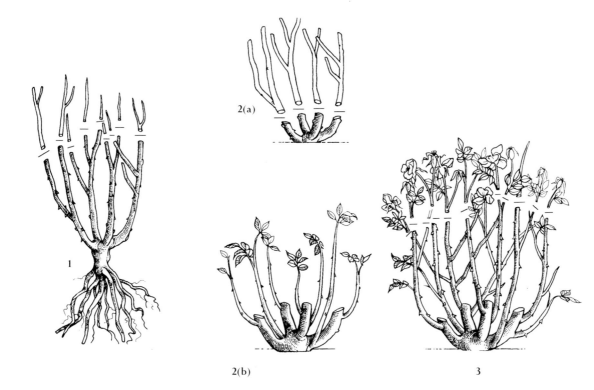

1

2(a)

2(b)

3

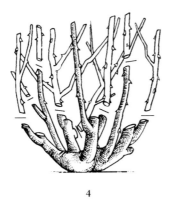

4

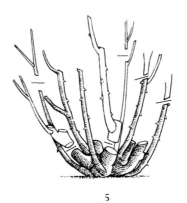

5

1  At planting, coarse and damaged roots are cut back.
   Main shoots are trimmed by a few inches
2  (a) In early spring all stems are cut back to 23cm
   (9in)
   (b) New growth appears in late spring
3  In autumn, cut all flowered growths back by
   15–23cm (6–9in)

4  In early spring, prune back year-old shoots by one-
   third of their length, any older shoots to 23cm (9in)
   and laterals to 15cm (6in)
5  In subsequent years, prune in early spring as in step
   4. Cut out any diseased and dead wood, and any
   stems likely to rub together or grow inwards

following summer, flowers will appear on short laterals from last year's growth. After the flowers fade all shoots are cut away at the base. If there are few basal shoots appearing, leave one or two of the flowered shoots but cut back their laterals to 10–12cm (4–5in). Tie in all new growth. Repeat the cycle each year.

**Climbers** Summer-flowering only, non-recurrent. The flowers are larger than in those of the true ramblers. The climbers produce few shoots from the base, the new growth coming mainly from 0.9–1.2m (3–4ft) above ground. Cut the stems back to a point just above the origin of a new shoot which has emerged from the old. Into this group has forced its way *R. filipes* 'Kiftsgate', an extremely vigorous form, climbing 9–12 (30–40ft) into a tree and bearing creamy white fragrant flowers most of the way. Pruning is almost impossible and fortunately not necessary.

**Noisette Climbers and Ramblers** All are recurrent, and suitable for wall training or pergolas. 'Gloire de Dijon' (1853) is the best example but there are poor forms around and it would be worth asking for a cutting from a plant you have seen to be of the best clone. Propagation under mist is easy – as a rule. This rose is certainly recurrent from early summer until autumn. A warning about pruning in the first year has been given (p132). After the first year all shoots can be shortened, leaving enough to allow horizontal training, if possible. Laterals are shortened to two buds.

**Large-flowered Climbers** Flower more than once but the later bloom seldom equals the first. 'Lady Hillingdon' (1917) responds well to early spring pruning but is shy of flowering unless grown in a sunny place. 'Mermaid' is rather tender; pruning may be delayed until mid-spring and need not go beyond tidying up. The flowers are single, sulphur-yellow, in clusters. 'New Dawn' repeats its blush-pink double blooms until early autumn and needs only light pruning. 'Helen Knight' (1977) seems more like a wide shrub rose than a climber, with good yellow flowers for two months in spring. The long arching shoots may be cut back to 90cm (3ft) when flowering ceases.

PILLAR ROSES

Repeat-flowering on wood of the current year. Usually of upright habit, not more than 3m (10ft) high. The pillar is best made of timber, failing the real thing of stone or good brick. Suitable plants include 'Aloha' (1949), deep pink, fragrant; 'Golden Showers' (1956), golden fading to cream, foliage dark green; 'Swan Lake' (1968), double white, flushed pink; and 'White Cockade' (1969), double pure white, good dark foliage.

For the first two years train the growths to surround the pillar and shorten laterals. Cut off leading

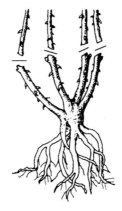

1 In early spring after planting, cut back shoots to 25–38cm (10–15in)

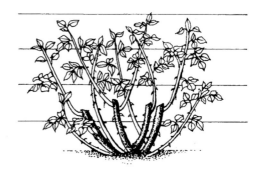

2 During the first summer, train new growth to wires as it extends. The plant will probably not flower this year

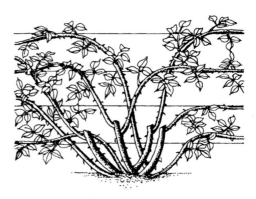

3 By the end of the first season, good growth has been made

## TRUE RAMBLERS

These flower once, on laterals of long basal shoots of the previous year

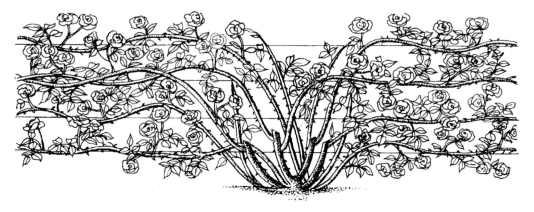

4  In the second summer the plant will flower well

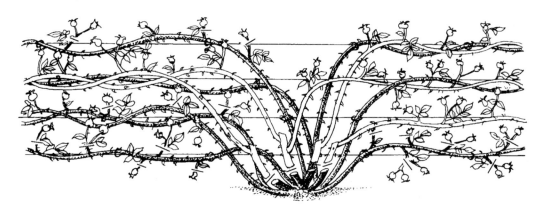

5  Flowered shoots are cut to the base as blooms fade, leaving
several to fill out the framework

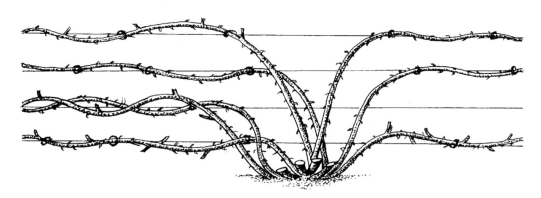

6  By the end of the season's growth, all stems are tied in ready
for the following year's flowering

MINIATURES

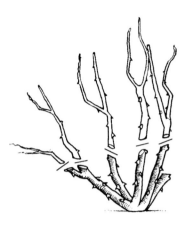

1  In early spring cut shoots back
to 10–15cm (4–6in)

2  Dead-heading means a visit to the plant two or
three times a day in the flowering season

3  In early spring, remove weak growth completely.
Cut back strong shoots to 10–15cm (4–6in)

POLYANTHAS

1  After planting, in early spring cut back strong
stems by one-third of their length. Remove any
weak stems completely

2  Flowering takes place in summer.
Summer prune

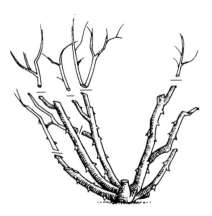

3  In early spring, cut back strong stems by one-half of
their length. Cut out old or diseased wood completely.
In subsequent years, reduce strong stems by one-third
of their length or rather less. Cut out completely any
weak stems from the centre to keep the bush open

shoots at the top of the pillar. Shorten laterals in early spring, to produce flowering spurs.

## STANDARD ROSES

Hybrid Teas and Floribunda roses are the usual choice for standard roses in formal designs, not necessarily with bush or shrub roses. The site must not be exposed since the head is liable to be top-heavy, overweighted on one side. On planting the stake must be strong and driven into the earth almost as far as the part which is above ground.

The base of the stem is not exactly elegant but is difficult to conceal without making access to the rose awkward. The weeping standard offers a solution. If a small-flowered (true) Rambler is used, the old growth is removed to a few inches after flowering. If a large-flowered hybrid such as 'Albertine' is chosen, it is cut back to a point immediately above the origin of a new lateral, but the weeping effect may be less easy to achieve. Strings attached near the tips of the long stems are then fixed to tent-pegs with slight tension. After two or three months they may be removed.

## ROSE HEDGES

At first you may hesitate at the idea of using roses for hedging. Roses are deciduous, never really evergreen, though the *R. sempervirens* sport 'Felicité et Perpétué' does its best. In winter they often look mournful, and

'Adélaide d'Orléans', bred in France in 1826, is a hybrid of *R. sempervirens* from southern Europe and, like the latter, is evergreen with plenty of foliage. The flowers are small, semi-double and abundant on a climbing stem up to 4.5m (15ft). In great demand after it first appeared, 'Adélaide d'Orléans' was then neglected; however it is still available from specialist rose nurseries

after pruning offer only a forecast of pleasure to come. As boundary hedges they may be effective deterrents to intruders, but better plants are available for that purpose – hawthorn or, more sophisticated, the Japanese bitter orange, *Poncirus trifoliata*. This is admittedly slow-growing, but impenetrable, bears fragrant flowers like orange blossom, and does not require pruning.

Only one group of roses springs to mind as hedge-forming: the Rugosas. Some of the best grow easily to a height of 1.2, 1.5, 1.8 or 2.1m (4, 5, 6 or 7ft) with the same spread, and here is a choice.
*R. rugosa* Many clones and a readiness to hybridize. A good form grows to 1.8–2.1m (6–7ft), its flowers scented and deep red, the hips globular and also red; plenty of them.
*R. rugosa* 'Alba' Similar but with flowers pure white.
'Blanc Double de Coubert', 1.8 × 1.5m (6 × 5ft). Pure white flowers, faint scent, hips few and poor. It

## CLIMBING ROSES, I

These flower on laterals from shoots of the previous year

1  The plant flowers in summer, once only. New growth arises
mainly around 1–1.2m (3–4ft) from the base

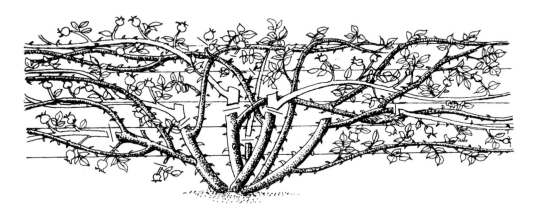

2  After flowering, flowered stems are cut back to the main
shoots which will replace them. These are trained horizontally

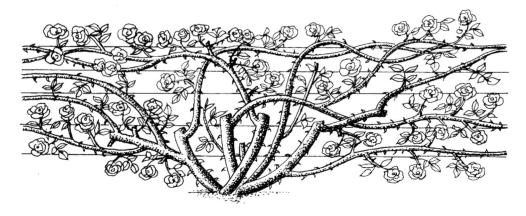

3  Flowering takes place the following summer along the new
leaders. Repeat step 2 after flowering

## CLIMBING ROSES, II

These climbing sports of the Hybrid Tea roses and Floribundas, and
Noisette-style roses flower on wood of the current year, usually repeating through the summer

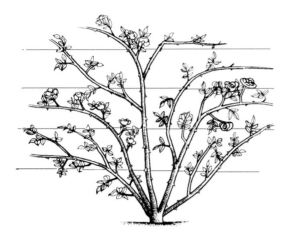

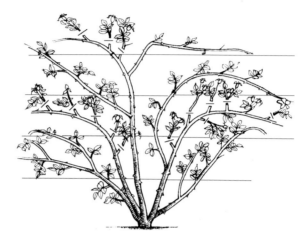

1  In the summer after planting, new shoots are tied to
their supports. A few flowers are produced

2  In winter, cut back flowered laterals to 15cm (6in).
Secure leading shoots to wires

3  In the following summer flowers
form on new shoots and laterals.
Summer pruning encourages
repeat flowering

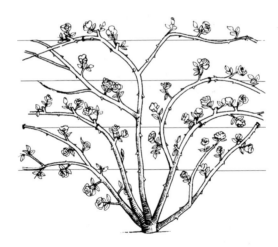

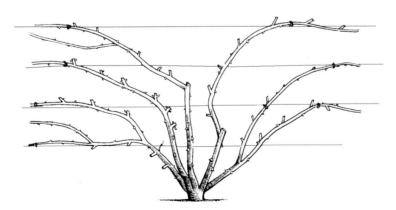

4  In winter, cut back laterals
to 15cm (6in). Repeat the cycle
in subsequent years

PILLAR ROSES

These are repeat-flowering on wood of the current year, and
have an upright habit to around 3m (10ft)

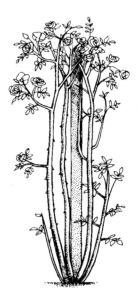

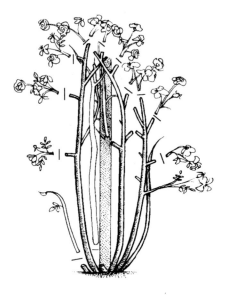

1 The plant is trained to surround the pillar.
Summer prune

2 In autumn, flowered laterals are cut back to two
buds. Cut out dead, diseased and weak growth

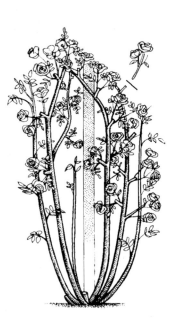

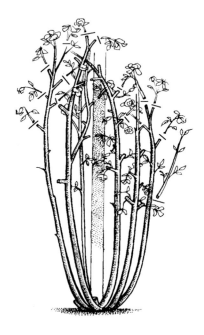

3 Flowering takes place on laterals of old
wood. Summer prune

4 In the second and subsequent autumns, cut
off leading shoots at the top of the pillar.
Shorten laterals sufficiently to keep the plant
more or less symmetrical

## STANDARD

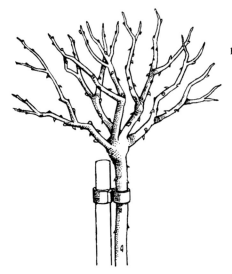

1 Standard rose at planting. The main stem is secured to a stout stake

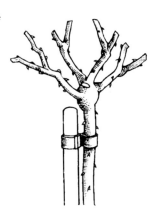

2 In late winter, cut back stems to 15cm (6in) or 3–5 eyes, rather less severely for floribundas, say 6–8 eyes. This is repeated in subsequent years

## WEEPING STANDARD

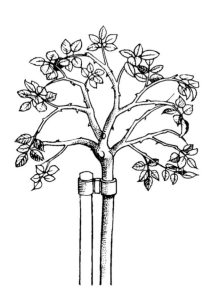

1 A weeping standard after grafting with a rambler such as 'Excelsa' or 'François Juranville'

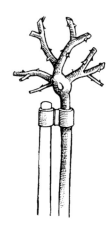

2 In early spring after planting, cut stems back to two or three buds. After flowering, cut back old growth to 5–7.5cm (2–3in) for small-flowered ramblers, or to immediately above the origin of a new lateral for large-flowered roses

tends to be bare at the base, but is recurrent for four months at least.

'Roseraie de l'Hay', 1.5 × 1.5m (5 × 5ft). Big semi-double, crimson-purple flowers, strong scent. A vigorous plant of dense habit. Hips negligible, but it flowers throughout summer; therefore remove dead flowers as soon as possible.

'Frau Dagmar Hastrup', 1.5 × 1.5m (5 × 5ft) but often lower. Pale pink flowers, faintly scented, over a long season. It is worth sparing about half the flowers from dead-heading to have a show of hips, which are like tomatoes and freely borne.

'Scabrosa', 1.5 × 1.2m (5 × 4ft). A dense, upright shrub, good dark foliage. Flowers much-scented, silvery pink (if there is such a thing) and freely carried.

On the whole it seems best to have a hedge of one sort only, not mixed, though that is tempting. Pruning of Rugosas is light trimming and that would make such a hedge easy to keep uniform, but not formal. Choose a rose which excels in scent.

# Herbaceous Plants

It may be unusual to include herbaceous plants in a discussion of pruning, but I have chosen to do so here as the secateurs and even occasionally the saw have worthy tasks to perform in the culture of annual, biennial and perennial plants. The usual techniques are explained below, together with some examples of plants which benefit from pruning and cutting back.

### 1. Dead-heading by removing individual blooms

Removing individual blooms as they fade helps to promote further flowering. It is thought that this spares the energy which goes into seed formation and allows the plant to direct it to further production of flowering heads. Examples include:

*Argyranthemum frutescens* (formerly *Chrysanthemum frutescens*) (French marguerite) This bushy, half-hardy perennial to 45cm (18in) has a woody base, attractive finely divided leaves and daisy-like flowers with white, pink or yellow petals, according to type, freely borne all summer. It can be grown from seed but is usually raised from cuttings under glass and is ready to be planted outdoors as soon as the risk of frost is minimal.

**Pruning** Individual flowers are cut off as they die. The benefit of this is seen particularly well in cultivars such as 'Jamaica Primrose' with a yellow centre (as all these daisies have) and soft, yellow flowers whose fading is predicted by the darkening to almost black of the centre. If you keep at the job the reward is flowering which continues from midsummer until late autumn.

*Dahlia* hybrids Popular flowering bedding perennials grown from tubers which can last for years if lifted and stored away from frost each winter. These are potted up in spring to start into growth and put out in the border in early summer, where they will flower from late summer until the first frosts,

producing plants ranging in height from 45cm (18in) for the single-flowered types to 1.5m (5ft) for the giant decorative types. The flower shapes and colours also cover a wide range.

**Pruning** A daily inspection for dying blooms and removal of all of them down to the foliage (leaving no stumps visible) is rewarded by repeat flowering. *D. merckii*, a hardy perennial in the south of England, is treated in the same way.

*Erysimum* 'Bowles' Variety' A sub-shrubby perennial that makes a superb bush of 60cm (2ft) long stems studded with wallflower-type, purple flowers in late spring. This plant is perennial in the milder areas though short-lived, especially in rich soil. Cuttings under mist root readily.

**Pruning** If each of the flowering shoots is cut right back to its origin as it fades, new stems will soon appear and flowering will continue well into autumn, though never as profuse as the first flush of flower.

### 2. Dead-heading the whole plant

On some plants this can result in a second flush of flowers being produced. Examples include:

*Astrantia* species Hardy herbaceous perennials that thrive in shade and have pleasant foliage from which their flower heads rise to 60cm (2ft). 'Rubra', a form of *A. major*, has plum-coloured flowers in summer and there are recent red cultivars of great promise.

**Pruning** If dead-headed after their first flowering in early summer, they rest until the onset of autumn and then produce a crop of flowers as good as the first.

*Delphinium* hybrids The majestic flower-spikes of delphiniums, up to 1.8m (6ft) or even more for the tallest types, in shades of blue, white, purple-pink and even red, are a fine sight in the herbaceous border in summer, but short-lived if left unpruned.

**Pruning** If the flowering stalks are cut right back after their first performance there is usually a second, less impressive but welcome display several weeks later. In the case of the Belladonna hybrids this repetition is uncertain, but the Elatum types are reliable.

*Nepeta faassenii* Excellent perennials for a sunny, front-of-border position, especially 'Six Hills Giant', possibly a hybrid, which produces a mound of stems about 60cm (2ft) high all covered in lavender-blue flowers in early summer.

**Pruning** All fade together and are cut well back in one rather tedious operation – particularly so in a border of 30m (100ft) – and by early autumn new growth is ready to repeat the flowering, which is less sumptuous than the first but still desirable. Discriminating cats chew the young growths and roll on them, but disdain the flowers.

*Viola cornuta* A useful and endearing plant with mat-forming evergreen foliage and diminutive pansy-like flowers of white or various shades of blue in early summer, reaching a height of 10–30cm (4–12in). The plants like moisture and if that is not available they should be grown in light shade.

**Pruning** Once flowering is over, the plants should be cut back with secateurs, or shears if in a large clump. Include the leaves and give a feed so that new leaves and flowers should form.

### 3. Cutting back flowerheads to prevent self-seeding

As well as allowing more energy to be diverted by the plant into vegetative growth and flower production, this will save the gardener valuable time spent removing unwanted seedlings. Examples include:

*Heracleum mantegazzianum* This huge, imposing plant 3m (10ft) high, with rounded umbels of white flowers up to 45cm (18in) across in summer, seeds itself ruthlessly. Though alleged to be biennial, it seems to survive for years where it is not wanted.

**Pruning** If it is a nuisance, cut back the main stem before the flowers develop – the Grecian saw makes this easy.

*Tanacetum parthenium* (formerly *Chrysanthemum parthenium*) (feverfew) This is an attractive plant, no more than 45cm (18in) tall and bushy, with white flowers from midsummer to early autumn. The golden-leaved form is particularly fine, but may be unwelcome in carefully designed colour schemes. Left to itself, this plant can produce seedlings 100 m (110yd) away in every direction.

**Pruning** Remove flowerheads individually as they

fade. More will appear, but be vigilant as it is easy to miss one or two and the results may be spectacular.

### 4. To delay flowering

This is useful in the culture of some choice plants that need to build up a strong root and shoot structure before being allowed to expend energy on producing flowers. Examples include:

*Meconopsis betonicifolia* If you do not garden on acid soil do not read further, but if you do and enjoy a rather moist climate you should be able to coax this desirable, short-lived perennial to produce its large, clear blue flowers from early to midsummer on a plant 0.9–1.2m (3–4ft) high.

**Pruning** Cut off the flower stems before flowering occurs in the first and even second year to encourage this plant to have a flowering life of three or four years.

### 5. Dead-heading to give the plant a good appearance

Some plants simply look ragged if old seedheads and foliage are left in place. The pruning here is only for cosmetic purposes, but just as important to keep the plants looking their best. Among the plants that are improved by this treatment are:

*Alchemilla mollis* The flowers appear in early summer and the plant is then most beautiful, with very small greenish-yellow flowers in sprays up to 45cm (18in) tall, over hairy rounded leaves of pale green. This is a great self-seeder and not at all easy to dig out from a rock wall, the sort of site where it will thrive.

**Pruning** Flowers should be cut off as soon as they fade, together with any leaves which show signs of age. New leaves will quickly form, but there will be no more flowers later in the year.

*Doronicum* 'Miss Mason' This easy-going perennial produces its bright yellow, daisy-like flowers in spring, on a plant up to 45cm (18in) high, after the daffodils.

**Pruning** The dead flowers are sheared off and the pleasant, heart-shaped shiny leaves are revealed.

*Helleborus foetidus* A long-lived, evergreen perennial that is notable for leaf and flower. The leaves are beautifully cut, almost divided and such a dark green as to appear almost black; the flowers are carried on the 30cm (12in) long stems in clusters of pale green with an edge of maroon in early spring.

**Pruning** Once flowering is over, the flower stems are cut to the ground and the evergreen leaves make a striking ground cover. If left, seedheads will form and the plant self-seeds.

*Helleborus orientalis* Cream flowers rise to 60cm (2ft) above cut leaves of grey-green in late winter

and early spring. This species is a variable plant.
**Pruning** It is treated in the same way as *H. foetidus*.

### 6. To remove foliage to display flowers

In some plants, particularly those with long-lived foliage, the leaves can eventually look rather tired. Removing them may be the best policy, particularly if there is a flush of flowers to admire instead. The most obvious example of this type of plant is:

*Epimedium pinnatum colchicum* This unassuming plant is almost evergreen and the leaves, in autumn, turn red and yellow. As winter ends you should begin to look beneath the canopy of foliage, up to 30cm (12in) high, for signs of emerging flowerheads. The flowers will eventually grow to 30cm (12in); they are yellow and pleasant but not exciting.
**Pruning** As soon as the new flowerheads appear, cut away all the old leaves with shears or secateurs. New leaves soon appear and make a pleasing ground cover for a year. All epimediums do this.

### 7. To collect seed of worthwhile plants

There is always satisfaction in raising one's own plants from one's own seed. It is worth trying this technique with plants such as:

*Hesperis matronalis* (sweet rocket) Although perennial, this traditional cottage garden plant is often treated as biennial because plants deteriorate fairly quickly and produce poor flowerheads as they age. They reach 90cm (3ft) tall and when raised from seed the colour varies from white to lilac on single flowers with good fragrance, which is most marked in the summer evenings.
**Pruning** After taking seed the flowering stems can be cut to the ground. The double forms are best avoided as they are unreliable (and not as beautiful).

*Hibiscus trionum*, syn. *H. africanus* This plant is tender but when raised from seed (which it produces in abundance) sown under glass in spring it can be planted in the open ground when frost no longer threatens, and will flower on a stem of 45cm (18in). The petals are white with a violet eye and the flowering season is long, lasting from midsummer through to autumn.
**Pruning** The seed pods are rounded and prominent, attracting light-fingered visitors who cannot resist them. The race to be there before these can be exciting, and can continue throughout the flowering period as the seeds ripen.

*Lunaria rediviva* (honesty) The perennial honesty is an unbelievably neglected plant, though introduced in 1596. It tolerates shade well and appreciates a good loamy soil. The flower heads rise to 60cm (2ft) in spring, the petals being a very attractive white with a blue tinge. Though it is a short-lived perennial it also self-seeds freely, so there is no difficulty in maintaining a good group.
**Pruning** Remove some of the white and papery seedheads once they have ripened in late summer but since they are decorative, you may decide to leave the rest in place.

*Salvia* All of the many species need well-drained soil. Most satisfactory from seed is *S. patens*, which occasionally survives the mild winters of recent years, reaching 60cm (2ft) and flowering from late summer to early autumn. The amount of seed varies but is greatest on the dark blue form, least on the pale 'Cambridge Blue'. A mauve form has appeared in the last few years and produces offspring of the same colour, as do the others.
**Pruning** Cover the seedheads with a paper bag gathered in at the open end before cutting them off to prevent the loss of too many ripe seeds.

*Verbena bonariensis* This sun-loving perennial plant reaches 1.2m (4ft) high with branching stems, each bearing a tuft of lavender-blue flowers, from early summer until autumn.
**Pruning** It seeds itself freely, and seed only needs to be collected as a gift for interested visitors. The plant can be cut down altogether in autumn and is hardy.

*Verbena rigida* Another perennial, this plant has violet flowers in the same period as *V. bonariensis* but reaches only 60cm (2ft). It is reasonably hardy, but it seldom lasts more than one frost.
**Pruning** As above.

There are plants which produce beautiful seedheads which might well be dead-headed if this habit is not known. *Actaea alba* has light green leaves and small cream flowerheads in late summer, unexpectedly turning into white berries, pea-sized on scarlet stalks up to 90cm (3ft) tall.

*Actaea rubra* is similar but the berries are scarlet and rise above the leaves.

*Arum italicum* 'Pictum' produces narrow leaves with a marbled effect of very pale green, waved at the edges, which appear in autumn and grow slowly through winter into spring, reaching 30cm (12in) long. The pale green flowers appear on a spike and are surrounded by a spathe, a large bract, which is a modified leaf and is green, like those of the wild arum (lords and ladies). The flowers and leaves disappear by midsummer and in early autumn spikes carrying bright red berries appear apparently from nowhere. When they finally disappear the whole cycle is repeated all over again. You may not feel that all this is worth waiting for, but many do.

# Fruit Trees & Bushes

The aim, in pruning fruit trees and bushes, is quite different to that of pruning ornamental trees and shrubs. Although productive plants can be very attractive in their own right, the pruning is intended to achieve maximum effective fruiting in the long term. This means that the approach adopted for pruning, say, a fruiting cherry will be quite different to that for an ornamental cherry, grown for its display of early spring flowers.

Preventing the spread of pests and diseases is important for any gardener, but it is even more of a priority with fruit trees and bushes than with ornamental. For this reason, garden tools must be kept scrupulously clean for pruning fruit and the blades well maintained and sharp, so that the risk of disease entering healthy cropping plants is reduced to a minimum.

## APPLES AND PEARS

It is said that no-one today wants a standard apple or pear tree for a garden, and commercial growers find the smaller and more compact forms easier to manage and more rewarding. A few orchards (or their remains) with old standard trees still exist and very beautiful they are, producing good clean fruits even after 80 years. We, however, must address ourselves to the smaller forms which have been made available by research at the John Innes Horticultural Research Institute, Merton, Surrey (opened in 1909, since moved) and East Malling Research Station in Kent (opened in 1913). After the Second World War these establishments were able to create a series of rootstocks which could transmit to the scion grafted on to them varying degrees of vigour and produce a plant either dwarf, semi-dwarf, half-standard or standard size. These were the Malling-Merton or MM Stocks. In general use are:

M27 Extremely dwarfing – for vigorous varieties in good soil, kept weed-free.

M9 Very dwarfing – for dwarf bushes, dwarf pyramids and cordons.

M26 Dwarfing for average conditions.

MM106 Semi-dwarfing – widely used for bush, cordons, espaliers. Crops in three to four years.

MM111 Vigorous – on poor soil makes rather small trees; on good soil a large tree, perhaps.

All these stocks have a bred-in resistance to woolly aphids, and resistance to various viruses in both stock and scion has been added by research at East Malling and Long Ashton Research Stations. Pears

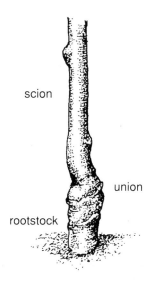

The trunk of a grafted fruit tree, showing the scion, union and rootstock

DISTINGUISHING WOOD BUDS AND FLOWER BUDS
ON FRUIT TREES

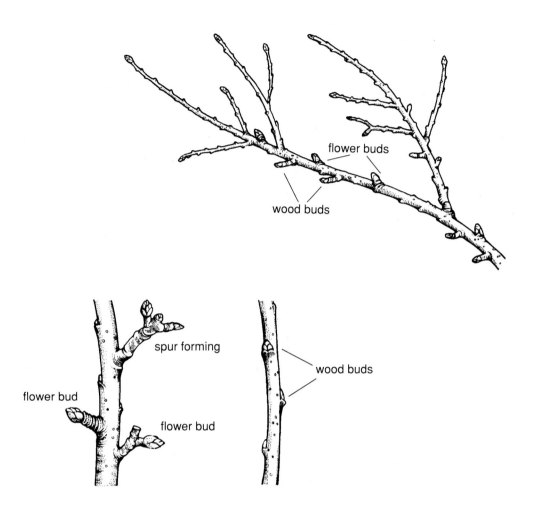

flower buds

wood buds

spur forming

wood buds

flower bud

flower bud

flower bud

flower bud

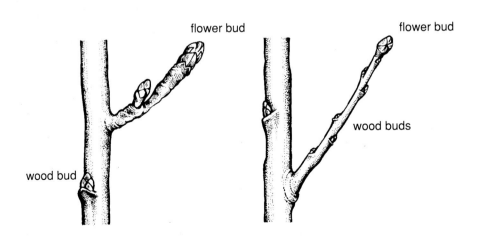

wood buds

wood bud

Spur pruning of mature apples and pears

After the fifth year, the growth of the tree slows down. By judicious
pruning it can be encouraged to produce large crops for many years

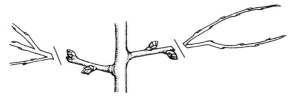

1  In late winter maiden laterals are cut back to
four buds

3  In the following summer fruit is borne on the buds
which have formed

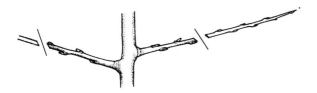

2  In late winter of the following year these shoots
are cut back to a flower bud

4  A spur system begins to form. Eventually it will
have to be thinned out

RENEWAL PRUNING

This depends on the ability of apples and pears to convert growth buds to flower buds
on two-year-old stems which have not been pruned

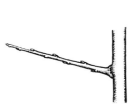

1  In the first winter a strong lateral is chosen, but left
unpruned

3  In the following summer to autumn, fruit is borne
on this pruned lateral

4  In late winter the fruited lateral is cut back to
2.5cm (1in)

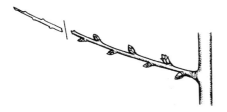

2  In late winter of the following year extension
growth is cut back to where it joins the old wood

5  At the end of the growth period a strong new lateral has formed – and the cycle continues

TREE FORMS

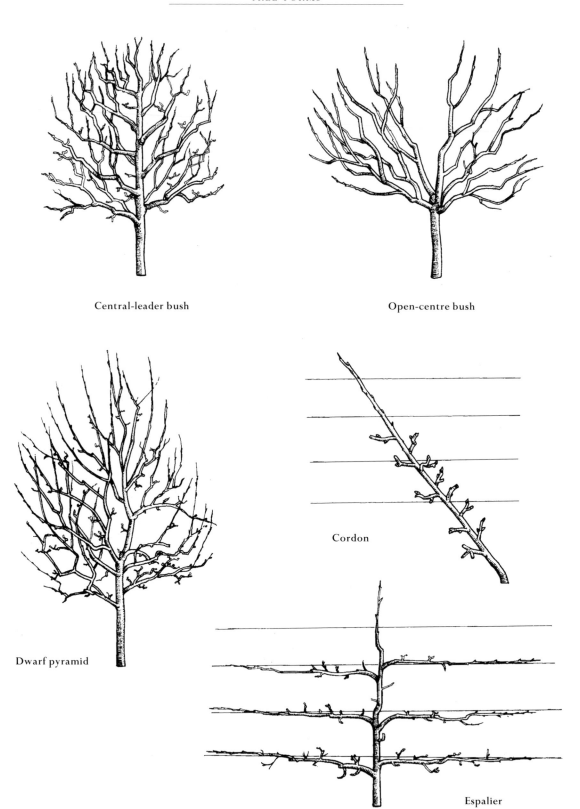

Central-leader bush

Open-centre bush

Dwarf pyramid

Cordon

Espalier

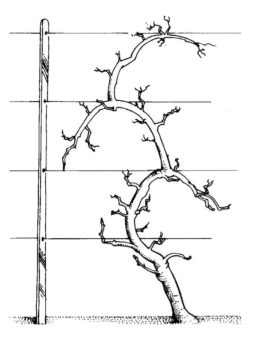

Arcure

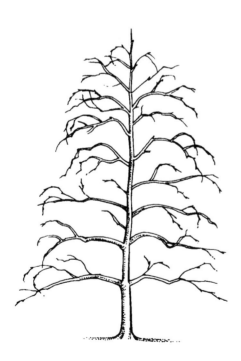

Spindle bush

**PAGE 154**
TOP Cordon pears: those to the left (probably Conference) are bearing well. There is vigorous new growth, and this will be cut back to 7.5cm (3in) in midsummer. Growth of sublaterals from existing side shoots is cut to 2.5cm (1in): this lets light and air into the rather congested centre of the cordon
BELOW Espalier pear: winter pruning has been carried out well, but the branches should have been spaced a little more widely

**PAGE 155**
Fan training seems to have lost favour in private gardens, but is highly successful in the hands of experts, as with the fan-trained Conference pear at the Royal Horticultural Society's garden at Wisley shown in this photograph

are grafted on to the Quince A rootstock for garden use or Quince C for commercial orchards. There are three main styles of cultivation for apples and pears:

**Bush** (see pruning diagrams pp158–9) This is the form of tree usually grown in private gardens, grafted on M26 as an open-centre tree with main branches radiating from a stem. When planting (in the dormant period) make sure not to bury the stock-graft union (if you do so the graft may put down roots and grow away undwarfed, defeating the object of selecting a dwarfing rootstock). Next cut back the maiden stem to about 60cm (2ft). At the end of the growing season (late autumn) there will be primary branches and in winter three or four of these are chosen, with as wide an angle as possible from the main stem and evenly distributed around it. These are cut back by half and any surplus or weak branches removed.

At the end of the next (second) season, secondary branches have formed and in winter all the leaders are cut back by one-half of their length, with any weak ones by two-thirds. Prune back any surplus laterals on the inside of the tree to four buds, to encourage them to produce spurs.

At the end of the third season repeat the pruning but leave laterals on the outer side unpruned. After this, formal pruning may cease if growth is satisfactory. If flower buds have formed on unpruned laterals, cut back to the highest flower bud.

From now on the virtues of the form of growth will appear. All parts are accessible for inspection, pruning and fruit-gathering.

**Cordon** (see pruning diagrams pp160–1) This has the advantage that the stems can be planted close to each

APPLES AND PEARS: BUSH TREE

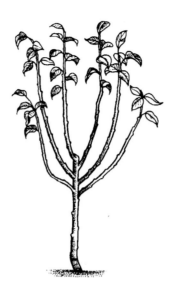

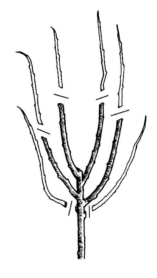

1  Maiden tree at planting in winter. Cut back by half

2  Vigorous new growth has resulted

3  By the following winter, strong branches have formed. Retain the best four, cutting them back by one-half of their length

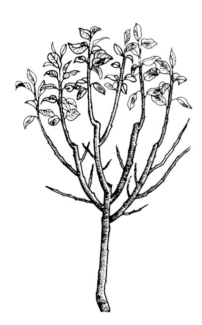

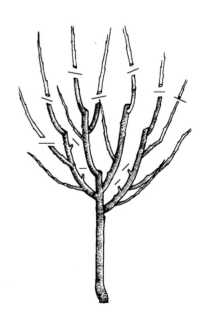

4  By the end of the second year, secondary branches have formed

5  Choose four more branches to become part of the framework. Cut back strong leaders by one-half of their length, weaker ones by two-thirds. Remove weak shoots

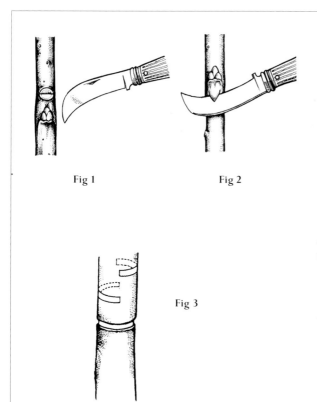

Fig 1                    Fig 2

Notching is the removal of a small triangle or semi-circle of bark above a dormant bud (Fig 1). It aims to stimulate the bud into growth by cutting off the flow of sap from the leaves and is carried out in late spring. It is used to influence the placing of active buds and to lessen the chance of unduly long stems without buds. Nicking, which is the same, is applied below a bud and has the opposite effect, inhibiting bud growth (Fig 2)

Fig 3

Bark ringing is intended to promote the production of fruit buds and to cut down that of growth buds. This is achieved by interrupting the flow of food and hormones from the leaves and upper buds in the phloem channel. A ring of bark 0.5cm (¼in) wide is cut out as deep as the hard wood 60cm (2ft) above ground level. This is done in late spring, making it possible for the ring to heal before growth ceases in autumn. A wider cut will probably kill the tree. If your courage fails, cut to offset semi-circles as in Fig 3, and that may suffice

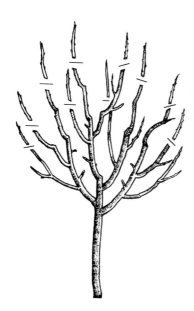

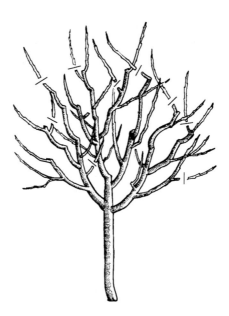

6  By the third year, the main leaders are established. In winter strong leaders are reduced by half the current year's growth, weaker ones by two-thirds

7  Mature tree in winter. Pruning of the leaders is no longer necessary, and laterals on the outer growths are left unpruned. Laterals at the centre are cut back to 5–7.5cm (2–3in), weak stems to 2.5cm (1in)

APPLES AND PEARS: CORDON

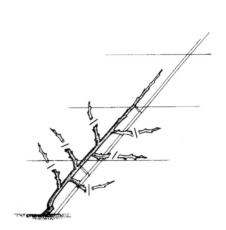

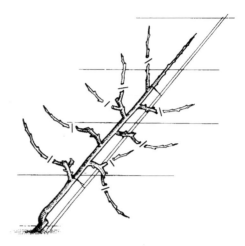

1 In the first winter, cut back any laterals
to four buds. Do not prune the leader

2 At the end of the first growing season, cut
back laterals to four buds, sub-laterals to
two buds

3 The following spring, remove flowers as
they appear

4 In summer, prune laterals to three leaves and the
basal cluster

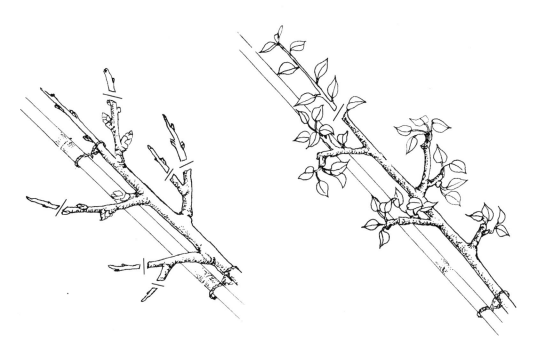

5 In winter, cut back pruned laterals to the
highest flower bud, or 2.5cm (1in)

6 In spring, once the leader has passed the top wire,
cut the extension wood back to its origin

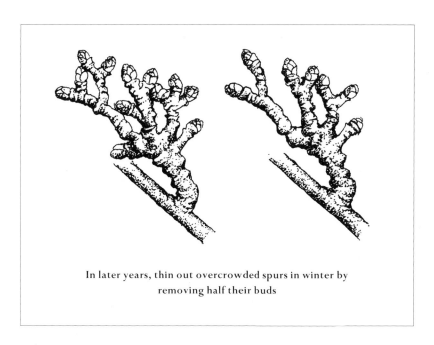

In later years, thin out overcrowded spurs in winter by
removing half their buds

APPLES AND PEARS: ESPALIER

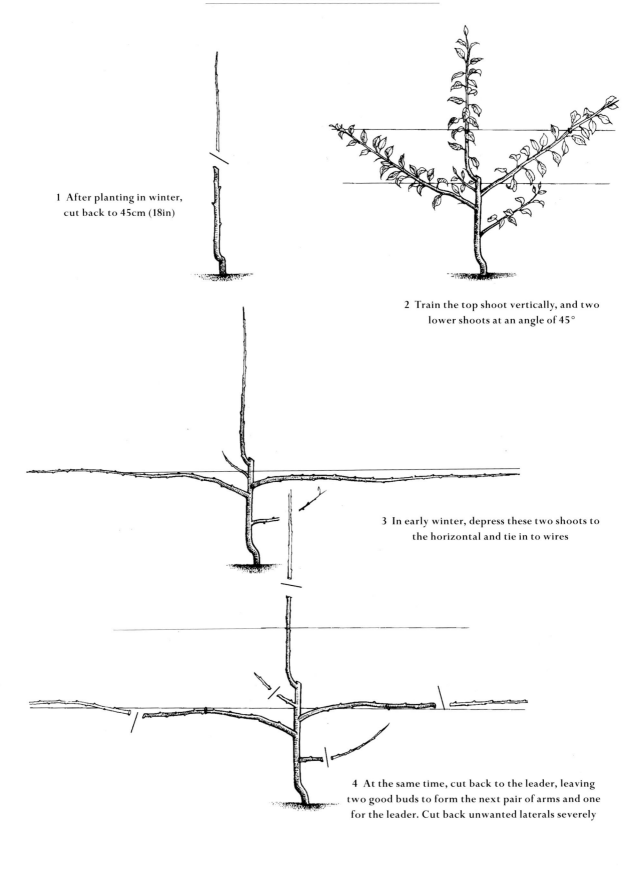

1 After planting in winter, cut back to 45cm (18in)

2 Train the top shoot vertically, and two lower shoots at an angle of 45°

3 In early winter, depress these two shoots to the horizontal and tie in to wires

4 At the same time, cut back to the leader, leaving two good buds to form the next pair of arms and one for the leader. Cut back unwanted laterals severely

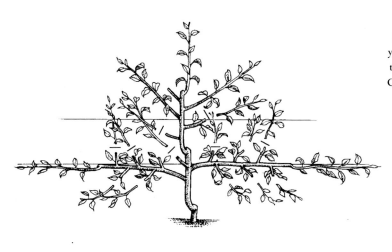

**5** In the summer of the second year, the second tier is trained in the same way at the first to 45°. Cut back laterals on the first tier to 15cm (6in)

**6** In the following winter, cut the central leader back to 45cm (18in) from the upper tier. Cut laterals on the main stem back to 15cm (6in), and horizontal stems by one-third of their length

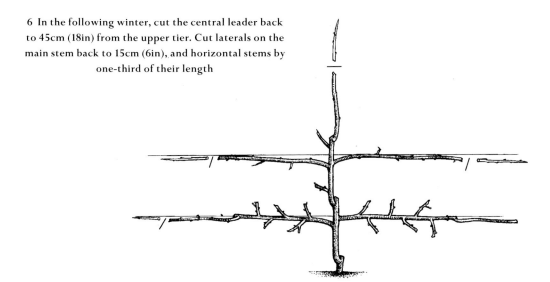

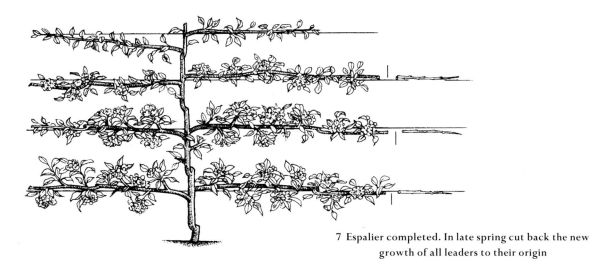

**7** Espalier completed. In late spring cut back the new growth of all leaders to their origin

APPLES AND PEARS: DWARF PYRAMID

1  At planting, cut back to 45cm (18in)

2  In the following winter, cut back the leader to 23cm
   (9in) of new growth, the side branches to slightly
   less

3  The following summer, cut back any laterals not
   required to 5–7.5cm (2–3in)

4  In the second winter, cut back the leader to a bud
   facing the opposite way from before, to leave about
   30cm (12in) of new growth. Cut back laterals to
   20cm (8in)

5  In the third and subsequent summers, prune laterals to 10cm (4in) and sub-laterals as far as the basal
   cluster

6  In winter, cut back the leader to leave about 30cm
   (12in) of new growth. Cut back branches as necessary to outward-facing buds to maintain shape

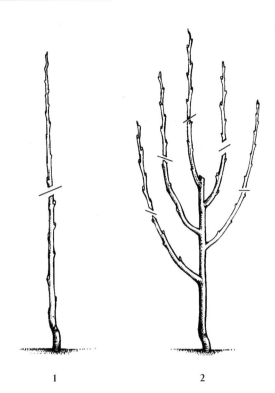

1                    2

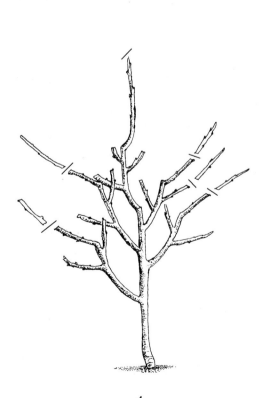

4                                    5

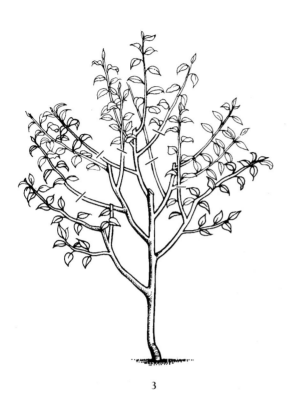

3

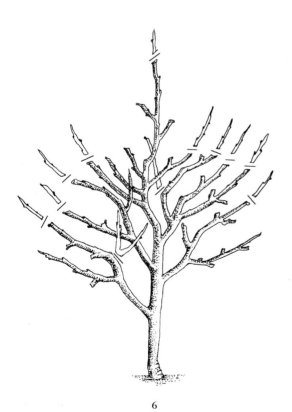

6

other and thus several varieties can be grown in a small space. A dwarfing rootstock is necessary and expert advice is worth seeking locally. The cordon is best grown at an angle of 45° from upright so that all parts of the plant are easily accessible. Bamboo stakes are tied to a wire fence and the cordon attached.

At the end of the first season cut back laterals to four buds and sublaterals to one bud. Do not prune the leader. In the spring of the second year remove any flowers as they appear and in midsummer prune laterals to three leaves and the basal cluster. In winter cut back laterals which were pruned in summer to the highest flower bud, if any; if not, prune them back to 2.5cm (1in).

In the spring of the third year, see whether the leader has grown beyond the highest wire – if so, cut away the new growth. In midsummer reduce laterals and sublaterals as before. In winter thin out any overcrowded spurs, and so on.

**Espalier** (see pruning diagrams pp162–3) This follows the same principle as the cordon but involves training an upright leader with evenly spaced branches trained out horizontally on either side. If starting with a maiden, plant in winter and cut back to 45cm (18in). Train the top shoot vertically and the shoots from lower buds at an angle of 45°. In early winter depress these shoots to the horizontal and tie in to wires stretched horizontally along the wall or support. In the next years the process is repeated until the three or four tiers are completed, keeping unwanted laterals from the main stem severely pruned as necessary.

An ingenious but simple variant of the espalier is the single-tier or **step-over** form, grafted on M27 rootstock and used alongside a path, perhaps in the vegetable garden, or as a double edge to a path. It is best with the same apple on each side, carrying a small burden of fruit; only the choicest.

A brilliant and beautiful extension of the espalier system is seen in the **arcure**, invented in Belgium and shown on p157. It seems to work well and is easy to manage.

Even in the smallest gardens, it is possible to grow apples and pears thanks to the development of the Ballerina or Columnar tree, which is upright and narrow, suited even to container growing. It was born in British Columbia in 1964, originally as the form 'Wijerik', a sport of 'McIntosh'. A number of varieties are available now, although they are more limited in number than the usual grafted forms. The ballerina tree grows as if an upright cordon and the fruit is borne on short spurs quite close together.

PLUMS AND DAMSONS: BUSH TREE

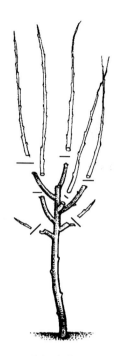

1  At planting, the leader was cut back to 1.5m (5ft) and the laterals to 7–10cm (3–4in). Now primary branches have grown

2  In early spring of the following year, choose four branches evenly distributed round the stem and cut back by one-half of their length. Cut back laterals to a few inches

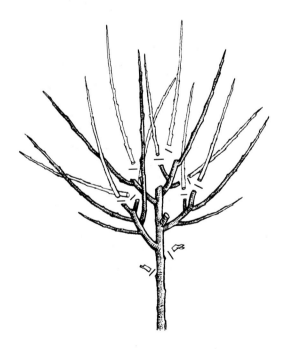

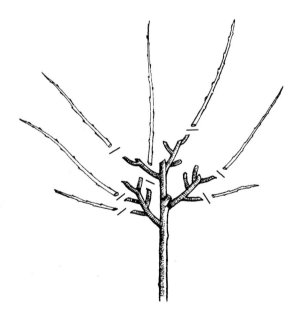

3  In winter of the third year choose four more branches and cut back all eight leaders by one-half of their length. Remove all low laterals

4  At this time, also cut back laterals on the inside of the bush to 7–10cm (3–4in). In subsequent years, if growth is strong and branches pointing in the right direction, pruning of leaders need not continue. Weaker growth should be pruned as in the third year

PLUMS AND DAMSONS: DWARF PYRAMID

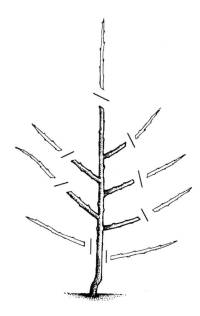

2  In summer cut back laterals to 20cm (8in), and
sub-laterals to 15cm (6in) above downward-
pointing buds

1  A feathered maiden is planted in winter. At bud
break in early spring, remove laterals up to
45cm (18in) from ground level. Cut back
laterals above this by one-half of their length

3  The following summer, cut back leaders to 20cm
(8in), and laterals to 15cm (6in)

4  The following and subsequent summers, cut
back branch leaders to 20cm (8in), and
laterals to 15cm (6cm)

SWEET CHERRIES: FAN

1  In early summer of the first year, select two strong
shoots and tie in to canes. Remove all other shoots

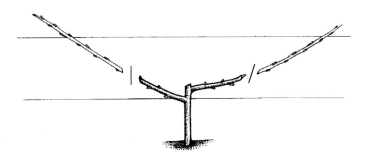

2  In the following spring, shorten each leader to
about 30cm (12in)

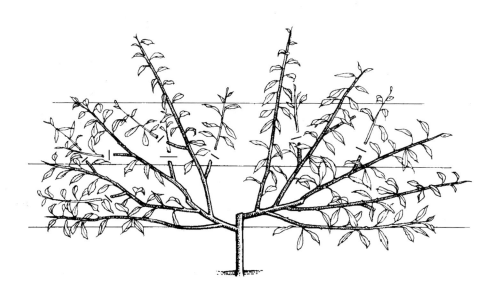

3  Tie in four to six strong shoots from each leader,
leaving the centre of the plant empty. Cut back sub-
laterals to 7.5–10cm (3–4in)

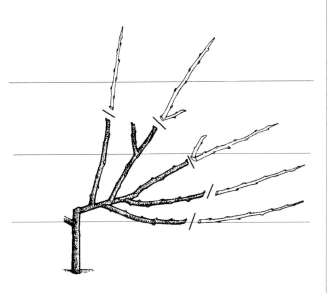

**4** The following winter, cut back all leaders to leave around 45cm (18in) of new growth

**5** In summer, tie in shoots and cut back sub-laterals to 7.5–10cm (3–4in)

**Fan** This method of training was originally devised to take advantage of the shelter and reflected warmth from walls. Sunny, sheltered walls are ideal for sweet cherries, apricots, greengages, peaches, nectarines and plums, as well as choice apples and pears, although most varieties of apple and pear will thrive on an open fan, trained against wires strained between posts, as may be seen to perfection at the gardens of the Royal Horticultural Society at Wisley, Surrey. Today, fan training has largely given way in private gardens to cordons and espaliers, which are more economic of space.

The technique is much the same for all the fruits mentioned above (see pruning diagrams left and pp170, 172–3). To support a fan-trained fruit tree, a wall should be at least 1.8m (6ft) high and 4.6m (15ft) wide. It saves time to start with a feathered tree, which should have a branch on each side about 30cm (12in) above ground level. Other branches are removed and the two remaining are cut back to 50cm (20in). In the following season try to develop four good laterals on each side, two growing upwards and one downwards, leaving the centre more or less open. Side shoots will be shortened to 5cm (2in).

### PLUMS

Plums are well suited to the average garden as long as they have a situation which is not exposed to cold winds and some protection from late frosts. Particular care should be taken to avoid frost pockets. Pruning has hazards, notably silverleaf disease, due to a fungus producing a toxic substance which circulates in the sap after gaining entry through a wound, most often that of pruning. The leaves appear silvery compared with those unaffected, and the infected wood reveals a dark central stain. That part of the tree will die. The only treatment is to remove all affected parts, cutting back until the cut surface is clear. Do this at midsummer as the risk of infection has by then diminished. All the removed wood must be burnt at once. Naturally the pruning of plums and other plants of the *Prunus* genus should be restricted to late summer and autumn.

Some plums can be grown from suckers, for instance 'Pershore Egg', 'Warwickshire Drooper' and 'Cambridge Gage', but most are grown on rootstocks on which the growth is fairly compact. Two are now recommended, 'St Julien A' and more recently 'Pixy'.

Plant a maiden tree in the dormant season. Cut the stem to about 1.5m (5ft), just above a bud. Primary branches appear in summer but no pruning is needed until early spring of the next year. Then cut back well-spaced branches by about one half, or rather more, to an outward pointing bud. Remove any surplus

## Fruiting spurs

**1** From the fourth year onwards, in summer cut out all breastwood and backward-growing shoots. Cut all sub-laterals to 15cm (6in)

**2** In early autumn, reduce all sub-laterals that were cut in summer to 10cm (4in), to create spurs on which flower heads will form in the following year

For early training, follow pruning instructions for bush plums and damsons, p166

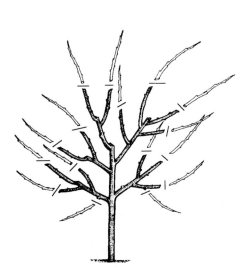

**1** In early spring of the third year, prune back all leaders by one-half of their length to outward-pointing buds to produce an even framework

**2** At bud break the following spring and in subsequent years, cut back some older branches to the origin of young shoots. Leave leaders unpruned

branches. Any laterals from the main stem are cut back to 7.5cm (3in) or so. In the third year prune as before in early spring, allowing some sub-laterals to develop, but cutting them back by one half. At the end of the season allow four more branches to remain but cut back laterals on the inside of the bush to 7.5cm (3in). Pruning then ceases.

Plums can also be grown as dwarf pyramids, in the same way as apples or pears. Damsons are grown in the same fashion as plums but with less severe pruning at every stage.

### CHERRIES

**Sweet cherries** These present a problem for the average gardener. They make large trees, 12m (40ft) or more across, and need a dwarfing rootstock, such as 'Colt'. New dwarfing rootstocks are currently undergoing trials but are not yet available. Also one must have at least two different plants which are compatible, as all these cherries are self-sterile and cannot produce fruit on their own. Fan training can solve the problem of space up to a point, and is carried out in the same way as for apples. Start with a maiden tree cut back to 30cm (12in). Pruning should be severe in the period of forming the framework (see pp168–9, 170).

**Morello cherries** These are much easier for the gardener than any of the sweet varieties. They are self-fertile, their growth is more restrained and they do perfectly well on a cool, shady wall. As they flower

A fan-trained Morello cherry: self-fertile, not too vigorous and does well on a north-facing wall. What more can you ask? As shown, it will flower profusely. If it fruits well, try to make sure that there is enough young wood to replace that which has fruited

1 A feathered maiden at planting. In winter to early spring cut the leader back to a lateral about 60cm (2ft) from the ground. The laterals below 30cm (12in) from the ground are removed, the rest cut to 10cm (4in) to outward-pointing buds

2 In the second winter to early spring, cut back leaders by one-half of their length. Leave a few promising short laterals unpruned

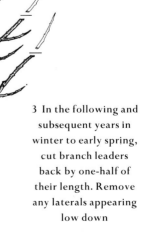

3 In the following and subsequent years in winter to early spring, cut branch leaders back by one-half of their length. Remove any laterals appearing low down

PEACHES AND NECTARINES: FAN

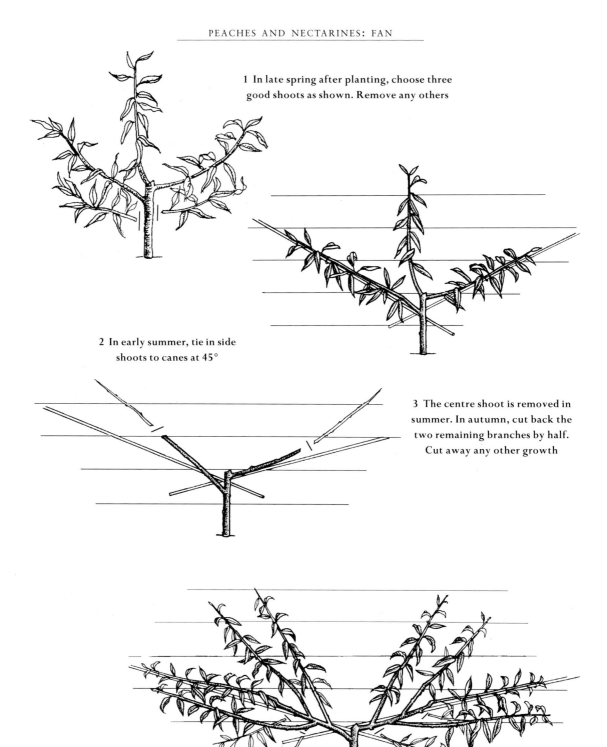

1 In late spring after planting, choose three
good shoots as shown. Remove any others

2 In early summer, tie in side
shoots to canes at 45°

3 The centre shoot is removed in
summer. In autumn, cut back the
two remaining branches by half.
Cut away any other growth

4 In summer of the second year, choose four good shoots from each main side
branch, the longest of which should be the lowest, so as to extend the fan.
Cut away other short laterals

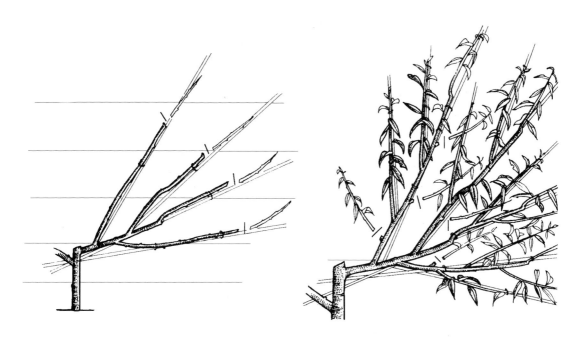

5  In late winter of the third year, shorten leaders by
one-third of their length

6  In summer, choose three shoots from each leader.
Cut out any others

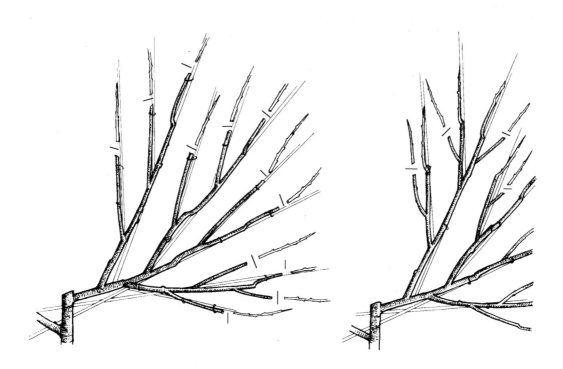

7  In the following winter, prune back the leaders
lightly by one-quarter of their length

8  In subsequent years, prune any laterals
needed to extend the fan by one-third
to one-half of their length

FIGS: FAN

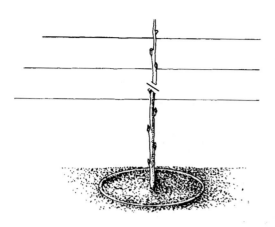

1 Plant a rooted pot plant in an open-based trough 30cm (12in) from the base of a south-facing wall. Prune to 35cm (15in), above a wood bud

2 By summer, laterals have formed and are tied to supports. Remove misplaced growth

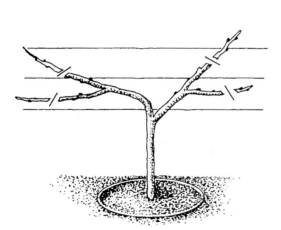

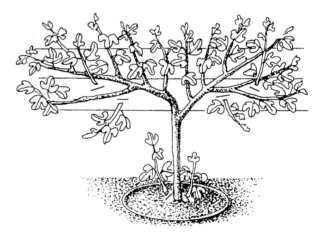

3 In early spring, cut back shoots by one-half of their length

4 In summer, tie in laterals and remove basal and misplaced shoots

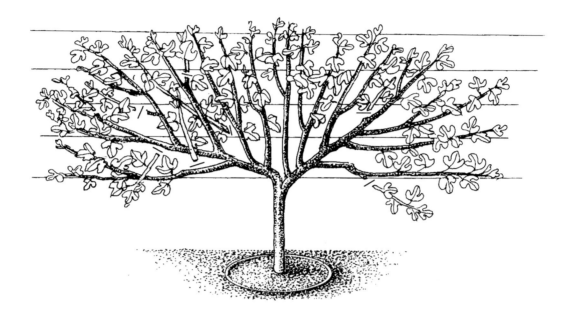

5  The following summer, tie in extension growths of the main ribs,
and cut them when they have filled the wall space

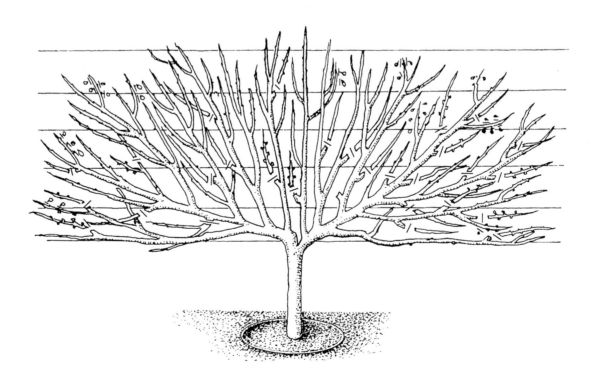

6  In autumn of the fourth and subsequent years, cut back the branches
which have fruited to one eye or bud. Remove any immature fruits
larger than pea size

FIGS: FAN

*continued from page 175*

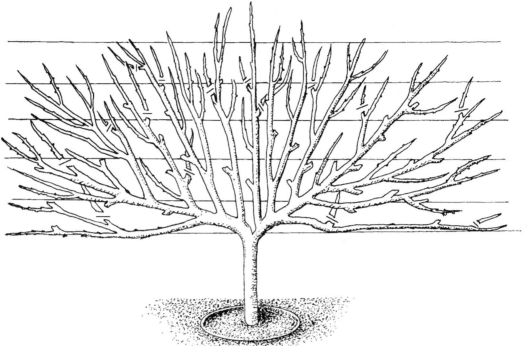

7  In early spring, cut out any surplus or damaged shoots

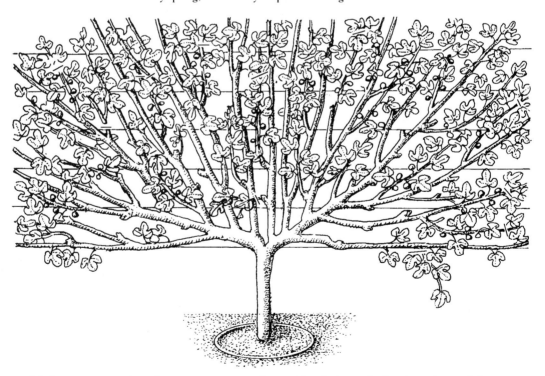

8  In late summer, embryo figs appear on young shoots. After fruiting, the best branches are left
unpruned and are tied in 15cm (6in) apart. Maintain a succession of fruit by cutting out some
old and unfruitful stems from time to time

on wood made in the previous year it is necessary to make sure that there is enough young wood coming on to replace that which has fruited. The early training of a bush tree is very like that of a bush plum, with an open centre. The bush is trained on a leg of about 90cm (3ft) and the leaders cut back in early spring for four or five years. Some of the older shoots are pruned to one-year-old laterals on young growth just appearing. In time, perhaps 10 years, the tree may need to be rejuvenated by cutting back main branches to within 1.5m (5ft) of their origin. Fan training is not often satisfactory.

## PEACHES AND NECTARINES

It is difficult to be enthusiastic about a fruit tree which is more likely than not to produce a small, even negligible crop in most years in Britain. It is not difficult to form a framework by using lateral growths from a feathered plant; cut back the leading shoots by one-half at the end of the first and second seasons. If a wall is available, fan training may be a partial solution, but peach leaf curl will always be a problem for plants grown in the open.

## FIGS

In Britain, figs ripen in sheltered positions in the milder areas but are mostly grown under glass. Think twice before embarking on fig cultivation. Figs are not hardy, are very vigorous, and need careful and detailed pruning. Their fruit is damaged by birds and wasps. The young shoots can develop a grey mould in a wet year and canker at any time. They must be watered frequently in dry weather. However, figs are self-fertile and in a climate with little or no frost are worth trying. The site must have all possible sun and the roots must be restricted if any fruit is to develop. An open-based trough 60 × 60 × 60cm (2 × 2 × 2ft) with its top just above ground level will do, with the sides made of paving or bricks, while the bottom should contain broken bricks or rubble to stop tap-roots forming. This trough is built against a wall which must be at least 3m (10ft) high and as much wide. The trough is filled with good soil and a well-rooted pot plant installed.

The plant is pruned back to 38cm (15in), cutting above a wood bud, in early spring. In summer tie in the laterals which will have developed, spacing them 45cm (18in) apart. Cut out any shoots coming forward from the wall, and any arising from the base. In the following spring cut back the shoots, now forming the framework, by about half of their length. In summer tie in the laterals to canes and remove basal shoots. The canes should be at least 45cm (18in) apart and laterals should be 23cm (9in) from each other.

In summer of the following (third) year, tie in extension growths and stop them when the framework covers the allotted wall space. In late summer embryo figs, the size of a pea, will appear on young shoots and the best of them will survive and ripen. This is more likely if they are near the base of the plant, so it may be worth picking off those that are near the tip rather than at the base of shoots as soon as they are seen, although this is time-consuming work. When the fruit crop is gathered only the best branches should be left unpruned and tied in after being spaced out to 15cm (6in), preferably more. From then on a succession of fruit and second-year growth should be maintained by cutting out some old and unfruitful stems from time to time.

## CURRANTS

**Red and white currants** These can be grown on cordons, espaliers and fans. Cordons are simplest. On planting, shorten the central leader by half and all the laterals to 2.5cm (1in). Next winter, and each subsequent one, repeat this shortening of the leader until it reaches 1.5–1.8m (5–6ft). In summer the laterals are pruned to about 10cm (4in), then in winter they are reduced to 2.5cm (1in) and will in time make fruiting spurs. Each winter the leader is cut back to a single bud, then in summer it and all laterals are reduced to 10cm (4in). And so on.

Bird damage is a serious threat to the crop of these currants and may delay the pruning programme. Both buds and fruit appeal to bullfinches, tits and sparrows. A fruit cage is the only really effective prevention and it is as well to group all soft fruits under one cage. The top of the cage can be covered by fish netting while the buds are forming, and the net can be removed at flowering time to be replaced as the fruits ripen. Insects avoid nets, which will prevent, or at least reduce, pollination.

**Blackcurrants** The cultivation of blackcurrants is completely different from the above. They produce the best fruit on one-year-old wood, though some less good on older wood. They need plenty of manuring. At planting, cut down the plant (which will be either one or two years old) to 2.5–5cm (1–2in) from ground level. Strong shoots will be made, up to 60cm (2ft) long. In the following autumn cut away the weakest of the shoots. In the next year, fruit is borne on all the shoots in midsummer, and then in the dormant season you should remove about one-third of the branches to the base as well as any weak shoots. One year later again remove about one-third of the branches and cut others to a point where there are vigorous laterals. Continue this annual routine.

BLACKCURRANTS

REDCURRANTS: BUSH

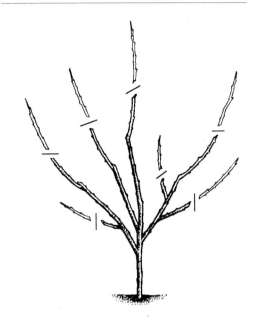

1 In late winter after planting, cut back all branches by one-half of their length, including the central leader

1 At planting, cut all shoots back to 5cm (2in). Do not prune in the following winter. In summer the bush will fruit on wood produced the previous year. New growths appear at the base

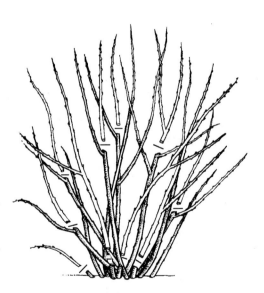

2 The following and subsequent winters, prune the leaders by one-half of their length. Choose strong branches to form the permanent framework and prune by half. Prune laterals to 5cm (2in). In the second and subsequent summers, cut back some laterals near the centre to let in light

2 In the following early spring, remove one-third of the branches which fruited the previous summer, down to the ground. Cut the remaining branches to vigorous new growth. Repeat this process each year

REDCURRANTS: CORDON

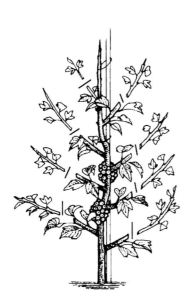

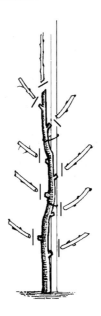

1  In the first summer, train the leader vertically, tying it in to its support. Cut back all laterals to 10cm (4in)

2  In the following winter, prune the leader by half the previous season's growth. Cut back laterals to 2.5cm (1in)

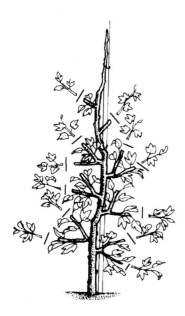

3  In the second summer, train the leader vertically,. Cut back laterals to 10cm (4in). Repeat steps 2 and 3 until the cordon has reached the required height

4  In the fully developed cordon, cut back the leader and laterals to 10cm (4in) in summer. Each winter, cut back the leader to one bud of the summer's growth and all laterals to 2.5cm (1in)

GOOSEBERRIES

Gooseberries are not demanding in their soil needs, but they can be very exacting for the pruner if the spur system is used. As they do not rate highly among fruits with most people in Britain, a simple method of culture is probably adequate. It produces more fruit than the spur pruning used in cordons, but the fruit will be smaller and have less flavour. I have to confess that an overdose of gooseberry fool as a schoolboy leaves the author with a lifelong distaste for the fruit.

The simple method is as follows:

At the end of the growing season, after winter planting, six or eight branches are chosen and cut back by half their length to buds which point upwards. In the winter of the second year, the leaders are cut back by one-half of their length, but laterals are left unpruned. After that there is no more pruning. Fruit is borne on two-year-old shoots and on spurs, if any form.

The close spur system used on upright cordons produces fruits of large size and better flavour. After planting in midwinter, branches are cut back by one-half of their length. At the end of the first growing season, the extension growth is cut back by one-half. Choose shoots to make new branches and cut them also back by one-half of their length. Cut back other side shoots to 5cm (2in). In the following summer clear the centre somewhat by cutting back laterals, to make it easier to gather fruit. Next winter, cut back leaders by one-half of their length and laterals to 5cm (2in).

RASPBERRIES

These need regular manuring and potash. The canes are supported by wires stretched between posts about 1.5m (5ft) high, only two strands of wire being necessary. For short people the top wire can be at 0.9–1.2m (3–4ft), with the canes arched over as the plants grow beyond this height.

Summer-fruiting raspberries are cut to about 25cm (10in) on planting in autumn or winter. There will be no fruiting in the following summer but new canes will appear in spring and the old stumps are removed. The canes are tied to supports as they grow, and any not required are removed at ground level. In the next early spring any shoots damaged in winter should be cut back to healthy wood. Flowering and fruiting occur in midsummer and any new growth is thinned to leave enough shoots to develop at 10cm (4in) intervals to fruit in the following year. In early autumn cut back the fruited canes to ground level and tie in the new canes.

Autumn raspberries are not just a poor relation. The varieties 'Autumn' and 'Zeva' have excellent flavour, their only problem being the weather in early autumn, which can be excellent or the reverse. They need the same supports and the same pruning in the first year as the summer-fruiting raspberries. In the second year all canes are cut to the ground in early spring and should fruit in early autumn. Then the pruning of the previous year is repeated, and so on.

GOOSEBERRIES

The simple method

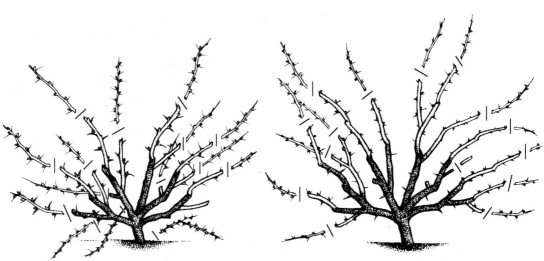

1 In autumn of the first year, cut back leaders by one-half of their length. Choose several well-placed laterals and cut these back by one-half of their length. Cut back all other laterals to 5cm (2in). Remove any suckers

2 In the second and subsequent winters, cut back leaders by one-half of their length. Cut back laterals to 5cm (2in)

## GOOSEBERRIES
### The spur system

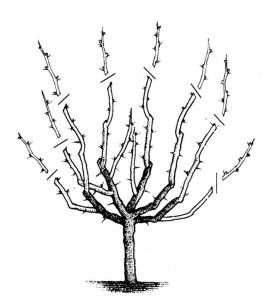

1 In autumn of the first year, choose eight well-spread branches and cut them back by one-half of their length, other side shoots to 5cm (2in)

2 In the second winter, cut back leaders by one-half of their length and laterals to 5cm (2in). No further routine pruning is required

### RASPBERRIES: AUTUMN FRUITING

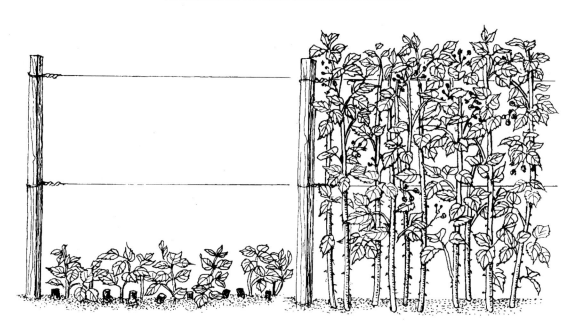

1 In the first year, treat as for summer-fruiting varieties. In the following early spring cut out all canes to ground level

2 The new canes will fruit in early autumn, Repeat step 1 each year

RASPBERRIES

1  In the first season after planting canes are tied in
10cm (4in) apart. No fruiting

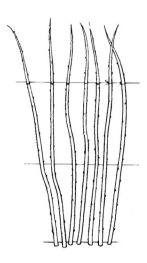

2  By autumn of the first year tying-in is complete

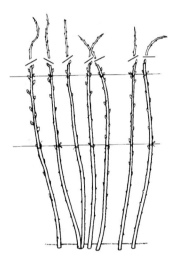

3  In late winter, dead or failing tops are removed

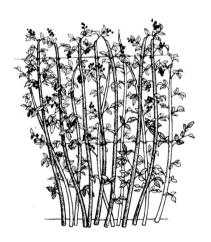

4  In midsummer, fruiting takes place on last year's
canes. New growth developing at the base is thinned
to 10cm (4in) apart

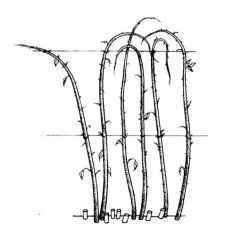

5  In autumn, cut all fruited canes
to ground level. Tie in new canes,
and if growth is vigorous loop the
canes over

## BLACKBERRIES

Some will feel that a good deal of the pleasure with blackberries is derived from gathering them in the wild on hedgerows, where the choicest are only just within reach and pruning is not required. This may be so, but for those who would like to include black-berries in their fruit garden, the easiest and most satisfactory system of training on wires depends on separating the canes that are flowering this year from those that will do so next year, and training one group to the left, the other to the right. This reduces hand-ling to the minimum. After harvesting, cut the fruited canes down to ground level.

**Loganberries** can be managed in the same way. They are less vigorous than blackberries and easier to train.

## BILBERRIES

Blaeberry, whortleberry, whinberry or blueberry, what-ever you call them, the fruit is in season from late summer to early autumn, and is used in pies, tarts, jam and jellies. The bilberry prefers an acid soil and produces shoots from ground level, or from a stool if pruned. The side-shoots flower on growth of the previous year and fruit freely, and no pruning is required in the first two years. Manuring is advis-able each year to produce berries of good size, while pruning after the first two years involves cutting away the older shoots after fruiting.

## MEDLARS

*Mespilus germanica* makes a tree up to 6m (20ft) with an irregular habit of growth, which is attractive but difficult to describe. The flowers are white or slightly pink, solitary and appearing in late spring. The fruits, 2.5cm (1in) wide, are brown and apple-shaped with an open eye, surrounded by the persistent calyx, the whole again difficult to describe but unforgettable once seen. The fruits are left on the tree until leaf fall, then stored until 'bletted' – meaning about to decay, as otherwise they are too hard to use. Pruning has little place but if vertical shoots arise from the branches, as they do at times, they should be cut away. The Latin name, *Mespilus*, derives from the Greek, meaning 'half a ball', which well describes the shape of the fruit.

## QUINCES

The quince is the Golden Apple of the Ancients, who looked upon it as the emblem of love and happiness. The fruit is either round or pear-shaped with yellow woolly skin and flesh. The seed coating contains a gum with mucilaginous and demulcent properties, which explains why it makes such good jam and marmalade. It was, and still may be, added to apple pies as a routine. It is an excellent garden tree, grow-

Triple cordons are ideal for gooseberry training, making the maximum use of the space available. Heavy crops may need thinning. In winter the side-shoots are pruned to three buds, and are shortened in early summer to five leaves. The variety shown here is 'Whinham's Industry'

ing no more than 6m (20ft) high, the head being dense because the branches grow in all directions. The removal of those that rub together is not easy and may damage the natural character of the tree. The flowers, white or pink, are 5cm (2in) across, solitary and produced in late spring. Quince is rarely dam-aged by frost. The only task is to attempt the control of suckers, which can be abundant.

## BLACK MULBERRIES

*Morus nigra* is a very long-lived tree seldom above 6m (20ft) high but much wider, rugged and gnarled when mature. The fruit clusters are dark red, about 2.5cm (1in) long. The taste when ripe is agreeable and the fruit can be used the same way as blackberries. Mulberry gin is said to be better than that made from sloes or damsons. No positive pruning is needed. The juice of the fruits stains clothes and skin.

LOGANBERRIES

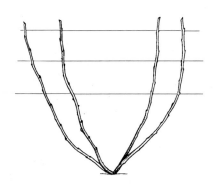

1 In the summer after planting, the stems are trained to wires as shown. In the following early spring cut back the tips so that canes are about 1.5m (5ft) tall

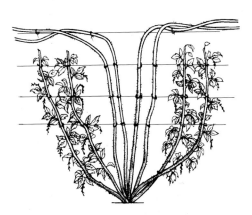

2 New canes are tied in to wires inside old canes as they grow during the summer. In autumn cut away the fruited (outer) canes

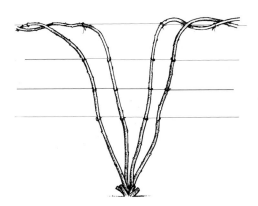

3 Tie in the new canes for fruiting the following year

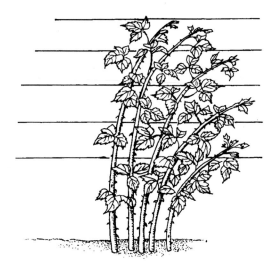

1 Tie all rods in to their supports. No fruiting

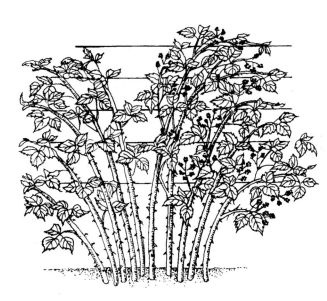

2 In summer, as new rods develop tie them in the opposite direction to the original set. In early autumn, fruit is borne on rods of the previous year

BLACKBERRIES

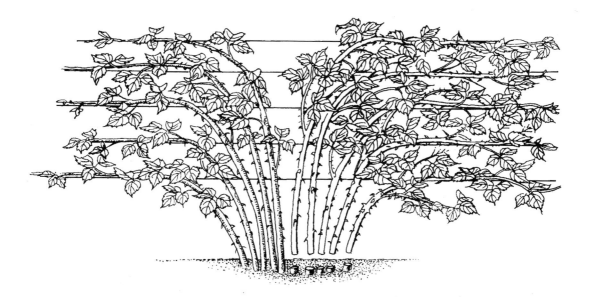

3  After fruiting, cut fruited rods to ground level

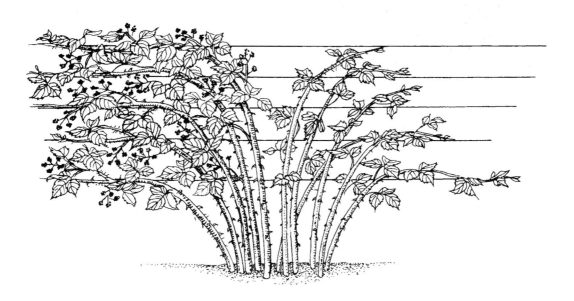

4  In summer, tie in new rods as they develop. In early autumn,
fruit is borne on rods of the previous year

# Glossary

**Acid** See pH.

**Acuminate** Tapering to a sharp point; of leaves, the margins of which curve inwards.

**Acute** Ending in a point; of leaves, the margins of which are convex.

**Adventitious** Growth that appears on a plant at a position which it does not normally occupy; as on pollarded trees, or at the top of blackberry canes when they come into contact with the soil.

**Alkaline** See pH.

**Alternate** Leaves, buds or stems which appear singly, alternating from one side to the other.

**Apex** The tip of a stem. The apical bud is the uppermost on a stem, the apical shoot the highest on a branching system.

**Axil** The angle between a leaf stalk and the stem from which it is growing.

**Bare-rooted** Trees or shrubs lifted in the nursery and delivered without soil round the roots. Containers have largely replaced this practice but they are often less satisfactory, leading to rootbound and inadequately watered stock. The bare-rooted plant, if well looked after, suffers little shock from transplanting.

**Bark** The surface layer of the trunk and branches of woody plants, protecting the phloem and cambium *(qv)*. It is usually composed of dead, corky cells to which addition is continuously made from within. Shredded bark is now widely used in making composts as an alternative to peat.

**Bark ringing** Used to encourage fruit trees to produce flower buds and to slow down growth. It involves cutting out a ring of bark not more than 5mm (¼in) wide round the trunk, about 60cm (2ft) above soil level in mid-spring. The effect of the cut is to sever the downward flow of food and hormones in the phloem and this stimulates the production of flower buds. A less drastic procedure is to remove a half-ring or semi-circle on opposite sides of the trunk at different levels. (See Fruit Trees & Bushes).

**Batter** The inward slope from base to top of a hedge, said to give a neater finish than a vertical surface, to prevent the hedge becoming top-heavy and to avoid damage from snow. There seem to be many fine hedges cut vertically which suffer no such problems.

**Bracts** Modified leaves found where a flower cluster or stalk arises, and in *Compositae* form part of the flower itself. Coloured bracts surround very small flowers on some *Cornus* and *Davidia*.

**Branch** A limb or shoot arising from the trunk of a tree, or a smaller division of such a limb. A primary branch arises from the trunk and a secondary branch arises directly from a primary branch.

**Breastwood** Shoots that grow forward from fruit trees trained on a wall or as espaliers. Such wood should be removed during summer pruning.

**Brutting** Partly breaking a one-year shoot at about half its length and leaving it to hang down. It is done to prevent late-summer growth after summer pruning and is typical of hazel-nut cultivation. The brutted shoots are reduced to a few buds in autumn.

**Bud** A condensed shoot which may contain leaves, flowers or flower clusters, usually protected by scales. Growth or wood buds are usually smaller than fruit or flower buds and are pressed against the stem. The difference, important to the fruit-grower, is fairly easy to discern with practice.

**Calciole** Describes a plant which tolerates or prefers an alkaline, limy soil.

**Calcifuge** A plant which will not tolerate alkaline soils, lime or chalk.

**Callus** Corky tissue which forms over any wound made on a woody plant and arises from the cambium *(qv)*. If a branch is cut from a tree the callus gradually covers the wound (if it is correctly made) and new bark forms.

**Cambium** See Vascular System.

**Chalk** Limestone, composed of calcium carbonate in a soft white formation, common in Britain. Calcifuge plants *(qv)* grow weakly and become chlorotic in a chalky soil.

**Chlorosis** Yellowing of leaves due to iron, magnesium or manganese deficiency. Iron deficiency is induced by very alkaline soil conditions; magnesium deficiency is usually due to it being leached from the soil by heavy rain (but also by excess potassium in the soil; manganese deficiency occurs in some sandy soils or clays). These three deficiencies can be corrected by adding the appropriate element, either directly to the soil or by spraying the leaves with ferrous sulphate (iron), magnesium sulphate (Epsom Salts) or manganese sulphate.

**Cladode (Phylloclade)** A stem which functions as a leaf and may look like one, but it carries the flowers, which shows that it is a stem. Examples are *Ruscus aculeatus* and *Colletia armata*.

**Clay** An earth composed mainly of aluminium silicate, the basis being very fine particles of sand. It does not break up when dry, retains water excessively and bakes hard in dry weather, but is quite fertile and retains fertilizers well. It can be improved by prolonged addition of leaf mould, compost or shredded wood.

**Clean** Of trunk or stem without shoots or branches.

**Clone** A clone is composed of plants all produced vegetatively from cuttings, budding, grafting or division from one parent plant, or a descendant using the same methods. These plants have the identical character of the parent. Seed will never achieve this uniformity.

**Coppicing** Cutting away new growths arising from the base of a tree or shrub. In gardening it is mainly used to produce coloured young growth of stems (and sometimes leaves) on some willows or cornus, but also to provide very large leaves for ground cover when using ailanthus, eucalyptus, catalpa, and paulownia. It can also be called stooling.

**Crotch** The junction of primary branches with the trunk of a tree. The branches are especially liable to break away if two limbs of equal size have formed the crotch.

**Cultivar** A plant variation which has originated in cultivation, not in the wild, and is sufficiently distinct to have a name of its own. If originating in the wild, such a novelty would be a 'variety' but the distinction is not always easy to make.

**Dioecious** Describes a plant that carries male and female flowers on separate plants. The pollination difficulty is solved in part by planting one male among several females (see Monoecious).

**Entire** Describes leaves with smooth margins.

**Epicormic** Such shoots (water shoots) are derived from adventitious *(qv)* buds which form beneath the bark of woody plants but move out with the cambium until they are near the surface. When the main shoot is damaged they erupt and grow out from the bark. They are common on fruit trees but very few conifers produce them. They seem to occur for no apparent reason on European limes, at the base of the tree.

**Eye** A dormant bud, normally on a grape vine.

**Fastigiate** Of narrow erect growth, for example, the Lombardy poplar.

**Feeding** The application of elements essential for plant growth. Nitrogen, phosphorus and potassium (potash) are the basis of fertilizers, often with the addition of very small quantities of a few other elements, notably copper, iron and manganese (trace elements), which should be used with caution as they may be harmful in excess quantity.

It is not easy to calculate the amount of a fertilizer to be used, which depends to some extent on the weather and moisture in the soil, but it is wise to follow the manufacturer's instructions, which are carefully calculated. Generally speaking, nitrogen stimulates growth and leaf production, phosphorus helps to produce active roots, and potassium stimulates flower formation and ripening of fruit.

**Form** Strictly applied, this means a plant which differs in some minor character, such as a white-flowered form of a red-flowered species. Form is one step lower than subspecies.

**Genus** A family of plants is composed of one or more genera. The similar members of a genus are species.

**Glabrous** 'Not hairy' (which is not the same as smooth). A glabrous leaf can be rough.

**Glaucous** Bluish-green or grey.

**Globose** Nearly spherical. Applied to fruits, shrubs and the crown of trees.

**Habit** Characteristic form of growth of a plant, for example, upright, weeping, prostrate.

**Hairs** Occur on leaves and stems and occasionally on flowers and fruits, as a cover or indumentum. Their main function is to insulate against heat or cold. The term 'hirsute' is used botanically for coarse, dense hairs; 'pubescent' means downy with short hairs barely visible, 'tomentose' means woolly or felted and 'villous' refers to long weak hairs.

**Hardy** Indicates a plant able to grow outside without protection all year round in a given area. In Britain there are obvious differences in hardiness between plants grown in the north and those grown in the south, and the Gulf Stream produces significantly warmer climates in coastal areas in Scotland and Northern Ireland. In the USA 10 zones of climate are recognized, reflecting their degree of hardiness.

The lie of the land can influence hardiness considerably, producing microclimates both benign and hostile. In Britain mild spells in winter followed by frost undermine confidence in the weather pattern in most years.

**Inflorescence** The flowering part of a plant. There are three categories:

1. **Cymose** A flower is produced at each terminal growing point and later flowers from lateral growing points.

2. **Racemose** Having an active growing point and able, in theory at least, to develop indefinitely with the youngest flowers at the apex.

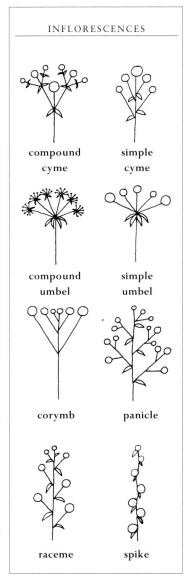

INFLORESCENCES

compound cyme

simple cyme

compound umbel

simple umbel

corymb

panicle

raceme

spike

3. **Mixed inflorescences**, not belonging to either of the above categories. The most frequent kinds are:

*Capitulum (racemose)* – a tight collection of stalkless flowers, seen in *Compositae*.

*Catkins* – a mixed inflorescence of stalkless flowers, seen in hazel.

*Corymb* – usually small flowers or flower heads, all about the same height. The flower stalks leave the main stem at different points (cf 'Umbel').

*Cyme* – a variety of inflorescence, all of which have growing points which end in a flower.

*Panicle* – a branching raceme in which each branch resembles an individual raceme. Branches may be alternate or opposite.

*Raceme* – an elongated inflorescence without branches. Each flower has a short stalk.

*Spike* – an inflorescence with a vertical axis and numerous stalkless or nearly stalkless flowers.

*Umbel* – an inflorescence in which the flower stalks arise from a central point at the top of the main stem. Umbels may be simple or compound.

**Lateral** A side-growth of any kind on a shrub or tree. Understanding of this term is vital to the pruning of fruit trees.

**Leader** The shoot which ends a branch and grows on in the same direction. The central leader continues the main trunk in a vertical direction and is not pruned, although it may be damaged inadvertently, whereas laterals are pruned.

**Leaves** Considered here from the point of view of one who is seeking to identify a plant or at least place it in a genus. The most common arrangements are shown on page 188. Leaves may have a stalk (petiole) and are then petiolate; if without a stalk, sessile.

**Leg** The length of the main trunk of a tree from the ground to the lowest branch.

**Maiden** A tree or bush in the first year after grafting or budding. This term is mainly used for fruit trees, but also roses. Feathers are the laterals of maidens (cf Whip).

**Microclimate** See Hardy.

**Monoecious** A plant which has both male and female flowers, able to function in fertilisation (cf Dioecious).

**Mouth** The open end of a bell or trumpet-shaped flower.

**Neutral** The point of the pH scale *(qv)* at which soil is neither acid nor alkaline: pH = 7.0.

**Nicking and Notching** See Fruit Trees & Bushes.

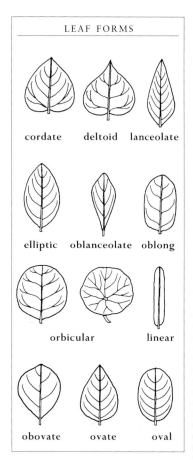

```
LEAF FORMS
```
cordate    deltoid    lanceolate

elliptic    oblanceolate    oblong

orbicular    linear

obovate    ovate    oval

**Petiole** A leaf stalk. On some climbers, such as clematis and nasturtium, the petiole will twine round the nearest support of a suitable size.

**pH** indicates hydrogen ion concentration and measures the acidity or alkalinity of soil, water or whatever. The scale is logarithmic so that the difference between pH 7.0 and 8.0 is much greater than that between, eg, 5 and 6.

**Phloem** See Vascular System.

**Pleach** Originally meant hedge-laying by bending stems of trees or shrubs, then cutting them half through and interweaving them, using posts as necessary. It now commonly refers to a screen or hedge formed at some height, 1.8–2.4m (6–8ft) from the ground by branching of trees the trunks of which are kept bare below this level. Limes or hornbeams are usually chosen for this purpose.

**Pollard** A tree which is cut back every few years to a main trunk, often 1.2m (4ft) or so from the ground.

**Raceme** See Inflorescence.

**Reversion** Correctly used for:

1. Variegated (qv) plants which revert to producing leaves of their plain form, usually green, for example, *Elaeagnus*

*pungens* 'Maculata', *Acer negundo* 'Variegatum'. Removal of reverted stems is necessary but is not a cure for the tendency.

2. A virus disease of currants, causing the leaves to become smaller than normal with fewer veins. If the diagnosis is confirmed the plant should be removed.

**Scion** A shoot or bud removed from a plant for the purpose of budding or grafting to another, the stock, which provides the roots.

**Shoot** The growth of an emerging seedling. When leaves or lateral growths appear it is known as a stem. Unfortunately the word is also used for lateral growths, twigs or branches.

**Shrub** A woody plant with many stems and no trunk. A large shrub may become tree-like and may be persuaded to act like a tree by removal of side branches from the most upright stem, for example, *Photinia davidii*.

**Species** Plants of one species have characters which distinguish them from any other and they breed true. Subspecies are one step less well-defined but in general resemble species.

**Spur** A short branch system which carries clusters of flowerheads.

**Standard** Loosely used for any tree grown with a bare stem. Trees are trained as standards for fruit-growing with 1.8m (6ft) stems, half-standards are trained with a stem of 0.9–1.2m (3–4ft) and shrubs, particularly roses, are often grafted on stems of 0.9–1.2m (3–4ft).

**Sucker** A word of ill-omen for gardeners, as it commonly refers to unwanted growths produced on the stock of grafted plants. This may overcome the desirable growth of the scion. The leaves on a sucker are often, but not always, easy to distinguish from those of the scion. These suckers must be removed, which is not an easy task. Advice to pull rather than cut them off is often valueless, as they are tenacious. Cutting off just below ground level tends to generate a forest of new suckers. One should attempt to trace each sucker to its origin on the rootstock by gently digging, finally cutting the sucker away completely.

**Tap root** A strong root growing almost or quite vertically downwards, presumably in search of water or nourishment. The black walnut, *Juglans nigra*, grown from seed is very quick to form a tap root and becomes very difficult to transplant within three years. Conifers behave in the same way.

**Tendril** A modified leaf or shoot. Some, such as those of ivy, branch and at their ends produce adhesive suckers which fix

them on to a surface. On vines, they are thready and twine, others wave about until they encounter something around which they can coil.

**Thinning** See Fruit Trees & Bushes.

**Trellis** A structure of light bars of wood or metal, crossing each other at intervals and fastened where they cross. Nowadays trellis is available in panels made of wood or plastic. If free-standing it needs support from posts at least every 1.8m (6ft) and can be partially draped with climbers. Against a wall it should be fastened to stand 2.5cm (1in) or a little more away from the wall surface.

**Type** Term used by long-suffering gardeners to differentiate a particular form of a plant from that more commonly grown, which they regard as the 'type'. Properly, the type is a plant described from the wild, the description being supported by a dried herbarium specimen. This 'type' plant may not be the commonest form of the species.

**Umbel** See Inflorescence.

**Variegated** Leaves usually, stems and flowers seldom, have markings in two or more colours in a variegated plant. The markings are, as a rule, white or cream, due to the absence of chlorophyll (which gives the normal green colouring), but other colours may be seen, as in the partially pink and white leaves of the climber *Actinidia kolomikta*. Variegated plants are weaker than their plain green originals, and they tend to revert back to green.

**Variety** A variation in a wild as opposed to a cultivated plant. It must be sufficiently distinct to deserve a name of its own.

**Vascular system** A system of tubes in plants consisting of two series:

1. The **phloem**, which conveys the foodstuffs made in the leaves to all other parts of the plant, including the roots, as necessary;

2. The **xylem**, which conveys water and minerals taken up by the roots to the leaves, where they are converted (with the aid of sunlight and the green pigment chlorophyll) to the complex substances needed for growth. This is the process of photosynthesis, as a result of which oxygen is given off into the air.

**Vegetative propagation** Propagation other than by seed. Methods include offsets, runners, division, cuttings, budding and grafting.

**Water shoots** See Adventitious.

**Whip** A young tree (up to two years old) with an erect stem and no laterals (feathers).

# Bibliography

Arnold-Foster, W. *Shrubs for the Milder Counties* (Country Life Ltd, London 1948)

Bailey, L. H. *The Pruning Manual* 18th Ed. (The Macmillan C. New York 1934)

Bazeley, B. *Tree Fruit Growing* (Wm Collins and Son, London 1990)

Beales, Peter *Classic Roses* (Wm Collins Co Ltd, London 1985)

Bean, W. J. *Trees and Shrubs Hardy in the British Isles* (John Murray, London; A–C 1970, D–M 1973, N–RL 1976, RI–Z 1980. Supplement 1988)

Brickell, C. *Pruning* (Mitchell Beazley, London 1979)

Bristow, Alec *How to Bring Up Plants* (Harvill Press, London 1983)

Brown, George E. *The Pruning of Trees, Shrubs and Conifers* (Faber and Faber, London 1972)

Curtis, C. H. and Gibson, W. *The Book of Topiarys* (The Bodley Head, London 1904)

Dallimore, W. *The Pruning of Trees and Shrubs* (Edward Arnold Ltd, London)

Dallimore, W. and Jackson, A. B. *A Handbook of Conifers and Ginkgoaceae* 4th Ed. (Edward Arnold, London 1966)

Fraser, H. *The Gardener's Guide to Pruning* (W. H. and L. Collingridge, London 1966)

Gibson, M. *The Book of the Rose* (Macdonald General Books, London 1980)

Grounds, Roger *The Complete Handbook of Pruning* (Ward Lock, London 1973)

Hadfield, Miles *Topiary and Ornamental Hedges* (A & C Black, London 1971)

Halliwell, Brian *The Complete Book of Pruning* (Ward Lock Ltd, 3rd Edition 1988)

Hudson, J. *The Pruning Handbook* (Prentice Hall, New York 1971)

Huxley, Anthony *Huxley's Encyclopedia of Gardening for Great Britain and America* (Universe Books, New York 1981)

Lacey, Geraldine *Creating Topiary* (Garden Art Press, Northiam, East Sussex 1987)

Lloyd, Christopher *Clematis* (Wm Collins, 1977).

Lloyd, Christopher *The Well-Chosen Garden* (Elm Tree Books, London 1984)

Lycett-Green, Candida and Lawson, Andrew *Brilliant Gardens* (Chatto and Windus, London 1989)

*The Plant Finder* Devised and compiled by Chris Philip, Editor Anthony Lord (Headmain Ltd, Lakeside, Whitbourne, Worcester 1991)

Prockter, Noel J. *Climbing and Screening Plants* (Faber and Faber, London 1973)

Rehder, Alfred *Manual of Cultivated Trees and Shrubs Hardy in North America* (Dioscorides Press, Oregon, 2nd Ed. 1940)

Reid, John *The Scots Gardener* (Glasgow 1683)

Robinson, William *The English Flower Garden* (John Murray, London 15th Ed 1933)

Sackville-West, Vita *In Your Garden* (Michael Joseph Ltd 1951)

# Acknowledgements

This book is a 'companion' to encourage the belief that a knowledge of the form and character of plant species and their cultivars is necessary for the rational practice of pruning.

I have tried to keep up with the changes in nomenclature which are announced each year. The Plant Finder, edited by Anthony Lord, is most valuable in this respect and I am grateful to him for help and advice. (Some believe that The Plant Finder is the greatest horticultural invention since the trowel.)

I have had valuable demonstration of the effects of pruning from Michael Hickson at Knightshayes and Roy Finch in Worcestershire. From Christopher Lloyd, too, at Great Dixter and through his writing, which shows the value of record-keeping every year. Topiary has gone almost beyond my experience, and I am grateful to Geraldine Lacey for her excellent advice. Anthony Huxley has been most patient at a very busy time, both in answering questions and advising me on how to avoid pitfalls.

Vivienne Wells was my first editor and was succeeded by Sarah Widdicombe, who has patiently guided me to the end, with John Youé as designer. I have almost enjoyed writing for them.

Wendy Pearce bravely agreed to convert my manuscript to a typescript, and did so with remarkably few spelling mistakes considering my erratic handwriting. Am I the last author to write a book?

My thanks also to Andrew Lawson for his wonderful photographs, which capture the essential character of their subjects so well, and to illustrator Maggie Redfern, for a difficult task stylishly performed.

And, finally, special thanks to Patrick Taylor, who advised throughout and encouraged me to persist despite the setbacks.

JOHN MALINS
*Tintinhull House, 1992*

# Index

Numbers in *italic* refer to illustrations